Sophocles' *Philoctetes* and the Great Soul Robbery

I0893574

Publication of this volume has been made possible, in part, through the generous support and enduring vision of WARREN G. MOON.

Sophocles' *Philoctetes* and the Great Soul Robbery

Norman Austin

THE UNIVERSITY OF WISCONSIN PRESS

The University of Wisconsin Press
1930 Monroe Street, 3rd Floor
Madison, Wisconsin 53711-2059
uwpress.wisc.edu

3 Henrietta Street
London WC2E 8LU, England
eurospanbookstore.com

Copyright © 2011
The Board of Regents of the University of Wisconsin System
All rights reserved. No part of this publication may be reproduced, stored in a retrieval system, or transmitted, in any format or by any means, digital, electronic, mechanical, photocopying, recording, or otherwise, or conveyed via the Internet or a website without written permission of the University of Wisconsin Press, except in the case of brief quotations embedded in critical articles and reviews.

Printed in the United States of America

Library of Congress Cataloging-in-Publication Data
Austin, Norman.
Sophocles' Philoctetes and the great soul robbery / Norman Austin.
p. cm. — (Wisconsin studies in classics)
Includes bibliographical references and index.
ISBN 978-0-299-28274-5 (pbk.: alk. paper)
ISBN 978-0-299-28273-8 (e-book)
1. Sophocles. Philoctetes. 2. Greek drama (Tragedy)—History and criticism.
3. Philoctetes (Greek mythology) in literature. 4. Trojan War—Literature and the war.
5. Troy (Extinct city) in literature. I. Title. II. Series: Wisconsin studies in classics.
PA4413.P5A95 2011
882′.01—dc22 2010044623

To My Companions of the Road

BOB BYARS

HENRY GREENHOW

LARRY KOJAKU

BOND JOHNSON

SIMON MARCUS

WILLIAM MULLEN

GORDON SIEVEKE

and to

THE CITY OF ATHENS,

in Pindar's words

"Pillar of Hellas and Citadel of the Daimon"

ἔτι τοίνυν καὶ αἱ θυσίαι πᾶσαι καὶ οἷς μαντικὴ ἐπιστατεῖ—ταῦτα δ' ἐστὶν ἡ περὶ θεούς τε καὶ ἀνθρώπους πρὸς ἀλλήλους κοινωνία—οὐ περὶ ἄλλο τί ἐστιν ἢ περὶ Ἔρωτος φυλακήν τε καὶ ἴασιν.

[All sacrifices and everything to do with divination—for these are the forms of communion between gods and humans—are concerned with nothing else but the protection and healing of Love.]

Eryximachus, in Plato's *Symposium*, 188b–c

Contents

Preface

I first read Sophocles' *Philoctetes* at the beginning of my professional career, while I was a graduate student at Berkeley. At that time I thought of the play as an antique, interesting but certainly enigmatic, something like a fragment of a pediment from some archaic temple. Several decades later, at the end of my career, I chose the play as the text in the last undergraduate class in Greek that I would teach at the University of Arizona. Then I discovered with some amazement that it was altogether modern. At this point when, with a maturer vision, I read Odysseus' words in the prologue of the play, where he explains to Neoptolemus that Philoctetes' screams, provoked by his snakebite, were so horrendous, so *sacrilegious*, that they prevented his fellow warriors from performing their religious rituals, I was electrified, as if I had touched a live wire. When I was a graduate student, the frontal lobotomy and electric shock were medically approved therapies for silencing a person's pain, therapies as much for the benefit of the patient's friends and family no doubt as for the patient. But at that time I was too little experienced in either life or literature to see that Philoctetes' expulsion from his community could be a trope for our modern therapeutic practices. I had yet to learn that now as in Sophocles' time decorum remains high among the religious virtues.

Philoctetes' excommunication is not the only modern element of the play. Equally modern is the metastasis of his disease from the body to the soul, as also the absolutism of his will, his defiant fixation on his anger and his sickness, his refusal to make the smallest compromise in the direction of health if such compromise is to include forgiveness of his enemies for the harm they have inflicted upon him. This is a story told and retold every day in every therapist's clinical practice.

Two years after I had read the play with the students in the classics program at the University of Arizona, I taught the play again, now in translation, in a course offered in the Humanities Seminars program at that university. The participants in the Humanities Seminars are members of the wider community, many of them retired but others still active in their profession, and all interested in lifelong learning. I devoted the full ten weeks of the seminar to the play, taking the participants through it section by section and explicating the English translations with my own hermeneutic interpretations of the Greek text.

In the fifth week, midway through the seminar and at the exact midpoint of the play, when Philoctetes falls into his epileptic-like seizure and utters the hellish sound for which he had been excommunicated ten years earlier, I was gripped by fierce abdominal pains, which necessitated an immediate rendezvous with the nearest emergency room. I was hospitalized for the next six weeks and was sent from one hospital to the next in search of the specialist with the right equipment, the right diagnosis, the right medication that could restore me to health. At several moments in that long pilgrimage, the prognosis was dire indeed, and I owe thanks to the many friends in my Tucson community and across the continent whose visits, cards, phone calls, and prayers, whether raised in temple, chapel, or church, surrounded me with tender affection and walked me back from the grave.

When recuperating at the house of my friend Bob Byars in the last days of my ordeal, I awoke one morning with a dream still strong in my memory, which had me writing a book about the play. My friend, told of this dream, immediately produced some sharpened pencils (my preferred writing instrument) and supplied me with a lined, yellow pad. With these in hand, I walked with slow and tentative steps (after six weeks spent in hospital beds) to the nearest Starbucks coffee shop, where I put down on paper the first words of what would eventually issue into this book.

Plato condemned ancient tragedy as pathological—poets representing characters behaving in pathological ways and thus encouraging the spectators to indulge in similar pathologies. For Plato, the ideal tragedy would focus only on the ideal hero, acting only in ideal ways. He had a great antipathy to tragedy because the tragic vision insists on an axiom that was anathema to him, that human suffering is at the very center of the cosmic design. Needless to say, given his paradigm, which had no place for suffering, tragedy would soon go out of business, and in its place we would have only hagiography. Whatever their reasoning, the tragic poets chose the other path and presented characters, some honorable but many considerably less than honorable, as casebook examples of various severe pathologies, thereby enriching our understanding of ourselves and our societies as complex conglomerates of confused and contradictory emotions and behaviors. In his *Philoctetes*, the last play produced in his lifetime (409 BCE), Sophocles has made pathology the central issue. My reading of the play centers on this pathology or rather on its complex of several pathologies.

My study is intended for classical scholars. The play, however, which has until recently rusticated in quiet neglect, has a value worthy of a larger audience than those able to read it in its original language, and my intention has been to make the play more accessible to those who might be drawn to it by their interest in the history of ideas, in literature, the theater, philosophy, religion, or medicine, since the play speaks to every discipline in what we broadly call the humanities.

I have structured this book as a series of chapters based on the structural divisions of the play itself. Since any complex play is a tapestry of meanings, it is impossible for an interpretation to adhere exclusively to a linear form. Ideas first broached in the prologue of this play are readdressed in the subsequent development of the plot. But a study that ignores the sequence of events in a tragedy may also miss the significance of that sequence. Each ode, each episode approaches the essential problems of the play at a different moment in their articulation. In naming the chapters of this study according to the ancient divisions of the tragedy itself, prefacing each chapter with a brief definition of the names given in antiquity to that section, I hope to assist modern readers who have not been tutored in the structure of ancient Greek tragedy and also to emphasize the essential nature of ancient Greek tragedy as a musical composition.

Undoubtedly, we will read the play with different eyes than those with which Sophocles viewed the traumas of his own age. Our task as critics and interpreters is to render Sophocles' meanings as faithfully as possible in a translation far removed from Sophocles' own time and culture. No text, however, whatever its provenance, is a closed document. Insofar as it represents a single moment in a dynamic process of its author's thought, it remains forever an open text, a thought caught on the wing. But even more important, its completion depends on us, the readers. To quote Harold Bloom, speaking of his own *Gnosis*, "in the deep reading of a poem what you come to know is a concept of happening, a realization of events in the history of your own spark or *pneuma*, and your knowing is the most important movement in that history" (Bloom, *Agon*, 8).

My almost lifelong association with the masterpieces of Greek and Roman literature has been an odyssey full of beauty, mystery, and danger. I am grateful to all those who have guided, assisted, or accompanied me on this voyage. I owe a special thanks to the three mentors who first set my feet on the road to Athens: to my Latin master, Gordon Martin, who in the Chefoo School on a mountain top in China taught me to love Latin conjugations; to the Reverend Robert Halliday, who, when I was in high school in Toronto, preparing to enter the University of Toronto, introduced me to the wonders, mysteries, and jubilation of New Testament hermeneutics; and to Professor Ronald Shepherd, who taught me the elements of Greek in my first year at the University of Toronto. There followed a series of professors at the University of Toronto and then at the University of California, Berkeley, who continued to open my eyes to the power of the Greek poets. In my teaching career, I also have countless students to thank, whose enthusiasm and concentration inspired me to delve ever deeper into the consciousness from which these texts grew.

It would be impossible to render due thanks to all the scholars, colleagues, friends, doctors, and nurses who have contributed in their various ways to the making of this book. I feel compelled, however, to acknowledge three who had the most direct influence in the care that I received in Tucson during my illness: first, Dr. Michael Boxer, who quietly assumed unofficial responsibility for my case and behind the scenes worked to ensure that I would receive the best medical care that Tucson could provide; then Nancy Bissell and Bob Byars, the friends who opened their homes during that semester, providing me with the home I needed away from home where I could feel nurtured and at peace. If sickness is part of the human condition, I can only pray that other sick persons can find the gracious affection that I found among my friends in Tucson.

I would also like to thank all the persons at the University of Wisconsin Press for the careful treatment they have given to this book at all stages of its production. In addition, I am especially grateful to Barbara Wojhoksi for her conscientious editing of the manuscript and to Naomi Linzer of J. Naomi Linzer Indexing Services for her professional skill and care in the preparation of the index.

I would be remiss if I did not also acknowledge the young servers at the various coffee shops in Tucson, Arizona, and Fort Lauderdale, Florida, whose coffee cups measured out this book from page to page. With special affection I remember the staff of Borders Bookstore in Fort Lauderdale, where most of this book was written through its various revisions. Seated on the deck outside Borders, bathed in the limpid Florida light, looking across the Middle River at the yachts tethered to their posts on the other side (sometimes with the *Odyssey* joining their lineup), the breezes rippling the waves and ruffling my feathers, an iguana liveried in green eyeing me with studied circumspection as he would stalk past on his morning watch, and now and then a ripe coconut suddenly released from the tree overhead and landing with a thump almost at my feet, in this happy landscape, with those charismatic angels hovering in the background always ready with a mocha or a cappuccino for the thirsty traveler, I could almost imagine I was sitting in the forecourt of heaven.

Sophocles' *Philoctetes* and the Great Soul Robbery

N
MACEDONIA
Struma R.
Abdera
Evros R.
Byzantium
Bosporus
PROPONTIS
Mt. Pangaeum
THASOS
SAMOTHRACE
Axios R.
Pella
CHALCIDICE
Mt. Athos
Cyzicus
Hellespont
Sestos
TROAD
ASIA
Simois R.
Troy
MYSIA
Scamander R.
TENEDOS
LEMNOS
Mt. Ida
Haliacmon R.
PIERIA
Mt. Olympus
EPIRUS
Mt. Ossa
Peneus R.
Larissa
Iolcus
Mt. Pelion
AEGEAN
SEA
LESBOS
Mytilene
Pergamum
LYDIA
PHRYGIA
Hermus R.
Buthrotum
Dodona
THESSALY
Pherae
PHTHIOTIS
SCYROS
Artemisium
Smyrna
Sardis
Pactolus R.
Mt. Tmolus
CORCYRA (CORFU)
Lamia
Spercheus R.
Oechalia
Trachis
EUBOEA
Euripos
Chalcis
Eretria
CHIOS
IONIA
Colophon
Meander R.
Ephesus
Acheloüs R.
ACARNANIA
Mt. Oeta
LOCRIS
BOEOTIA
Delphi
Mt. Parnassus
PHOCIS
Thebes
LEUCAS
AETOLIA
ATTICA
SAMOS
Mt. Mycale
Miletus
CARIA
ANDROS
ICARIA
Gulf of Corinth
Ceryneia
CEPHALLENIA
ITHACA
Sicyon
Megara
Athens
Mt. Cyllene
Corinth
DELOS
PATMOS
ACHAEA
Nemea
Mt. Erymanthos
Mycenae
Saronic Gulf
CEOS
CYCLADES IS.
SPORADES IS.
Halicarnassus
ELIS
ARCADIA
Argos
ARGOLIS
PAROS
NAXOS
COS
Cnidus
ZACYNTHOS
Olympia
Lerna
PELOPONNESUS
Alpheus R.
SERIPHOS
IONIAN
SEA
MESSENIA
LACONIA
Eurotas R.
Sparta (Lacedaemon)
Pylos
MELOS
THERA
RHODES
0 50 100 miles
0 50 100 kilometers
CYTHERA

Introduction

Sophocles was an extraordinary man who lived in an extraordinary time. He was born in Athens in 497/496 BCE and died in 406 BCE, his life span coinciding with the greatest century in Athenian history. He was a major presence in the city in politics, religion, and the theater through the period of its expansion, and he died as the greatness of the city was collapsing because of its own imperial ambitions.

In the sixth century, Athens was a notable city, but it did not enter its greatness until the fifth century. Greatness came to the city through its victories in the Persian wars. In 490 BCE King Darius of Persia was decisively beaten by a much smaller Athenian force on the plains at Marathon, and he was forced to return to Susa, the capital of Persia, in great disgrace. Ten years later, in 480, the Athenian fleet, commanded by Themistocles, inflicted a calamitous defeat on Persia in the sea battle fought in the narrow straits between Athens and the island of Salamis. Athens soon grew to become the superpower of the Greek world. Partly through a robust imagination stimulated by its victory over the Persians, partly through the vision of Athens's chief politician, Pericles, and his astute manipulation of the Athenian citizenry, and partly through the wealth that poured into Athens from trade and the taxes imposed on the other Greek cities as protection against the Persian threat, Athens vaulted into the position as the chief city of both Greece and the whole Mediterranean, surpassing every other city in the region, indeed all these cities taken together, in art and architecture, drama, philosophy, and political theory.

Among the greatest achievements of Athens in this century was the institution that today we call Greek tragedy and comedy. These should more properly be called Athenian tragedy and Athenian comedy since, however similar they may have been in their origins to rustic rituals in other cities, as civic institutions they became a phenomenon wholly Athenian. When today we talk of Greek tragedy, we mean performances produced at the Theater of Dionysus in Athens in the fifth century. The three greatest poets of the tragic theater lived in this century—Aeschylus, Sophocles, and Euripides—and Aristophanes, the greatest poet of the comic stage, was their contemporary.

Aeschylus was born in 525 BCE and died in 456/455. His first victory in tragedy can be dated to 484. Modern scholars consider that he probably had 79 plays produced in the Theater of Dionysus, of which 7 have survived. Sophocles was born approximately a generation later. Legend has it that he was one of the youths chosen to dance in celebration of the Athenian victory of Salamis. As a youth he was no doubt a member of the chorus in other dramatists' plays and in time became a playwright himself. Ancient testimony credits him with some 130 plays, reduced by modern consensus to perhaps 123. Since tragedies were produced as tetralogies—three tragedies with a satyr play included as the day's final performance—he must have had his plays produced in the theater over thirty times in the course of his long career. It was also said that he won some twenty-four victories in the tragic festivals—these victories, awarded for the tetralogy as a whole, would account for some 96 of his plays. These figures testify to a prodigious career and a prodigious talent. He won the first prize for his *Philoctetes* in 409, when he was eighty-seven. It was his last play produced in his own lifetime. He wrote one final play, *Oedipus at Colonus*, but did not live to see it produced. It was performed in 401, four or five years after his death.

From this large corpus of Sophocles' work, a canon of seven plays was formed in late antiquity, and all seven have come down to us, his *Philoctetes* being one of them. In this play, as in other Sophoclean plays, the personal and the political are tightly intertwined. Every play by Sophocles has two questions as its central themes. The first is the personal: what is it to be a human? The second is equally important, sometimes made explicit and sometimes treated more implicitly: what is it to be a citizen living and participating in a community of citizens?

The labyrinthine network of connections between personal psychology and political ideologies has given us some of the most profound observations on human consciousness. To read Greek tragedy is to study history, but it is also to go deep into our own consciousness. The poet's mission, as Umberto Eco has stated it, unlike the objective of the scientist or the mathematician, is not to give us *the* meaning to life's enigmas, or even *a* meaning, but rather to shower us with a "surplus of interpretations."[1] The language of ancient tragedy is rich and layered in contradictions, and the strong reader, to borrow Harold Bloom's term, must aim to be as strong a reader as the strong text demands.

This play is informed with the sense of the threat of the collapse of Athenian power. In 472 BCE in his *Persians*, Aeschylus celebrated that great moment in Athenian history, the victory over the Persian fleet at the Battle of Salamis. From that moment Athens grew in stature year by year, but its proud successes began to falter as its imperialism ran up against opposition and mutiny from the other Greek cities. In 415 Athens suffered one of its worst disasters in its defeat by the Spartan forces at Syracuse. In 409 the glory of Athens was already a thing of the past, though the full consequences of its collapse were not yet as recognizable to the Athenians themselves as they are to us today. But all Athens was in a state of great anxiety, and the *Philoctetes* is one of the documents that testify to that anxious state of mind. The melancholy fear that Athens, once at the hypocenter of the explosion of new ideas in the century, had lost or was on the point of losing its soul permeates the play.

Philoctetes was a minor character in the epic tradition. He is mentioned briefly three times in Homer, once in the *Iliad* and twice in the *Odyssey*, and other poems in the epic repertoire fill in the story. He was bitten on the foot by a snake guarding the shrine of a goddess near Troy, at a place named Chrysē in this play. The wound was chronic. It did not heal but continued to suppurate, causing Philoctetes such pain that his cries prevented the Greeks from performing their necessary sacrifices. The Greek leaders had Philoctetes taken to the island of Lemnos and abandoned there. They then proceeded to Troy to wage war to retrieve Helen, who had been abducted from her Spartan home by the Trojan prince Paris. Ten years into the war, with no end in sight, Odysseus then captured the Trojan seer Helenus and from him extracted a prophecy that the Greeks could not capture Troy unless they brought two men to the field—Neoptolemus the son of Achilles from Skyros, where he was being raised while his father was at Troy; and Philoctetes from Lemnos. With Achilles dead, Neoptolemus was no doubt to take his place and be a second Achilles, and Philoctetes was now needed because he owned the bow and arrows of Heracles, which were invincible.

Philoctetes had been given these weapons by Heracles himself when he granted to Heracles his terrible wish to be immolated after Heracles realized that he was dying from the poison that his wife had applied to the robe in which he was celebrating his most recent great victory. Heracles had his son build the pyre, but his son refused to bring the torch to set it alight. Instead, Philoctetes, Heracles' comrade, agreed to perform this terrible act of kindness and received the bow of Heracles as his reward. After Philoctetes was brought back to Troy, the camp physician, Machaon, son of Asclepius, healed his wound. With a single arrow, Philoctetes then killed Paris. With both Hector and Paris dead, Troy soon fell to the Greeks. Thus Neoptolemus, only a boy when his father went to war, and Philoctetes, quarantined for the ten years of the war, emerged at the very end as the conflict's great heroes, sharing the glory of those final moments of the Greek victory.

Each of the three great dramatists composed his own Philoctetes play. Aeschylus produced his in the 470s BCE; Euripides, a younger contemporary of Sophocles, produced his version some forty years later, in 431; and Sophocles produced his thirty years later, in 409. The other two Philoctetes plays have not survived, but we have the good fortune to possess an essay written by the rhetorician Dio Chrysostom in the first century CE comparing all three plays.[2] From Dio we can infer that although the other two dramatists had made a significant contribution in transferring the story to the Athenian stage, Sophocles' contribution was far superior to theirs, ensuring that his would become the canonical version and theirs would slip quietly into oblivion.

Sophocles' *Philoctetes* has not enjoyed the popularity of his Theban plays. The choral passages of this play fall short of the majesty that makes the choral odes of his earlier plays so memorable. The play itself hardly fits the paradigm that we associate with Greek tragedy, and Heracles stepping in as the deus ex machina has been criticized for imposing by divine fiat a resolution on the otherwise intractable human issues. Thus the play has been relegated to the study, a document with more value for students of Sophocles' thought than for the stage. But in recent years the play has moved from the periphery as its originality has become more apparent. Its issues—the psychological, the social, and the medical, all closely intertwined—are as much the challenges of our modern societies as they were for the Athenians of the late fifth century.

1

The Problem of Translation

Triton incomplicate with that
Which made him Triton, nothing left of him,
Except in faint, memorial gesturings,
That were like arms and shoulders in the waves,
Here, something in the rise and fall of wind
That seemed hallucinating horn, and here,
A sunken voice, both of remembering
And of forgetfulness, in alternate strain.

Wallace Stevens, "The Comedian as the Letter C"

To read any text is to enter a hermeneutic labyrinth. This is true even for a modern text, but the challenge is magnified when our text is both ancient and a classic. In the case of Greek tragedy, as we delve deeper into the differences between the two media, between the printed text and the public stage, and the two epochs so far removed from each other, problems loom up sufficiently formidable to make us fear that even at our best we can be only antiquarians, decoding texts shaped by a worldview as foreign to us as the language in which they have been transmitted. Yet, in spite of the cultural impediments, we continue to read Sophocles' *Antigone* believing that it has more than antiquarian value. How then should we read such a text so as to do justice both to its spirit and to our own?

In addressing the hermeneutic problem, Hans-Georg Gadamer leads off with the German word *Bildung* (which is retained as "Bildung" in the English translation of his *Wahrheit und Methode*). The word, which at the simplest level means "form" or "formation," among German thinkers has come to mean "culture," and for its definition Gadamer quotes Wilhelm von Humboldt: "But if in our language we say Bildung, we mean something both higher and more inward, namely the attitude of mind which, from the knowledge and feeling of the total intellectual and moral endeavor, flows harmoniously into sensibility and character."[1] To which Gadamer adds: "The rise of the word Bildung in this sense calls rather on the ancient mystical tradition, according to which man carries in his soul the image of God after whom he is fashioned and must cultivate it in himself."[2]

The seismic shift that affects our modern reading of an ancient text has been the influence of the Enlightenment, which has brought with it an ideology based on science and the scientific method. This point of view is as deeply embedded in our thinking, planted in us almost at the moment of our birth, as the analogical and allegorical methods were embedded in the prescientific mentality of the classical age. The scientific method has its uses in our study of the material world, but as Gadamer argues so well, the investigative method required for the natural sciences cannot serve as the model for what he calls *Geisteswissenschaften*, "the human sciences" or "the forms of knowledge that pertain to the human spirit."[3] The natural sciences focus on the objective world and search within phenomena for some general law to account for their nature and behavior. But the "human sciences" are focused only secondarily on the external and the objective. Their field is the subjective; their quest is to understand human experience from within.

Gadamer writes of how each of us, looking out on the world, sees it from his or her own horizon. The horizon of ancient thinkers differs significantly from ours, yet we cannot expect to ignore our own horizon in order to place ourselves in Sophocles' situation. Even if that were possible, it would be neither useful nor desirable. If we mistakenly hoped to interpret the ancient texts in this way, working solely from within their situation, this attempt could, in fact, produce "an actual deformation of knowledge."[4] Gadamer uses the analogy of an ordinary human conversation. If, in such a conversation, our sole aim is to place ourselves in the other person's situation, then this would be no true conversation but rather only a means with which we aim to learn the other person's horizon, much like a conversation between a doctor and a patient. In such a conversation, we make "our own standpoint safely unattainable."[5] If a true conversation is between the two parties, "I" and "Thou," in this simulated conversation we would have removed the "I" from the dialectic process.

At the same time, however, in withdrawing from a conversation, letting ourselves be guided solely by the aim of understanding the other person's situation, we have also made that person inaccessible. The loss for us, if we apply this method to our study of the ancient texts, is that "we have given up the claim to find, in the past, any truth valid and intelligible for ourselves. Thus this acknowledgement of the otherness of the other, which makes him the object of objective knowledge, involves the fundamental suspension of his claim to truth."[6] Applying the scientific method to works of the human spirit thus removes both the "I" and the "Thou" from any meaningful contact and interaction.

The true "human science" calls on us, in reading an ancient text, to fuse the two horizons, both ours and the ancient poet's.[7] Our encounter with the tradition requires us first to acknowledge the tension between the texts of that tradition and our modern worldview. Our task, Gadamer writes, "consists in not covering up this tension by attempting a naive assimilation but consciously bringing it out."[8] Following the Hegelian dialectic, Gadamer acknowledges that the ancient text is alien to us and what is alien we must freely acknowledge as such; reaching out to the alien, however, requires us to undergo a process of self-alienation. If, however, it remains forever alien, then it has lost any meaning for us, since its reach can extend no further than the horizon of its original author. In the end, if we have allowed for both horizons, we return to ourselves with our own horizon changed and enlarged. Gadamer quotes Hegel's assertion that the world of antiquity is well suited for this hermeneutic project "in that this world is remote and alien enough for us to be able to bring about the necessary separation of ourselves from ourselves, 'but it contains at the same time all the exit points and threads of the return to oneself, for becoming acquainted with it and finding oneself again, but oneself according to the truly universal essence of spirit.'"[9]

Sophocles' *Philoctetes* has objective value as a document reflecting one of the most significant moments in the history of Western thought. But its true value is subjective. Every element in the play is made part of the apparatus to illuminate a moment in the story of our evolving human consciousness. We must first admit that the play is certainly alien to us in many of its features. The greatest discrepancy between its worldview and ours can be summed up in the single word "religion." We can glimpse the scientific method in its infancy in the Hippocratic essay on the "Sacred Disease" (epilepsy), where the author argues that this disease is no more sacred than any other.[10] Like any other disease, it can be traced to natural causes. Perhaps Sophocles, having himself a strong bent toward medicine, might have heard something of such theories. But if so, they play no part in his etiologies of the soul's disease. We might infer from his *Philoctetes* that he would hold the opposite opinion, that every disease is sacred. He does not see material phenomena nor does he look for material etiologies. Every cause is for him spiritual and every event is teleological. Accident and chance have no place in his cosmology. One of the most powerful words in the play is *kairos*. We might translate it loosely as "opportunity" but its more accurate significance is "timing," and timing in this play always signifies the conjunction of human time and sacred time. Everything that occurs in Philoctetes' life comes about at its proper moment, as Neoptolemus asserts to the chorus. Philoctetes on Lemnos was living in sacred time. "None of these things is a marvel to me," Neoptolemus says in response to the chorus's perturbation at Philoctetes' suffering; "for if I am thinking aright, that suffering that came to him from Chrysē is divine [*theia*], and his present suffering here, separated from anyone who could care for him—it is not possible that this is not the concern of some god, so that he might not aim the invincible weapons of the gods against Troy until the time [*khronos*] should be fulfilled when it is pronounced that Troy must be conquered by these same weapons" (vv. 191–200).[11] The message could not be said more transparently: every element of the old myth as it is enfolded into this drama is included for one reason only, to signify the divine.

Religion, especially the polytheism of pagan Greece with its superstitions and taboos, is the great obstacle that blocks our entry into the mind of the Athenian tragedians. We can read Shakespeare without recourse to religion, but that is an oddity, which George Santayana has addressed in a challenging essay on Shakespeare's lack of religion.[12] "For Shakespeare," Santayana writes, "in the matter of religion, the choice lay between Christianity and nothing. He chose nothing." The consequence is that the "cosmos eludes him."[13] If we were to ask Shakespeare the significance of everything he displayed in his dramas and poetry and the outcome of it all, Santayana observes that Shakespeare could hardly say more than to quote the words of his character Macbeth:

> It is a tale
> Told by an idiot, full of sound and fury,
> Signifying nothing.

But how are we to put religion aside when we approach Sophocles? We certainly cannot say that he composed his many tragedies to document that the world we inhabit signifies nothing. As Santayana continues: "The will of man fulfills the decrees of Heaven. The hero manifests a higher force than his own, both in success and in failure."[14] In the modern secular environment, religion can be studied as a social phenomenon, but social theory cannot take us into the experience itself. Religion has disappeared as the necessary precondition for tragedy. That the sound and fury of our world signify nothing may come as freedom to the modern existentialist, but existentialism in itself cannot take us far in our reading of Greek tragedy.

In writing about our fusion of horizons, Gadamer notes that within a tradition the process of fusion is continuous and, we might add, virtually unconscious, "for there the old and the new continually grow together to make something of living value, without either being explicitly distinguished from the other."[15] Sophocles' attitude toward the Homeric mythology offers us a good paradigm of this principle. All his extant tragedies, including his *Philoctetes*, are based on the epic tradition as if the values of that Homeric storehouse were essentially the same as his own. Nothing, however, could be further from the truth. But so continuous are the horizons between one epoch and another when the tradition is in full force that Sophocles never had to contemplate the problem of the horizon at all, or to concern himself with misreading a hallowed text.

The tragedies presented on the Athenian stage were always religious events. They were staged at the religious festival in honor of Dionysus. The priest of Dionysus sat in the place of honor. The citizens assembled on the hillside to watch the performances should be more properly called not spectators but participants, witnesses, if we like, of the sacred event, their presence as sacred as the drama enacted on stage. Gadamer reminds us of the "idea of sacral communion which lies behind the original Greek idea of theoria. Theoros means someone who takes part in a mission to a festival."[16] How then is a modern reader, coming to the play in silence and reading it in solitude, cut off from any connection with the communal religion in which the play was situated, to do justice to the play's religious meaning?

Sophocles' *Philoctetes* comes to us equipped with the customary divine armature of Greek tragedy. Six deities are given their parts in the play: the goddess Chrysē, Zeus, Asclepius, Heracles, the supreme Daimon whom Philoctetes invokes at the end of the play, and the sea nymphs whose blessing the chorus invokes as it brings the play to its close. Of the six, one makes his personal intervention at the end of the play to announce to Philoctetes that he is not entitled to a private decision at odds with his destiny but must bend his will to conform to the will of Zeus. In addition to its mythological characters, the play is replete with religious terms. We are given first the commonplace words to signify the deity: *theos* (god) and *theion* (divine). The play also employs a series of other terms charged with religious significance: *moira* (destiny), *tykhē* (fate), *atē* (curse), *hamartia* (wrongdoing), *dysphemia* (utterance of evil omen), *phthonos* (divine jealousy), *proskynesis* (act of veneration), *sebas* (reverence), *eusebeia* (act or attitude of religious reverence); *kēr* (demon); *nemesis* (divine retribution, used in the adjective *nemeseton*, likely to provoke nemesis); *araiou Dios* ("Zeus who hears men's curses," to borrow Webster's translation, here in the genitive case). To these should be added *kairos*, which in this play certainly signifies a sacred time.

Two important terms in this play pertaining to the religious sphere are *psychē* and *daimon*. The conventional translation for *psychē* as it is used in this play is "mind," though I prefer to translate it as "soul," a meaning justified both by the history of the word's development in the fifth century and by its context in this play. The word *daimon* is used in this play to signify both the great deity, otherwise unnamed, invoked by Philoctetes at the end of the play, who directs all human affairs to their proper end, and the lesser *daimon* who accompanies every individual human being from birth to death and directs and controls that person's fate. It is generally translated as "fate" and thought of as something impersonal, but "fate" is a weak translation for each individual's personal *daimon*, one of those indicators pointing to "ancient mystical tradition" of which Gadamer writes, in which individual human beings carry in their souls an image of the divine.[17]

The *Philoctetes* was performed at a religious festival, and it is throughout a religious play. The snake that had bitten Philoctetes on the foot is the guardian of a sacred shrine. The snakebite is punishment for a religious offense. Thus his wound is a sacred wound and he himself, to use the Latin word, becomes *sacer*, both sanctified and made taboo. Philoctetes' ten years of deprivation and pain on Lemnos are set within a divine timetable. Heracles' bow is a sacred object; Neoptolemus calls the bow and its arrows "the invincible weapons of the gods" (v. 198). Lemnos itself, an island dominated by an active volcano and with a mysterious history and fabled healing properties in its volcanic soil, is a sacred site. The very soil of the island, to which Philoctetes must prostrate himself and worship before his departure, is sacred. The cave that Philoctetes makes his home is also a sacred site, made sacred by his suffering. The bond created between Philoctetes and Neoptolemus is a sacred covenant. The prophecy given by the Trojan seer Helenus telling of Philoctetes' eventual healing and the glory awaiting him is a glimpse granted to a human into the nature of the divine order. Heracles, himself a god and sent to Philoctetes by an even greater god, intervenes personally to reorient human action on its divinely ordained trajectory.

Each of the religious terms in the play presents its own challenge to the modern reader, but beyond the vocabulary the play itself is so suffused with a religious presence that any commentary seeking to situate itself within the environment of the play is obliged to use a variety of terms that have been hallowed in religious tradition, concepts like hubris, repentance, forgiveness. The chorus brings the drama to a close with three verses that a casual reader might perceive as merely formulaic:

χωρῶμεν δὴ πάντες ἀολλεῖς,
Νύμφαις ἁλίαισιν ἐπευξάμενοι
νόστου σωτῆρας ἱκέσθαι.[18]
(vv. 1469–71)

[Let us go then, all of us assembled here,
But first praying to the Sea-nymphs
To arrive as the Saviors of our homecoming.]

The penultimate word in the Greek text of this play is σωτῆρας, "saviors." This is a drama of being *saved*. In this respect, it is very different in its concept from those works we customarily call tragedy, in which the protagonist is not saved but plunges blindly into his or her own doom. Gadamer writes of the Romantic movement that the "support for a new mythology . . . gives the artist and his task in the world the consciousness of a new consecration. He is something like a 'secular savior' (Immermann), whose creations are expected to achieve in a small way the propitiation of disaster, for which an unsaved world hopes."[19] Readers of Sophocles' *Philoctetes* who have some awareness of the disaster in which the Athenians were living at the time this play was produced must sense that Sophocles hoped to be a savior of this sort, remaking the old myth in such a way as persuade his fellow Athenians to change course and ward off the imminent catastrophe. The last word of this play is "to arrive," and the one other word in the final verse of the play is νόστου, genitive of the noun νόστος, which, as Douglas Frame has demonstrated from its use in the *Odyssey*, has a strong religious sense, signifying to return from the dead, to return to life.[20] "May the Nymphs come to us as the Saviors of our homecoming." So ends the play, when the savior who introduced himself to us at the beginning of the play has proved to be spurious and has been displaced in favor of the true saviors. The *Philoctetes* is a mystery play, and these last verses of the play are the choral benediction to announce that the service is concluded.

How is the modern interpreter to annotate an ancient text when, as Wallace Stevens puts it, Triton himself has long since vanished and even the language available to describe him can at best be only "faint, memorial gesturings"?

We face one hurdle in the mythology and religion of Sophocles' play and yet another when we turn from the religious language to the more secular language of the play, to such words as *sophos*, *logos*, *technē*, *physis*, *mythos*. These words may seem merely ordinary to us, but they were at the center of a worldview as deeply implicated in the conflict of the play as its religious orientation. The conflict staged among the characters in the play is the condensation of a debate that could be heard every day in Athens, in every corner of the agora and in the symposia hosted by the city's intellectuals. Underlying the conflict among the human characters is the deeper conflict about the meaning of *mythos*, as if Sophocles feared that the word were on the verge of becoming *myth* in our sense of the term, mere fable, a relic transmitted from a more superstitious age but now to be rejected as irrational and detrimental to human reason. Heracles by his appearance at the end of the play reinstates *mythos* as signifying a sacred text.

The first and simplest challenge is to find the adequate equivalent in our own language for a word frequently used in the play that has various, even contradictory, meanings. The word *sophos* is used numerous times in the play and in every instance is accompanied by controversy and passion. The word and its derivatives are under contention throughout the play. Neoptolemus and Odysseus are given a moment in the play when they become engaged in a debate on the meaning of the word, each of them possessing a horizon that the other does not and will not share. A translation must inevitably settle for one English equivalent or another, but each time we select one of the word's meanings in preference to the others, we shield ourselves, and if not ourselves then certainly our readers, from the vortex that swirls around that word in the original text. Between Odysseus and Neoptolemus is a war fought for the ownership of the word *sophos*: What is it to be *sophos* in fifth-century Athens? Who has the legitimate claim to be called *sophos*?

The greater challenge, however, is to catch the temper of the times in which the play was first produced. When Aeschylus produced his *Oresteia*, Athens was at the height of its power. The third play of that trilogy, the *Eumenides*, is suffused with the pride of an Athenian poet celebrating his city's finest political institution. When Sophocles composed his *Philoctetes*, however, Athens was a ruined city, even if its ruin was not yet as apparent to Sophocles as it is to us. Four documents testify to the high level of anxiety in Athens in the last years of the fifth century. Two are comedies—Aristophanes' *Frogs* and his *Clouds*. The third document saturated with political anxiety is this play, Sophocles' *Philoctetes*. The fourth is Plato's *Apology*. Socrates' trial was held only ten years after the *Philoctetes* was presented in the Theater of Dionysus, and we can assume that most of the citizens who served as jurors at his trial had only ten years earlier sat on the slopes of that other theater on the other side of the Acropolis as witnesses to the performance of *Philoctetes*. In the *Apology*, Plato has Socrates conjecture that Aristophanes' *Clouds* had a significant influence in generating an atmosphere of prejudice against Socrates. Who knows how the *Philoctetes* too might have contributed to that general suspicion and fear in Athens? We cannot help but be struck by the coincidence that the language used in the *Philoctetes* to indict Odysseus is exactly the language used by the Athenians to condemn Socrates and have him put to death.[21]

In a casual reading of this play, we might easily overlook the emotional vehemence of its vocabulary. We may respond to the characters' anxieties, but the words used to express those anxieties are so commonplace that we can scarcely respond to them with the same passion that Sophocles expected them to arouse in his Athenian audience. With Gorgias and Plato as our hermeneutic mentors, however, we can better comprehend that the dialectic of this play is built around some of the most inflammatory terms in the intellectual discourse of fifth-century Athens. When Odysseus discloses that the plot of the play hinges on the robbery of Philoctetes' soul, we cannot fail to see that the soul Sophocles has in mind is the soul of Athens itself.

Just as we learn to fuse the two horizons, the ancient and the modern, so in this play we recognize Sophocles doing likewise, both writing himself into the tradition and writing against the tradition. T. S. Eliot approaches what the Germans call *Bildung* in his own way when he reminds us that no poet stands alone but can be appreciated only through his relations to the long succession of dead poets. When a new work of art is created, it affects retroactively all the works preceding it. "The existing monuments," Eliot writes,

> form an ideal order among themselves, which is modified by the introduction of the new (the really new) work of art among them. The existing order is complete before the new work arrives; for order to persist after the supervention of novelty, the *whole* existing order must be, if ever so slightly, altered; and so the relations, proportions, values of each work of art toward the whole are readjusted; and this is conformity between the old and the new. Whoever has approved this idea of order . . . will not find it preposterous that the past should be altered by the present as much as the present is directed by the past.[22]

We humble readers are in that same line of succession that links one writer to his or her predecessors. When we come to Sophocles' play, our consciousness revises Sophocles' meanings as radically as Sophocles revised Euripides and Euripides revised Homer. Faced with this paradox, which is the primary hermeneutic principle, that to read a monument of the past is to both deconstruct it and reconstruct it into a form that was nonexistent before our reading, we must come to our task as translators and commentators with some humility and reverence but at the same time with a certain daring. To read a strong text like Sophocles' *Philoctetes,* we must be as bold as Sophocles yet not so bold as to forget that we are but spectators jotting down notes as we stand in the gallery contemplating a masterpiece now almost three thousand years in the making. To end as I began, with Gadamer: "Poetry, too, often becomes a test of what is true, in that the poem awakens a secret life in words that seem used and worn out, and tells us of ourselves."[23]

2

The Strong Poet

Tradition versus Originality

> He did not want to compose another *Don Quixote*—which would be easy—but *the Don Quixote*. It is unnecessary to add that his aim was never to produce a mechanical transcription of the original; he did not propose to copy it. His admirable ambition was to produce pages which would coincide—word for word and line for line—with those of Miguel de Cervantes.
>
> Jorge Luis Borges, "Pierre Menard, Author of Don Quixote"

> Aeschylus, who once was unfairly defeated, as Theophrastus said or Chamaelon in his work on pleasure, said that he had dedicated his tragedies to Time, knowing that it would bring him the appropriate honor.
>
> Athenaeus, *Deipnosophists* 8.39

Harold Bloom has meditated throughout his distinguished career on the theme of the strong poet and the strong reader. Many poets may have a measure of greatness by his assessment, but few qualify as a strong poet.[1] The poet who is destined to become strong is beset by two powerful but contradictory forces: by the anxiety of influence matched by an equally powerful solipsism. This poet must have the conviction, common no doubt in some degree to all people but acutely alive in the poetic temperament, that he is original, indeed, aboriginal, that with his birth the world was born.

But, alas, this poet is not aboriginal. He is a latecomer. Other poets have come and gone. Among these forebears is one, or one more than any other, whose genius was so aboriginal that it threatens to smother the ephebe's genius even before it shows its first leaf. Bloom envisions the ephebe poet discovering his true calling via a primal scene, an oedipal confrontation between the ephebe and his powerful ancestor. The ephebe begins as a good son, but at some point solipsism will have its way and the ephebe must slay his father, the murder in this case taking the form of a misreading of the great predecessor's poem. The ephebe must gather all his resources to shed the influence of his father and prove to himself that he is no latecomer but indeed the world's first poet. The ephebe, if he is to become a strong poet, must know that he and he alone is stout Cortés, that before his arrival no other Cortés, stout or otherwise, ever stood silent on that peak in Darien to gaze upon the Pacific. He must be the first to witness the world.

While Bloom may speak of the oedipal confrontation as the crisis necessary to determine forever the strong poet's vocation, he fastidiously steers clear of any banal application of Freudian analysis in the critical reading of one poet's influence on another. What writers might experience as anxiety is for Bloom usually the consequence rather than the cause. "The anxiety of influence," Bloom argues, "*comes out of* a complex act of strong misreading, a creative interpretation that I call 'poetic misprision.'"[2] As he further explains this dynamic relation between the newer and the later poet, whether the later writer internalizes the anxiety hardly matters: "the strong poem is the achieved anxiety."[3]

Bloom's thesis, though he derived it from his readings of modern British and American poets, provides insight into the nature of the competition among the tragic poets of ancient Athens. Little attention has been given to this aspect of Athenian tragedy. It has been treated as if it were merely incidental to the process by which the plays were selected for public performance, but surely the competition among the tragic poets must have been as fierce as in any other arena of public service. The poets must surely have felt the anxiety of influence at least as strongly as William Wordsworth felt the influence of John Milton.

Certainly Sophocles must be considered a strong poet if we apply the usual criteria. He achieved distinction at an early age, and his talent and his honors continued unbroken until he took his last breath in 406 BCE. As a youth, we are told, he danced naked and oiled around the victory trophy set up by the Athenians after the Battle of Salamis (480 BCE), accompanying himself on the lyre.[4] Later, in his career, when he produced his *Nausicaa*, he himself acted the part of Nausicaa (the winsome maiden whom Odysseus courts in the *Odyssey*), and his fine performance in playing ball (as Nausicaa does in Homer's story) went down in the history books.[5] As chorus boy, actor, composer, and choreographer, he enjoyed a career hardly matched by any other dramatist in the history of European letters. He competed year after year and won first prize time after time.

But is prodigious talent a sufficient criterion for Sophocles to earn the right to be called a strong poet in Bloom's terms? Can we talk of the contrary pressures of the tradition and his own originality as we might deduce them in the British Romantic poets, in Shelley, Keats, Wordsworth? Tradition so dominates ancient Greek poetry that even to broach the idea of creative anxiety seems to indulge in pointless anachronism. The anxiety is unmistakable in the Hellenistic poet Theocritus, who in his *Idyll* 16, addressed to Hieron II, tyrant of Syracuse, laments the poetic vacuum of his own day, when patrons could brush off poets with "Homer is enough for us."[6] But can we detect anything like this Alexandrian anxiety in Greek poetry at its zenith, when the poet was revered as a prophet and a sage?

Certainly Pindar's glorious epinician poems are fraught with the anxiety of competition, both the anxiety of the young athlete competing so desperately for his elusive victory and the poet's own anxiety as the man commissioned to memorialize in sublime poetry the victor's great moment of triumph. But Pindar casts his anxiety as a supreme confidence in his own genius, which allows him to scoff at his strongest rivals as if they were but vulgar crows cawing at the lordly eagle. His anxiety passes without much notice since it is bundled with the anxiety of the athlete, and it is so often expressed that it passes for a mere trope: as with athletes, so with poets; we all compete, each in our own field.

In Plato we discern a more conspicuous example of an anxiety of influence so intense that it puts many modern readers into a state of amazement. The father whom Plato sets out to kill at the crossroads was the fountainhead of the whole Greek poetry tradition, Homer himself. In several places in the *Republic*, Plato mounts an attack on the tragic poets as his great opponents, but his greatest hostility is directed against Homer, whom he classifies as "the most tragic" of the poets. Homer was the source of myth, and myth was the foundation of religion. The *Iliad* and the *Odyssey*, Gregory Nagy writes, "manage to incorporate and orchestrate something of practically everything that was once thought worth preserving from the Heroic Age."[7] Eric Havelock was the first scholar to understand Plato's animosity as deriving from the anxiety of influence.[8] Analyzing the revolutionary impact of literacy in classical Greece, he came to see that Homer, as the supreme poet of the oral culture, exerted a deeply hypnotic effect on thought and belief in classical Greece. Philosophy, or rather discursive reason as it was practiced by Socrates in fifth-century Athens, was a mode of thought in direct competition with the tribal knowledge incorporated in the epic. This must be the most extreme case of the anxiety of influence ever experienced in the history of Western literature.

At first glance we might detect no trace of this Platonic anxiety in Sophocles. Where Plato made Homer his archenemy, Sophocles seems to have done the opposite, placing Homer on a pedestal such as can hardly be comprehended today. Homer, or more loosely the whole epic tradition, was his muse. Sophocles' dependency on Homer was so egregious that it would be considered a major defect in a modern dramatist. A modern playwright who took every plot and character from Shakespeare would win no plaudits from the Critics' Circle today.

Borges's story "Pierre Menard, Author of *Don Quixote*" is a witty caricature of the anxiety of influence in its most acute state. His Pierre Menard is a strong reader. None could be stronger. He is the ideal reader whom every author hopes will read the author's words exactly as the author wrote them without introducing what Bloom calls his own "poetic misprision." Monsieur Menard sets out to rewrite that peerless novel, Cervantes's *Don Quixote,* not as some late copyist, but exactly as Cervantes wrote it, yet without impersonating Cervantes. He must remain himself, Pierre Menard, a man of his own time with his own unique sensibilities. Why would anyone undertake such a Herculean task? We might understand a Spaniard drawn to this challenge, the narrator says, but why a French poet from Nîmes, a symbolist, "essentially devoted to Poe, who engendered Baudelaire, who engendered Mallarmé, who engendered Valéry, who engendered Edmond Teste"?[9]

The joke here is that our Monsieur Menard must rewrite *Don Quixote* for the very reason that those names just listed—Poe, Baudelaire, Mallarmé, Valéry, Edmund Teste, each name engendering the next—have intervened between Cervantes and himself. Cervantes's *Don Quixote,* Monsieur Menard argues in defense of his project, "is an accidental book, *Don Quixote* is unnecessary. . . . To compose *Don Quixote* at the beginning of the seventeenth century was a reasonable, necessary and perhaps inevitable undertaking; at the beginning of the twentieth century, it is almost impossible."[10] Monsieur Menard's ambition is nothing less than to improve upon, indeed replace, the original genius with his own genius, more brilliant and certainly more original than the original.

The narrator of the story claims that M. Menard's project is superior to Cervantes's accomplishment since it issues from the thoroughly modern mind of a French poet steeped in the influence of the French symbolists. In such a competition the modernist must emerge surely as distinctively superior to a seventeenth-century novelist who did not have the benefits of a course in French symbolist poetry. Pierre Menard overcomes the most formidable obstacles to produce a work absolutely original yet marked by absolute fidelity to the original. Alas, the challenge is so enormous that M. Menard manages to produce only a few short fragments of what would have been the greatest literary achievement of all time. In those fragments, however, we see first that M. Menard has indeed written a new *Don Quixote* exactly as it was first written but, oh, what a great misreading!

Borges's Pierre Menard may be far removed from Sophocles, yet if we study even in a single play like the *Philoctetes* the extent and manner of its Homeric borrowing, we sense under the imitation an obsession, a spirit similar to M. Menard's need to be absolutely true both to the original text and to his own genius at the same time. To grasp the full implication of this burden that weighed on Sophocles, we need to frame our investigation within the broader agonistic spirit of classical Greece. The Greeks were driven by the acute anxiety of competition.[11] On the battlefield warriors fought to kill or be killed, but this battle also carried over into competition with each other, to be "always the best," as the hero Peleus admonishes his son Achilles in the *Iliad*, when sending his son off to war at Troy. The *Iliad* gives the tragic consequences of such intramural competition, when the two antagonists, Agamemnon and Achilles, are willing to see their own armies destroyed to satisfy their injured honor. War, whether against foreign powers or between two neighboring Greek cities, was an almost continuous way of life in the whole historical period. The competitive virtues were necessary, or thought to be necessary, for survival. Behind the competitive spirit, Nietzsche writes, "we immediately look into that pre-Homeric abyss of a terrifying savagery of hatred and the lust to annihilate."[12]

In peace the competition shifted to other grounds, notably to the athletic festivals. Behind their idealizations, these contests were often brutal affairs, which could be degrading to the spirit of the young athletes desperate for victory. In the greatest athletic competitions there was no second or third prize. There was only the winner, radiant in his brief moment as victor; all the other competitors were losers, shamed by their defeat. The same agonistic spirit reached into every aspect of poetic and musical performances: "The Greek knows the artist only as engaged in a personal fight."[13] The Theater of Dionysus in Athens was but one more field for such competition, which affected every aspect of the dramatic performances and every person connected with the events. We would be surprised if this civic institution were any less competitive than any other sphere of Athenian political and cultural life, especially since the very idea of tragedy was competition to the death. P. E. Easterling has written of how a star system grew up around the actors, and Simon Goldhill has noted that when a man was selected to serve as the *chorēgos* to fund one of the performances, this gave him a splendid opportunity for self-promotion.[14] Paul Cartledge observes that the competition at the dramatic festivals of the Dionysia and the Lenaea, among playwrights, actors, and *chorēgoi*, and within the plays themselves, "corresponded exactly to the one-off, everything-at-stake character of a Greek pitched battle by land or sea."[15]

In 449 BCE a ceremony called the *proagon* was instituted, a spectacle that opened each year's festival, when the poets and their actors were presented to the entire assembled crowd. In 416 BCE the poet Agathon won the first prize in that year's dramatic competition, and Plato's *Symposium* purports to record the conversations held at the symposium given that night by Agathon himself to celebrate his victory. In this dialogue Socrates has high praise for Agathon's bearing at the *proagon* held on the previous day, complimenting him for his courage when he mounted a platform to face a crowd of some thirty thousand spectators without the least trace of fear.[16] Goldhill describes the ceremony as a "nerve-wracking experience."[17] Perhaps it was not nerve-wracking for Agathon, whom Socrates praises for his wisdom, which was resplendent on that occasion. But certainly it must have been daunting for any poet to stand before that vast crowd about to render its judgment on the plays in which the poet had invested his reputation and all his creative energy for the past several weeks or even months.[18]

Before the poet was presented to the theater at the *proagon*, his play had already been through a twofold competition. First, it was submitted to an elected city official, the eponymous archon, who would choose the plays to be produced at the next dramatic festival. Aspiring poets would submit a trilogy on a tragic theme. At some point a fourth play was required, the so-called satyr play, which was a burlesque treatment of some aspect of the serious themes of the tragedies that would precede it in performance. The tetralogies that were selected by the archon for performance were then funded by a system of taxation called *leitourgia* (English derivative, "liturgy"), in which a wealthy citizen, called the *chorēgos*, was selected and assessed a contribution to support an individual playwright's performances. No doubt these benefactors had their own personal agendas, which they might want to see addressed in performances funded at their expense. Then, in the performance itself, the plays were judged a second time, now by a group of anonymous citizens, selected in an elaborate system of voting, who would represent all ten tribes of Attica. At the end of a winnowing process, from the ten citizens five were selected by lot to judge the plays and award the prizes for first, second, and third place in the year's competition. First prize was a generous monetary compensation. A successful tragic poet with ambition and talent might, like a victorious athlete, achieve an almost godlike status in Athens. But who today can recite the countless names of those ambitious poets who failed even to have their plays accepted by the deciding archon? The evidence suggests that Sophocles managed the stress of these ordeals with considerable panache. He emerged again and again as the winner in the competitions in the Theater of Dionysus (some twenty-four times we are told), and so high was his standing among his fellow Athenians that they declared him a hero after his death, gave him a hero's title, *Dexios* (for receiving Asclepius into his own home at the time when the cult of Asclepius was introduced into Athens), and provided him with a hero' cult. Nothing in the history of the British or American theater is remotely comparable to this achievement. What stage director can list twenty Tony Awards for productions on the New York stage? What movie director can boast of twenty Academy Awards for best movie of the year?

The tragic poets competed against their own contemporaries, but they were also competing with their predecessors who might have treated the same mythical material in earlier years. In the case of the three great tragic poets—Aeschylus, Sophocles, and Euripides—their lives spanned the whole of the fifth century, and for some years in the midcentury the lives and careers of all three overlapped. In some years Sophocles would have competed with Aeschylus, when Aeschylus was the grand old master and Sophocles an ephebe still struggling to win his first crowns. We might imagine three William Shakespeares (or four, if we include Aristophanes) alive in sixteenth-century London and all crowding the Globe Theater at the same time. Sophocles, we are told, won first prize in his very first competition, in 468 BCE, with Aeschylus coming in second. We wonder who felt the greater anxiety at the voting that year, Aeschylus, then in his fifties and at the peak of his career, or Sophocles making his debut as a dramaturge at the age of twenty-seven.

Who can say how many times Sophocles competed with Aeschylus? The records are sketchy, with great gaps at various points. Certainly he would have competed frequently with Euripides, who was closer in age, since their artistic careers ran parallel for many years. The competition among these three poets took a strange turn when Aeschylus died in 456 BCE. So high was the status that Aeschylus enjoyed in Athens during his life that a decree was passed after his death that his plays alone could be performed posthumously. This presented a peculiar challenge to the living poets, Sophocles and Euripides among others, that in any given year they might be submitting to the archon works that might be in direct competition with some highly successful play of the great dead poet. For some fifty years after the death of Aeschylus, Sophocles might be competing against him as if he were still a living contemporary. It would be as if plays could be produced in seventeenth-century London only if selected by a prominent member of Parliament, and an ambitious neophyte, rising into his career thirty years after Shakespeare's death, might have to submit his *King Lear* in the same year that some stage director had decided to reenter Shakespeare's highly successful *King Lear*.

Since no tragedies were produced in the Theater of Dionysus except through this dire process of competition, with the poets drawing on the same sourcebook for their plots, the imperative was inevitably to be recognized as traditional and original at the same time. In the case of Sophocles' *Philoctetes,* the challenge was exacerbated because when he produced his play in 409 BCE, two great masters, Aeschylus and Euripides, had already produced their versions of the same story. Sophocles may have seen both productions—Aeschylus's play produced in the 470s and Euripides' play in the 430s, when Sophocles would have been in his fifties and an accomplished dramatist himself. Many of the spectators who witnessed Sophocles' *Philoctetes* in 409 BCE would have seen Euripides' version produced twenty years earlier, and some no doubt had memories that went back to Aeschylus's production forty years before.

One aspect of the anxiety influencing the dramatists of the fifth-century was that they could not, indeed dared not, invent a new plot. It was tried once as far as we know, but it was not an experiment that gained traction in ancient Athens. Agathon, the talented, handsome poet whose victory in the tragic festival of 416 BCE is celebrated in Plato's *Symposium*, produced a play called *Anthos* or *Antheus* ("Blossom" or "Flower").[19] In his discussion of plot (*mythos*) in tragedy, Aristotle argues that a plot should meet our criteria for plausibility and probability. Events that have not happened may be plausible, but their possibility remains moot. An event that has occurred, however, meets both criteria. This is his defense of the practice of using what we today call "myth." He admits that a poet could construct an entirely new plot that would meet our criteria for both the plausible and the probable, and gives as his example Agathon's *Anthos*, a play in which no name is familiar, whether of event, place, or person, "yet it gives no less pleasure for that."[20] History has not been kind to Agathon. Were it not for his appearance in Plato's *Symposium* and his florid speech given that evening on the beauty of Eros, he would have faded into the fog of time. In the *Symposium*, he is presented as a facile orator, "poetic" in a superficial and sentimental way. His *Anthos*, his first victory as a playwright, might have had some of the same characteristics. We cannot help but suspect that Agathon, a latecomer to a scene that had already witnessed its greatest triumphs, was experimenting with pouring new wine into old vessels, but without much success.

Drawing on factual history, history as we understand it, was tried a few times in the early years of tragedy, but it too was an experiment that soon burned out. Aeschylus's *Persians*, produced in 472 BCE, took as its subject the Athenian victory over the Persian fleet at the Battle of Salamis in 480 BCE. This was a decisive victory for the mainland Greeks and a disaster for Xerxes. The king, enthroned on the heights of Salamis to watch his great fleet engage with the Athenians, saw his own fleet destroyed, and with its destruction went all serious ambition to conquer Hellas. Xerxes himself survived the day and limped back to Susa in disgrace. Here indeed was a story made for tragedy. It had everything: spectacle, emotions, a parable with a moral, and it was both plausible and probable. Aeschylus has made Xerxes his protagonist (although Xerxes does not appear until very late in the play and does not have much to say except dire lamentation), and he has set the scene in Susa, the Persian capital, where Atossa, the queen mother, and the whole court await news of the expected victory. But the survivors straggle home in pitiful condition, with a story not of conquest but of humiliating defeat. This was the very paradigm of the tragic plot, the downfall of a great man through hubris and the inevitable nemesis. Such a performance would be for the Athenians a most comforting affirmation of their own virtue and of their gods' favor. But the play was set in a foreign land with a foreign cast of characters. How often could a play focused on the tragic fall of the king of Persia or of some Egyptian pharaoh win the critics' approval in the Athenian theater?

Yet to reverse the plot to highlight an Athenian disaster was not an acceptable alternative. Phrynichus tried this experiment a few years before Aeschylus celebrated the downfall of King Xerxes. He took as his plot the fall of Miletus, a major Greek emporium on the coast of Anatolia. The incident was, as in Aeschylus's *Persians*, part of the continuing conflict between the Persian Empire and the city-states of Greece in the early fifth century. A great sea battle was fought between the Persians and an alliance of Greek city-states offshore from Miletus, at Lade Island in 494 BCE. The Greeks suffered a devastating defeat. Their fleet was mostly sent to the bottom of the sea; Miletus was destroyed, with most of the male citizens killed and the women and children sold as slaves. Phrynichus produced his *Capture of Miletus* very shortly after the defeat, perhaps in the following year (493 BCE).

Phrynichus made the Greek defeat the subject of his tragedy. It was a mistake. The play itself was a disaster. The Athenians, many of whom would have had family and friends in Miletus, were greatly agitated and took the damage to their emotions as a personal affront. The function of tragedy is indeed to arouse the emotions, but this was tragedy pressing on a raw nerve. "The audience fell into tears," Herodotus reports, "and fined the dramatist 1000 drachmas for having recalled to their memory their own personal disaster, and they ordered that no one at any time should ever use this drama again."[21] Some years later (476 BCE), Phrynichus made his amends by taking the opposite approach in a play called *Phoenissae* ("The Phoenicians"). It, like Aeschylus's *Persians*, celebrated the defeat of the Persians at the Battle of Salamis, and for this play Phrynichus won the prize. Clearly, the Athenian audience enjoyed having its emotions roiled provided the drama celebrated Athenian courage and pointed the finger of accusation at Persian hubris. But how many foreign disasters could the dramatists find that could celebrate the pathos of some majestic hero *with whom the audience could identify*?

The fine levied against Phrynichus for selecting as his theme a tragedy that directly impinged on the Athenian losses at Miletus was an expensive lesson for aspiring poets. Emotional turmoil is essential to tragedy, but the poet must work his emotional triggers with caution.

The tragic poets, as they were beginning to lay out their own territory somewhere in that space between epic and lyric, came to see that their dramas would play better when the emotions were distanced in the collective unconscious, which we call myth. "A sound tradition had saved Tragedy from journalism," J. T. Sheppard declares with a scholar's approval for the eternal over the ephemeral.[22]

Here was the dramatist's straitjacket. The plot (*mythos*), as Aristotle insisted, is the essential element of tragedy. If it is to arouse strong emotions, it must be emotionally compelling, yet contemporary events were to be avoided since they might incite emotions that would throw the whole theater into turmoil and the benefits of catharsis would be lost. The Athenians audiences must have felt a certain kind of aesthetic comfort when they took their seats and could expect to have their emotions stimulated by some deadly contest in the myths of the distant past.

All roads lead back to Homer. The mythical characters presented in the tragedies were as persons of flesh and blood in the fifth-century Greek consciousness. First, they were assumed to have once been living persons, many of them considered to be the founders of various Greek cities or to be the ancestors of the first families of Greece in the historical period. Epic poetry had breathed into these putatively historical persons a second life through what Plato understood as the witchcraft of mimesis, which made the long dead and the imaginary come to life again. Then these heroes were given a third life in the cult sites that sprang up throughout the Greek cities in the Archaic period, where they were worshipped in annual festivals, immortalized now and endowed by their worshippers with powers to bring blessings to the community. In the tragedies presented in Athens at the Theater of Dionysus, these persons of myth and cult assumed a fourth existence, with their stories reactivated and played out on the stage before a huge audience hungering for the kind of reality that only mimesis could provide.

This was a peculiar bondage to the distant past. The equivalent today would be the necessity imposed on a modern British playwright to find every subject in some marginal characters taken from Shakespeare or from the Arthurian cycle. In like fashion, Arthur Miller, to find his Willy Loman, would have to comb through sacred Scripture for a story from ancient Judaea that might suggest Brooklyn of the 1950s. We read the ancient dramatists hardly aware of the challenge imposed on the poets by the anachronism that the plot must be antique, the manners of the characters obsolete, yet the play itself should be wholly of its own time. This was exactly M. Menard's dilemma.

We circle back to Homer again. Since tragedy was a civic institution, the pressure on the dramatist was enormous, exerted not only by the public at large but more pointedly by the archon who made the selection for each year's performances, by the *chorēgos* whose largesse funded the performances, and by the anonymous judges from the various tribes who awarded the prizes. If the dramatists were competing with one another, with a complex system of citizens adjudicating their ideas and their productions, at the heart of the competition was Homer. Though they competed year after year against one another, their greatest agon was with their father, Homer himself. To earn the coveted first prize, Sophocles must copy Homer but not be a copyist. The rhapsodes were the copyists, reciting the Homeric poems with verbatim fidelity to the authorized text. But Sophocles was not a reciter; he was in his time and place a priest and a sage. He must be the interpreter, apparently speaking for Homer but in fact speaking to us through Homer. The result is that in his *Philoctetes* he did what no one had done before, neither his two rivals in the fifth-century theater, Aeschylus and Euripides, nor even the master, Homer himself.

Thanks to the generous if capricious hand of Providence, we possess a document from antiquity that illuminates the issues of tradition and originality with respect to the three great dramatic poets and their treatments of the Philoctetes myth. We could wish for more incandescence. This light is fitful at best, yet in the abyss of time even the fitful gleam can be a miracle. Dio Chrysostom, may his name live forever, was a Greek from Bithynia (Bursa in modern-day Turkey), living in the first century CE, when Bithynia was a province at the outer reaches of the Roman Empire. He was a sophist and rhetorician who achieved high status in Rome, but for some political intrigue in 82 CE was banished by the emperor Domitian both from Rome and even from his own home province.[23] Thus deprived of home and civilization, Dio wandered for years like some Eastern gymnosophist at the very fringe of the empire, in the Balkans and Asia, and in his exile discovered a new career for himself, like many a vagrant before and after, as a sage. Eventually the decree of his banishment was lifted by the emperor Nerva, and Dio flourished again under the emperor Trajan. He became a writer and lecturer. He was given the name Chrysostomos, "Gold Mouth," in recognition of his great oratorical abilities.

Dio had in his personal library in Prusa three Philoctetes plays, one by each of the three great dramatists. One morning, feeling poorly, Dio, after taking a few turns around the hippodrome in his carriage, decided to spend the rest of the day reading all three plays at one sitting. He then wrote an essay comparing the three plays.[24] No one would call this essay a *strong* reading. Nevertheless, it is a gold mine. Rhetoricians before Dio had articulated their theories of literature, but Dio's essay is not theory. It is simply an educated man's personal reading of the same theme dramatized by the three greatest poets of ancient tragedy. Since the Philoctetes plays by Aeschylus and Euripides are no longer extant, Dio's essay has a double value for us. It allows us to see how each dramatist took a simple story and shaped it into a drama for the Athenian stage and also helps us to trace the means by which each of the poets made his own contribution to the story. Dio's brief essay intimates how the three poets managed the tensions of their bondage to Homer and the competition among themselves.

The Philoctetes myth comes to us from Homer, through one brief reference in the *Iliad* and two even briefer allusions in the *Odyssey*, with further details supplied from other poets of the epic tradition. In the Homeric poems Philoctetes is a marginal figure, but Aeschylus was the first to discern in his story the potential for drama. Philoctetes, wounded by a snakebite, sequestered on the island of Lemnos for ten years, then brought back to Troy and, so the story went, killing Paris with a single arrow—now there was a theme for tragedy! But Aeschylus found his drama in the least likely place, on the island of Lemnos, in the solitary heart and soul of Philoctetes. The myth in the tradition speaks of no great conflict at Lemnos when Diomedes was sent out to fetch Philoctetes to Troy, but Aeschylus saw a situation charged with dramatic tension. The fall of Troy now depended on the Greeks' ability to restore friendly relations with an alienated man whom they had rudely cast out from their midst ten years earlier. Aeschylus called his tragedies fillets taken from Homer's great dinners, and his *Philoctetes* is a good example of what he meant.[25] Aeschylus saw in this character, barely visible in the epic, the makings of a tragic protagonist, brought to a fateful decision: whether he was to hold fast to his sense of personal injury at his mistreatment or could be persuaded to forego his resentment and join his comrades at Troy to complete their mission.

Aeschylus, finding his story as hardly more than a line item in the Homeric tradition, must develop it and shape it in such a way as to make it his own, while doing nothing to undercut Homer's authority. His one innovation is to have Odysseus dispatched by the Greeks at Troy as their ambassador to negotiate with Philoctetes on Lemnos. This seemingly minor alteration in the traditional plot was to have a lasting influence on the Philoctetes story. In the traditional story, the prophecy extracted from the Trojan seer Helenus had stated that Greek victory depended on the Greeks bringing two men to Troy: Neoptolemus, the son of Achilles, from Skyros in Greece; and Philoctetes from Lemnos. Odysseus is sent to Skyros and Diomedes to Lemnos, and each accomplishes the mission assigned to him. Aeschylus lifts Odysseus from the Skyros section of the prophecy and inserts him into the Lemnos episode, and Diomedes is quietly dropped from the story. If the Lemnos episode were to be transformed into drama, it needed character. Diomedes, as we see him in the *Iliad*, is a good soldier but without much character. On the other hand, what Homeric hero is more endowed with character than Odysseus? Homer's Odysseus is also, among his many gifts, a *speaker*. This feature alone gives Aeschylus a sound reason for tampering with the original plot. Tragedy called for speakers, and Diomedes is no speaker. But replace him with Odysseus and we have at once the necessary speaker and in consequence the essentials for drama, provided we endow Philoctetes with an opposing character. The stage is set: an angry cripple pitted against the most brilliant speaker in all of Hellas, the mission being to persuade the crippled outcast to forego his hatred and to let bygones be bygones for the higher good of the whole.

Aeschylus's alteration of the Homeric story is completely Homeric. Who is more Homeric than Odysseus with his rhetorical skills? Any Athenian watching Aeschylus's play as it was performed in the 470s would recall one of the best-known scenes of the *Iliad*, in book 9, when Odysseus is sent to enlist the angry Achilles back into the Greek cause. We cannot say much about the character that Aeschylus gives to Philoctetes, but with Odysseus made the antagonist in his play, we can infer that his Philoctetes must have been endowed with some of the lineaments of Homer's angry Achilles. To insert Odysseus into the plot and make Philoctetes a second Achilles—this is a creative rereading of the tradition. Even as Aeschylus modifies the Homeric story, he makes it yet more Homeric; his *Philoctetes* is now an adaptation of the great agon between Odysseus and Achilles in book 9 of the *Iliad*.

Some forty years later Euripides presented his version of the story on the Athenian stage. What could he to do improve on Homer and Aeschylus? He follows Aeschylus's precedent in keeping Odysseus in the story. To drop Odysseus would be unthinkable once Aeschylus had introduced him into the plot. But he reverts back to the old plot by adding Diomedes again, as Odysseus's partner. Whatever his reason for reinserting Diomedes into the plot, this device too is thoroughly Homeric. Diomedes had been the Greek delegate to Lemnos in the original myth. Furthermore, Odysseus and Diomedes are often associated in the epic tradition as in the night adventure of the *Iliad*, book 10. The plot still needed something more, however, if it was to bear Euripides' signature. His invention is to have Odysseus, when pleading the Greek cause to Philoctetes, claim that the Trojans, having learned of his intentions, are sending a delegation of their own to intercept his mission and win Philoctetes to their cause. No doubt Euripides adds this amusing device to the plot to heighten the tension of the negotiations; at the same time it allows him to give voice to the ideology of the virtues of Hellenism over barbarism as he does in several other plays.[26] Dio writes of Euripides' play that it was more "political" (*politikos*), and surely this topic—Greece versus Troy—would have contributed significantly to the political debate of the play. We can assume that Euripides, to aggravate the conflict, must also have made Philoctetes even more intransigent than he had been in Aeschylus. Philoctetes must have been rebarbative in Aeschylus or there would have been no conflict, but Euripides makes him so hostile that Odysseus can appear before Philoctetes only in disguise, which Euripides attributes to Athena's gracious intervention.

When Sophocles came to compose his *Philoctetes*, he had three contenders in his sights—first the two tragic poets of his own time, Aeschylus and Euripides, but beyond them the all-powerful Homer, a distant planet to be sure, but still more influential than any other. How could Sophocles persuade the archon who would decide the play's future that he had something new to say on this already well-worked theme? We might agree that at this point Aeschylus and Euripides had given life to Philoctetes such as he had never enjoyed in Homer. He was no longer merely a name on the margin of epic but truly a *character*. But Sophocles, to succeed, must go one step further. His *Philoctetes* of course must be relevant to the crisis of its day, in the last years of the fifth century, yet like the plays of his predecessors, it too must have Homer's signature on the approval line. Sophocles would compete for two crowns, the first being the prize awarded by the judges at both the beginning and the end of the contest, and the second being the wreath he must win from Homer's ghost to mark him as Homer's truest interpreter. Sophocles managed these conflicting aims with outstanding success. He was, if we may say so, more Homeric than Aeschylus, more Homeric than Euripides, yet distinctively more original than either of them. When

Dio placed the three Philoctetes plays side by side, he could not decide which dramatist deserved the prize. But we suspect that Sophocles' innovations ensured that his play was preserved while those of his competitors eventually fell into obscurity. Sophocles had created a new kind of drama. Whatever the issues raised by the other two dramatists, Sophocles took them all to a deeper level and no doubt developed others that were barely glimpsed by Aeschylus or Euripides.

Following the now inviolate precedent, Sophocles keeps Odysseus as a main character in the plot. He also follows Aeschylus in removing Diomedes altogether—unlucky Diomedes, destined to remain always peripheral to the story once Aeschylus had replaced him with Odysseus. But in Diomedes' place, Sophocles adds an altogether new character, Neoptolemus, son of Achilles. This was a brilliant move and at a single stroke made Sophocles the master of the story forever after. Sophocles is credited with adding the third actor to ancient Greek tragedy (that is, allowing for three speaking parts on stage simultaneously), and here we see that invention put to use with magnificent effect. Sophocles gives his Odysseus the ethos that the other dramatists had given him, so we infer, but he introduces a strange paradox. His Odysseus is recognizable as the Homeric Odysseus, while at the same time he is an Odysseus as never yet seen on stage. The plot of this play requires that Odysseus, for all his oratorical skills, be a failure, and precisely in the field of oratory. He must be a failed rhetorician. To achieve this effect, Sophocles has invested the ethos of Odysseus with such a horde of negative traits that he forfeits any possibility of winning the victory in this agon.[27] Odysseus does not have the capacity to overpower Philoctetes physically. His only chance of success is through rhetoric, yet this very hope is blighted because of his character. In Homer, Odysseus is clever, charming, duplicitous, but such ambivalent attributes do not seriously undermine his status as a hero. It is the opposite here. As Odysseus is rewritten for this role, so Philoctetes must be rewritten too. Sophocles has made his protagonist a man with two obsessions: one, his necessary preoccupation with his own disease; the other, his moral loathing for Odysseus. No detail, no incident from the tradition is omitted if it can be used to heighten Philoctetes' loathing for this paradigm of depravity. In making Odysseus morally repulsive, Sophocles invents his necessary motive for the third actor, introducing Neoptolemus into the plot to do what Odysseus cannot achieve in his own person.

With Philoctetes seething with moral indignation at the character of Odysseus, a personal meeting of the two men is out of the question. In the plays of Sophocles' two predecessors, Odysseus, however odious he may have been, is still the principal negotiator for the Greeks. In this play he must stay out of sight altogether. He must manipulate rather than act. His must be action at a distance. Thus from the very first moment of the play a strange oscillation is introduced into the plot. The most highly skilled Greek diplomat, sent out on a desperate mission calling for the most delicate diplomacy, with Mycenaean hegemony hanging in the balance, can be successful in his diplomacy only if he can find someone else to speak for him. He must act and not act at the same time, appear but not appear, be overwhelmingly present in his absence and absent in his presence. He is the artistic director and at the same time the director manqué, the consummate actor but as an actor a failure. Odysseus is given only one action in the play, to persuade Neoptolemus to put aside his more noble ethos and to achieve an end that Odysseus cannot achieve in his own person. This one act, though momentous for the play as a whole, is also Odysseus's great failure. He is also given only one brief appearance on stage, in the exodos, when he demands that Neoptolemus hand over the bow to him and threatens to carry off Philoctetes by force. Here too he is a failure. This Odysseus is a failure both as a doer of deeds and as a speaker of words.[28]

While Sophocles' addition of Neoptolemus to the plot is his most radical innovation, yet even here we detect Homer's influence. Neoptolemus was already in the traditional story, as the other person named in the prophecy given by Helenus; thus Philoctetes and Neoptolemus are linked in the tradition from the beginning. In fact, with Achilles dead, three men were needed to bring the Trojan War to its end: Odysseus, Philoctetes, and Neoptolemus, the three men who form the triumvirate of this play. The dramatic value of having the son of Achilles teamed with Odysseus on this delicate mission is obvious: Achilles and Odysseus are the two most significant Greek characters in the Homeric epics. But Sophocles takes invention much further. In all three Philoctetes plays, Odysseus must be persona non grata if the play is to have its serious agon. Each dramatist found his own solution to this problem. In Aeschylus, Philoctetes fails to recognize Odysseus, and Dio accepts this as plausible, given the effect that the ten years of pain and solitude might have had on his perceptions. Euripides, more sensitive to the issue of plausibility, resorts to a bare-faced Homerism in having Athena disguise Odysseus so that when he meets Philoctetes, while he must be recognizably a Greek, hence odious to be sure, he would be less odious than he would have been had his true identity been discovered.

Sophocles' strategy is the most ingenious. His Odysseus too must have his disguise, as in Euripides' play, but in this case *Neoptolemus is his disguise*. Scholars have noted the originality of using Neoptolemus in this plot but have not recognized that his raison d'être in this plot depends entirely on the ethos given to Odysseus. This is the three-actor principle taken to a new level of complexity, which by contrast makes Euripides' stratagem to have Odysseus disguised by Athena and inventing a story of a Trojan delegation pressing hot on his heels seem merely jejune.

Sophocles makes another deviation from the customary practice in having his chorus composed of sailors from Neoptolemus's ship. The tragic chorus was usually made up of members of the protagonist's community, a male chorus for a male protagonist, a female chorus for a female protagonist (as in Euripides' *Medea*). Philoctetes' solitary state presents a conundrum. As the protagonist, he needs his chorus, but how can he have his chorus yet be cut off from human society? Who is his community? The other two dramatists found simplistic solutions to this problem. Each has his chorus made up of Lemnian men, since Philoctetes was a resident of Lemnos in a manner of speaking. Dio informs us that Aeschylus has his chorus of Lemnians appear as needed without any excuse or explanation. Euripides, dressing up this implausibility with a cosmetic facade, has his Lemnians make excuses for staying away from Philoctetes for the past ten years.

Sophocles, however, has made the island uninhabited, hence no Lemnian residents exist to become the chorus of his play. Yet this play too must have its chorus if it is to earn a pass from the eponymous archon. The solution: with Neoptolemus added to the plot, the chorus can be transferred to him, composed now of the Myrmidons whom he would have inherited from his dead father, Achilles, and sailing under his command. This is a more reasonable strategy than having a chorus of Lemnian men who have ignored Philoctetes until Odysseus arrives from Troy, but it goes beyond realism and like Sophocles' other adaptations has far-reaching consequences. For Neoptolemus to be given a chorus, while Philoctetes is deprived of his, is to give Neoptolemus some of the attributes of the protagonist. This choice creates a second oscillation in the play. Who is the protagonist, Philoctetes or Neoptolemus? The play moves its center of attention from one to the other, and the chorus moves too with the shifting tides in the dramatic situation. At the beginning of the play the chorus is submissive to Neoptolemus's will, but in its final ode, when the chorus has been left on stage with

Philoctetes while Odysseus and Neoptolemus return to their ship, it becomes Philoctetes' community. Sophocles satisfied the customary requirements but in a completely new way.

Sophocles makes one other significant adaptation in the story. Lemnos in historical times was an inhabited island, and we can assume that when Odysseus put Philoctetes ashore on the island, it was not as ruthless an act as Sophocles has made it. Philoctetes could have survived with some rudimentary assistance from the local population. Both Aeschylus and Euripides treat the island as inhabited, even if the inhabitants have done little to alleviate Philoctetes' condition, but Sophocles drastically intensifies the protagonist's loneliness by making the island both devoid of any other human inhabitant and fiercely hostile to human habitation. Is any other hero in ancient Greek tragedy made so *existential*?

Peter Rose has argued that in making this change Sophocles uses the play to explore the ideas of social evolution that were being articulated by the fifth-century sophists.[29] Philoctetes is presented as Homo sapiens living at the lowest level of human culture, using stones to make fire, knowing nothing of agriculture, a hunter using only the most primitive tools, with no human company to share his labor or to work together for the common good. The political parable of the play, as Rose sees it, is the need for a human society working as a whole—the fifth-century polis comes to mind—to invent new technologies for the improvement of the human condition. This is a valid reading of the play, but certain psychological aspects are equally important since the conflict is played out on both levels simultaneously, the social and the personal. But it is important to recognize that the arid nature of the island is the environmental image of Philoctetes' own arid nature as it has become in his isolation.

Robinson Crusoe, cast up on a deserted island, discovered that a whole chest of useful goods had also washed ashore when his ship was wrecked. In the chest were various tools and, most important for a good Christian man, the Holy Scriptures. This equipment enabled Mr. Crusoe to create his own agriculture, build himself a home, and deepen his own religion. He was also blessed by Providence with another castaway on his island, his Man Friday, who would serve as his factotum and his whole religious congregation. By contrast, Philoctetes, when cut off from his community, is deprived not only of a genuine human livelihood but also of his religion. In his time religion was not to be found in texts that a man might take with him on a long sea voyage, nor in a hermit's retirement to some cave on Mount Athos, but in the social forms of worship. When his friends expelled him from their society, they expelled him from his religion.[30]

Sophocles has amplified and revised the traditional myth in such a way as to make it his own. At the same time, however, it remains entirely Homeric. The story itself, the protagonist, the site, the idea of an embassy sent to Lemnos, these are all elements taken from Homer. But his debt to Homer was far greater than merely the story line. In passage after passage of the play, we see his Homeric borrowings, sometimes in the briefest allusion, sometimes much more conspicuously. Almost everything said or done in the play is based on something to be found in the epic tradition. Sitting on the slopes of the theater beneath the Acropolis, with our Homeric texts in hand or certainly in our memory, we would nod our approval at every turn of the events unfolding before us. When Odysseus outlines for Neoptolemus the plot with which he is to rob Philoctetes of his soul, he takes it without embarrassment from Homer. The lie will be modeled on the anger of Achilles in the *Iliad*, when Achilles, insulted by Agamemnon, withdraws from the battlefield and threatens to take his Myrmidons back to Greece. It is also modeled on the story of the anger of Ajax when the arms of Achilles are awarded to Odysseus rather than to him. Neoptolemus is to impersonate the two Homeric characters, Ajax and Achilles. And of course, he must also impersonate the Homeric Odysseus. This newly minted Neoptolemus could hardly guess that his persona was to be a pastiche of three entirely separate Homeric personas. This is a clever use of the tradition, to make Homer the father of the story, but to wander out from the center in ever-widening circles, always keeping the father of the story within calling distance.

But homage to Homer is not the chief reason for this imitative practice. For all its Homeric atmosphere, a closer analysis reveals that this plot is really a new invention. Sophocles has borrowed a few items from the tradition. From Homer he has borrowed the principal character, Philoctetes, together with his snakebite, the suppurating wound, his exile on Lemnos, and the prophecy given by Helenus. From Aeschylus he has borrowed Odysseus as the delegate sent out from Troy. From Euripides he has borrowed the idea of disguise and the device of a second and fictitious mission being sent out from Troy to Lemnos.

These borrowings, obvious and ubiquitous, lead us easily to overlook the novelty of this play. Neither Odysseus nor Neoptolemus had any part in the Lemnos episode of the original story. These are not two characters taken from the old story for this modernized adaptation. Rather, they are two entirely modern characters taken off the streets of Athens and made to pass themselves off as authentic Homeric creations. We might as well call them Democritus and Pausanias, so little have they in common with the old story. They are put into Homeric dress, made to speak in Homeric accents and to show themselves as familiar with the well-loved Homeric poems as we are. But under their disguise we recognize them for what they are, two Athenian gentleman of late fifth-century Athens, the one a sophist, the other his pupil being sent out on his first run.

Here is the paradox: in tragedy, free invention was anathema. Thus the characters made to act their parts on the fifth-century stage must be copiously outfitted, head to foot, with Homeric accoutrements. The play must always be a period piece. Even Philoctetes himself is a Homeric character only in a manner of speaking. He had never been to Troy, having been separated from the action before the war began. Yet he must be read back into the story. When, in the first episode, he asks Neoptolemus how a character named Thersites is faring at Troy, it strains our credulity to suppose that Philoctetes would know anything at all of this man. Philoctetes' interest in Thersites has as its main objective to take us directly to the *Iliad*, book 2, to the only scene in which Thersites makes an appearance, when he raises his unholy ruckus against Agamemnon's leadership. We can sit back in our seats, reassured to see that Philoctetes has been reading the same text of the *Iliad* that we have in our possession.

As Philoctetes and Neoptolemus converse in this play, discussing the events and persons at Troy, we grasp the principle. They must read themselves retroactively into the Homeric narrative in order to authenticate themselves. These characters playing their parts on the Athenian stage, if they are to be made credible, must gain their credibility from Homer. They must convince us that they are real persons; but *real* here means persons made real first by Homer's art and then in the hero cults established in the Greek cities to celebrate their larger-than-life reality. Myth adds weight and substance to the ephemeral. In legitimizing his characters by making them simulacra of Homeric prototypes, Sophocles legitimizes himself.[31]

Did the dramatists never chafe at the anachronism that their plays must be Homeric through and through? Did their every creative thought have to pass through Homer's wicket? Modern criticism of ancient tragedy concentrates on the political ideologies that sustained the institution of tragedy in Athens, and today we peruse the texts for their allusions to specific historical events or for the poet's personal views on politics or religion.[32] The quest is a legitimate exercise. But given the necessity of this art form, that it must be rooted in an obsolete world, the tragedies' allusions to their own time must be indirect and opaque. We are much more impressed by the sheer mass of tragedy's obsolete architecture: kings and queens with absolute power, ruling by divine fiat, dynastic families blasted by some inherited curse, and the whole Homeric paraphernalia of gods wreaking havoc on human lives to instill submission in their human worshippers.[33] All roads lead back to Homer. "The most important feature of early Greek tragedy . . . is that tragedy was a substitute for Homer."[34] If this is not the anxiety of influence, we need another term to express much the same thing. But tragedy was no substitute for Homer, any more than theology substitutes for worship. There was no substitute for Homer. Homer towered above all other poets. He stood on a peak on Parnassus to which no other poet could ever aspire.[35] Tragedy did not substitute for Homer but rather served to enhance Homer. It breathed its own life force into those heroic icons whose cults were so much a part of Greek religion. What Greek, seeing this play, would not feel more pious toward Heracles, Philoctetes, and Neoptolemus, each of whom had his own significant cult, and even toward Odysseus, who was certainly a hero of myth and cults? And what spectator, seeing Sophocles' *Philoctetes* performed in the Theater of Dionysus in 409 BCE, would not leave the theater believing that he had witnessed the conflicts of living men? Peter Burian, taking the term from Charles Segal, refers to the "megatext" of Greek myth as "a system whose signifiers are closely aligned to the central values (and therefore the central conflicts) of a culture."[36]

Bloom writes that the anxiety of influence is not to be traced by collecting instances of the poet's borrowings from the master poet; it has little to do with resemblances in any obvious sense.[37] Rather, the ephebe's new creation is a response to what is clearly an obsession with the ephebe's father. Clearly, for the tragic poets of Athens, Homer was their father. They and the culture in which they grew were obsessed with Homer to a degree that seems almost incomprehensible to us.

The tragic poets were so beholden to Homer that they were to some degree, willingly or unwillingly, exponents of a bygone paradigm of human life, yet in their compulsion both to be true to Homer and at the same time to rewrite Homer, their creative misreadings brought into being a new kind of text. Imagine an *Odyssey* in which Odysseus failed in his every enterprise! Without the tragic poets' revisions of the tradition, Homer himself would not wield the authority that he exercises even down to our own day in the modern college curriculum.[38] Pouring new wine into the old vessels, the tragic poets could best validate themselves by validating Homer. At the same time, however, being strong poets, in their veneration they also created a second Homer, his double, an anti-Homer. On first reading, no story of ancient tragedy could seem more Homeric than the story of Aeschylus's *Oresteia*. Yet George Thomson, understanding the trilogy as wholly a fifth-century Athenian phenomenon, puts the case in a nutshell: "Thus, by concluding with the Panathenaic festival, the poet has brought his story out of the darkness of antiquity into the brilliant light of the Athens of his day."[39] The darkness Thomson speaks of is, of course, Homer; the brilliant light of day is Aeschylus. We latecomers are the beneficiaries of these misreadings of Homer by the strongest poets of all Hellas after Homer, having inherited our Homer in two strong forms, first as epic and then as tragedy.

3

The Prologos

(Verses 1–134)

The Function of the Prologos

The prologos in ancient Greek tragedy is the part "spoken before" the entrance of the chorus into the theater. In its origins tragedy was a choral performance, that is, a dance with music and words centered on the pathos of some great legendary or mythical hero.[1] At some point a speaker was separated out from the chorus who was to become in time the first actor. *Hypokritēs*, the Greek word for the actor (later to become our "hypocrite"), meaning "interpreter," points to the original role of this individual, as the person who "interpreted" the events of the performance to the audience.[2] In time this individual moved from being the interpreter to become the protagonist of the tragedy; later a second actor was added, and tragedy moved away from being a purely choral performance to become a conflict enacted between two characters with the chorus progressively diminishing in importance. Later still, a prologos was added to serve as an introduction to the play, in which a character could step out of the drama, or in some cases a god would appear, to specify the myth on which the drama was based and to indicate the direction of the plot.

For the prologos of this play, Sophocles uses a dialogue between two of the three characters in the play, Odysseus and Neoptolemus, to give us the necessary information not only in reference to the myth but also about the strategy to be employed in this play itself. Odysseus here has two personas. He is first the informant who tells the young Neoptolemus, who has newly arrived at Troy, the information that he needs in order for him to play his part in the plot and alerts us to elements that Sophocles has added to the traditional myth. But he also has a second function, as the character who will precipitate the plot. Once he has set that plot in motion by giving Neoptolemus his orders, Odysseus retires from the stage to watch the action unfold from the wings, much like the god in certain other tragedies, for instance, Athena in Sophocles' *Ajax*, who makes an appearance in the prologos to inform us that we are about to witness the tragedy that issues from her own divine machinations.

This prologos opens with Odysseus and Neoptolemus arriving at the island of Lemnos, a short distance by ship from Troy. Neoptolemus, the son of Achilles, has been brought from Greece to join the Greeks at Troy and has been assigned to Odysseus as his assistant to bring the wounded warrior Philoctetes back from Lemnos to Troy. The two men have just arrived from Troy, where the Trojan War is still in progress; they have moored their ship in the harbor and are now walking up the path from the harbor to the cave that has been Philoctetes' only home for the past ten years. When the prologos is completed, Odysseus will exit, and the sailors who have been left at the harbor will enter the theater to join Neoptolemus and function as his chorus. Philoctetes has not yet made his appearance; his absence gives Odysseus the time required for him to brief Neoptolemus.

As Odysseus explains the situation, Philoctetes is so consumed by his hatred of the Greek commanders, and especially of Odysseus, that Odysseus dare not be seen; hence he must remain out of sight and the whole burden of the mission must fall on Neoptolemus's shoulders. Using force against Philoctetes is out of the question as long as Philoctetes holds the bow of Heracles, and persuasion would be equally futile. To carry out his orders and accomplish the mission, Neoptolemus is told he has no alternative but to trick Philoctetes into compliance with their wishes. Neoptolemus is an ephebe, a youth just entering into manhood, with the innocence and naïveté of youth, and at the same time assumed to be endowed by nature with the heroic virtues of his father, Achilles. Odysseus explains the trick: Neoptolemus is to create a bond between Philoctetes and himself by feigning a hatred as intense as the hatred of Philoctetes for the two sons of Atreus and for Odysseus. He is to claim that he became so enraged when the armor of his father, Achilles, which should have been his rightful inheritance, was awarded to Odysseus, and has been so abused personally by Odysseus that he has withdrawn from the Greek army at Troy and is now sailing back to Skyros. Once a friendship between him and Philoctetes is established,

Neoptolemus can lure him onto the ship, whereupon the true destination will be revealed, when it will be too late for Philoctetes to reverse the course of action.

Neoptolemus balks at the assignment. As a hero in the Achilles mold, he would willingly use force if necessary, as his father would have done, but he will not resort to some underhanded trick. Sophocles thus frames his drama with the classical distinction between the two great heroes of the Homeric tradition: Achilles, the hero of direct force, the best warrior in open battle; and Odysseus, the master of indirect force, the hero who wins by schemes and subterfuges when open warfare is inconclusive.[3] Odysseus, being the expert in persuasion, overcomes the young man's scruples and persuades him that a brief moment of shame will be redeemed by the glory that Neoptolemus will enjoy in perpetuity. Besides, Odysseus insists, Neoptolemus as an ephebe must remember his duty to obey those set in command over him. Thus several conflicts are outlined: the first, between Odysseus and Neoptolemus, to be followed by another between Neoptolemus and Philoctetes, which in turn will lead into the conflict between Philoctetes and Odysseus. Equally important for the drama are the inner conflicts in the conscience of the two characters, Neoptolemus and Philoctetes.

The conflict among the three characters of this drama highlights a second level of conflict, which is a war of words. This play is as much about language as it is about character. It is situated at the center of the intellectual and political debates in fifth-century Athens. It is easy for modern readers to follow the play of character since the ethical issues are as much ours today as they were the most pressing issues in Sophocles' time. But the drama of words is less accessible to us, especially in translation, unless we are familiar with the philosophical climate and the spiritual crisis in late fifth-century Athens. The linguistic conflict may even escape translation altogether because certain important terms in this play are used in several different, even contradictory senses. Yet no Athenian hearing this play in 409 BCE could have escaped the bite in the vocabulary of the prologos. It introduces terms that are the foundational blocks of the play itself, but these are also the very terms roiling the political atmosphere of Athens.

Athens in the last years of the fifth century was in turmoil. Thanks to various influences, some accidental and some deriving from clever strategies and ruthlessness in the political sphere, Athens had catapulted to a position of extraordinary power, to become in the fifth century the greatest city of its time. It had become the hub of Greek culture. Sophists and philosophers from all over Greece were drawn to the city as to a magnet. It had become the point of confluence where all ideas could mingle and compete. But such grandeur came with a price. Athenian success led to its own demise. In the first years of the fifth century, Athens had assumed a position of supremacy in Greek affairs because of its stunning victory against the Persians at the Battle of Salamis in 480 BCE. Athens began to celebrate itself as the champion of civilization. But by the middle of the century Athens's boast to be the capital of all Hellas had become brazen and hollow. While the city might still be a democracy at home (democracy in its own terms), beyond its boundaries it had become a tyranny, as ruthless as any of the surrounding empires. The progressively more repressive external policies led to the Peloponnesian War, begun in 431 BCE, with Athenian hegemony challenged by an alliance of dissident cities under the leadership of Sparta, Athens's most powerful competitor. This was a protracted and indecisive conflict until 415 BCE, when Athens suffered a disastrous defeat at Syracuse from which it never recovered. When this play was produced in 409 BCE, Athenian power was already finished, though its demise may not have been as obvious to the Athenians as to later analysts. Five years later, in 404 BCE, the war was concluded, and Athens was doomed. While it continued to enjoy its privileged status as the cultural capital of the Mediterranean world, it never regained its power as a political force.

As the fateful war continued year after year, the worst excesses of the Athenian democracy came to the fore. Democracy and demagoguery became almost synonymous in the political arena. Power in this democracy, whether in the political arena or in the law courts, now depended on a person's oratorical powers. Rhetoric became the higher form of education. A new theory of language emerged concerned less with truth than with persuasion. The intellectuals, the self-styled sophists, boasted that they were adept in both the theory and the practices of this new science of language. Sophocles' *Philoctetes* is a play about that new theory of language.

Strong Words in the Prologos

Many of the key words introduced in the prologos had become the most controversial signifiers in the philosophical discourse of late fifth-century Athens. These I call the strong words. As such, they call for our strongest possible readings. Anything less would be to diminish the force of the play as it would have been heard in the Theater of Dionysus that afternoon in 409 BCE. The principal words I have chosen for commentary are

δυσφημία (*dysphemia*, an utterance of evil omen)
σόφισμα (*sophisma*, a clever strategy)
λόγος (*logos*, word, language)
σοφίζομαι (*sophizomai*, to devise a clever scheme)
γενναῖος (*gennaios*, wellborn)
σώμα (*sōma*, body)
καινός (*kainos*, new)
φύσις (*physis*, nature)
τέχνη (*technē*, craft, skill, art)
ψυχή (*psychē*, psyche, soul, self)
ἐκκλέπτω (*ekkleptō*, I steal)
σοφός (*sophos*, skilled, clever, wise)
ἀγαθός (*agathos*, good)

DYSPHEMIA

Odysseus explains to Neoptolemus the circumstances that led to Philoctetes' expulsion from the Greek army:

ὅτ' οὔτε λοιβῆς ἡμῖν οὔτε θυμάτων
παρῆν ἑκήλοις προσθιγεῖν, ἀλλ' ἀγρίαις
κατεῖχ' ἀεὶ πᾶν στρατόπεδον δυσφημίαις,
βοῶν, ἰύζων.

(vv. 8–11)

[It was not possible
for us to perform in a calm way our sacrifices
and libations, but he overwhelmed the whole camp
with his *wild cries of ill omen*, shouting and groaning.]

The Greek word for his "cries of ill omen" is *dysphemiai*, plural of the noun *dysphemia*. If the function of tragedy is to arouse our anxieties, *dysphemia* takes us to the core of some of our deepest social and personal anxieties. With this word Odysseus lays the ground for the rest of the play that is to follow. He uses it to defend his own conscience and to justify the army's need to treat Philoctetes with a ruthless cruelty. Philoctetes' shouts of pain were *wild*, *inhuman*; they nullified the army's religious observances. They were not just abrasive, like some breach of decorum; they threatened religion itself. We might consider translating *dysphemia* as "blasphemy," but it was not the content of his cries that was blasphemous but rather the sick man's *noise*, which gave his fellows a religious justification for his ostracism.

Raised in the modern humanistic environment, we are unlikely to respond to the word *dysphemia* with the same horror that it might arouse in the hearts of fifth-century Athenians. Most of us, especially those who are likely to read this play, do not live our lives governed as the Greeks were by a host of malevolent influences. Their religion was for the most part apotropaic, a set of rituals to avert such influences from human life. Modern readers might consider the army's expulsion of Philoctetes as merely callous, but Odysseus's use of the word *dysphemia* indicates that a religious horror was the deciding motive here.[4]

Religion is a social construct, at least in ancient Greece.[5] The central principle of religion was to propitiate the demonic forces of nature and enlist the benevolence of the kindlier powers. The open violence of ancient sacrifice has been masked in modern liturgies; "sacrifice" is hardly more than a trope, a pious figure of speech. Not so in antiquity. Sacrifice was a noisy and bloody affair.[6] It seems a peculiar incongruity that Philoctetes' groans and screams would interfere with the orgiastic excitement of bloodletting at every sacrifice. The great City Dionysia, the festival at which the tragedies were performed, opened with a huge public sacrifice, which must have been such an orgy of noise, blood, and smell as to make Philoctetes' screams scarcely audible. But noise must be properly sanctified if it is to become the sweet sound of success. We are fortunate to have information theory as a guide to the meaning of this word. "A noise," Jacques Attali writes, "is a resonance that interferes with the audition of a message in the process of emission. . . . Noise does not exist in itself, but only in relation to the system within which it is inscribed: emitter, transmitter, receiver. . . . Noise had always been experienced as destruction, disorder, dirt, pollution, an aggression against the code-structuring messages. In all cultures, it is associated with the idea of the weapon, blasphemy, plague."[7] Dysphemia is unsanctified noise.

The antonym of *dysphemia* is *euphemia*, which the lexicon defines as "the use of words of good omen or the avoidance of words of bad omen." *Euphēmē*, used in prayer or sacrifice, was a call for the good utterance that would contribute to the event's success. All rituals of sacrifice, as Walter Burkert puts it, "must be attended by the right word. Any evil, wrong, coarse, or complaining word would be harm, *blasphemia*, and so the good speech of the participants consists in the first instance in holy silence. Out of the silence there rises up the apostrophe to an Opposite, an invocation and entreaty: the prayer."[8] The intention of *euphemia* was far bolder than a pious apostrophe to the gods. It was nothing less than enchantment. Words, if correctly spoken by the right person at the right moment, could be a potent spell to conjure a god's very being into existence out of the primal chaos. Hence *euphemia*, when practiced in the course of a sacrifice, was translated into "holy silence," silence being the best precaution against any careless or ill-timed utterance, against, in short, *dysphemia*. Philoctetes' noise threatened to invalidate the rituals of sacrifice. Even worse, it might conjure malicious demons where gods were needed to bless the enterprise.

What of the "noise" of the animals being slaughtered at a sacrifice, of the ululations of the women, the triumphant shouts of the men? These of course were music, for the sacrifice itself was music.[9] The screams of the women and the bellowing of the bulls would be woven into the harmonics of the victory song performed by the lissome youths celebrating the sacrifice. Tragedy itself was the noise of that great civic sacrifice to Dionysus raised to a higher level of consciousness, sublimated into music. Philoctetes was deeply, perversely, dangerously *unmusical*.

SOPHISMA

Odysseus moves to speak of the plan he has in mind to deal with this distraught man. He calls his plan a *sophisma*, a noun derived from the adjective *sophos*, "clever or wise," clever strategy or calculation. Thus *dysphemia* is balanced by *sophisma*. Since Philoctetes' presence is now needed at Troy, his ravings are to be offset by *sophisma*:

ἀκμὴ γὰρ οὐκ μακρῶν ἡμῖν λόγων
μὴ καὶ μάθῃ μ' ἥκοντα κἀκχέω τὸ πᾶν
σόφισμα τῷ νιν αὐτίχ' αἱρήσειν δοκῶ.
(vv. 12–14)

[We have no time for long speeches,
or he may learn that I have arrived and then I would spill
the whole *sophisma* with which I expect to capture him.]

Not a word is said about the man's pain. Our focus at this early point in the play is entirely on taking possession of Philoctetes' bow, which the seer Helenus had told the Greeks was essential for their victory at Troy. Getting it to Troy requires a strategy that calls for Neoptolemus, untainted as yet by any previous participation in the war, to be sent in to manipulate Philoctetes as Odysseus would do if he could.

The simplest translation for *sophisma* is "clever strategy." Carl Phillips gives us "the very plan" (v. 20 in his translation), and Hugh Lloyd-Jones gives us "scheme," but "plan" is too clean for what Odysseus has in mind and even "scheme" is hardly adequate. T. B. L. Webster in his note to verse 20 points out that the adjective *sophos* so often has the negative connotation of crafty "that a translator could take σόφισμα as sinister if he wished." Our difficulty in a play like this, where language is the issue in every scene, is that the words spoken by a character are spoken by two persons simultaneously, first by the character as a persona within the play as if he were totally autonomous, but behind that character is another person, who speaks to us as our poet. When Odysseus uses the word *sophisma*, we might even suppose him to take a certain pride in his cleverness, though certainly we are to understand his cleverness as entirely sinister.

To get at the range of connotations in the word *sophisma*, we must trace our steps back to the adjective *sophos*. The Athenians would hear in Odysseus's *sophisma* the words *sophos* (wise) and its derivative *sophia* (wisdom). Immediately, they would be alerted to the first question of the play: what is it to be wise? Odysseus proposes a definition such as could be heard in the speeches and debates of the politicians, the rhetoricians, and the sophists of the day. The indictment against Socrates charged him with impiety, but the real charge against him, as Socrates himself understood, was that he was *sophos*, "wise," as the sophists were now defining the term.

In Homer, our earliest linguistic source, *sophos* has not yet become "wise" in the more abstract sense but denotes skill, any special kind of skill. Although applicable to any person proficient in some way, the adjective privileged one group above any other: the poets, whose skill, as the makers of the song, made them masters of the cultural institutions of Archaic Greece. Their skill and their authority were derived from divine inspiration. Of all the skills, the poets' came closest to being wisdom. But in the Archaic age a new skill emerged to challenge the poet's wisdom. Those whom we today call philosophers grounded their skill not in divine wisdom but in reason itself. Thus in the fifth century *sophia* bifurcated in two discrete and competing directions, being on one hand the traditional skill of the poet and on the other the skill of the new rationalists. Plato's quarrel with the poets centered on this word: who was truly entitled to be called *sophos*, the poet or the thinker? When Odysseus uses *sophisma* here, speaking now as a fifth-century sophist, surely we are to understand that from his point of view his plan is *rational*. It would not depend on divine intervention, as did the strategy of deception in Euripides' *Philoctetes*, which required Athena's assistance. This is the kind of plan a *clever* person might devise for dealing with a sick man.

Odysseus's *sophisma* is glossed by two later passages in the play. The first is in verses 421–52, when Neoptolemus has put the plan into action and it has accomplished its purpose. Philoctetes is now bonding well with Neoptolemus, for the two men have found themselves on common ground in their hatred of Odysseus. Neoptolemus has claimed that, like Philoctetes himself, he has been abused by the commanders of the Greek army, and by Odysseus most of all. But how could such a thing happen? Philoctetes wonders. Surely the noble warriors in the army would not have allowed the son of Achilles to be so abused. Philoctetes begins a roster of such men. Where was Ajax? But Ajax was already dead, he learns from Neoptolemus. Little could Neoptolemus know that he himself has been given Ajax's story to serve as his disguise, nor could it be told in the present context, where nobility is the issue, that the noble Ajax had committed suicide in this selfsame contest for the arms of Achilles that Sophocles has now transferred from Ajax to Neoptolemus.

Philoctetes responds with outrage that such a noble warrior would be dead while the two scoundrels, Diomedes and Odysseus, remain alive. He brings forward another name, Nestor:

‹φεῦ·› τί δ'; ὁ παλαιὸς κἀγαθὸς φίλος τ' ἐμός,
Νέστωρ ὁ Πύλιος, ἔστιν; οὗτος γὰρ τάχ' ἂν
κείνων κάκ' ἐξήρυκε, βουλεύων σοφά.

(vv. 421–23)

[What is this? That good and ancient man, and my personal friend,
Nestor of Pylos, surely he is still alive? This man would have
restrained their evil ways, giving wise counsels.]

Here certainly we are to understand *sopha* (neut. pl. of the adjective *sophos*) to mean "wise," when Philoctetes uses it to signify the counsels of the man whose seniority and benevolence had made him by general agreement the wisest member of the Greek military command. But Nestor, Neoptolemus continues, was in a bad way since the death of his son Antilochus. This news that Antilochus is dead provokes Philoctetes into another explosion at the injustice that two such noble men are dead while the villain Odysseus lives on.

Nestor's mention of the name Odysseus brings Neoptolemus in turn around to the main subject of this brief exchange. In his response to Philoctetes, he uses *sophos* twice in a single sentence, but now with respect to Odysseus, and in neither case can it be translated as "wise":

σοφὸς παλαιστὴς κεῖνος, ἀλλὰ χαὶ σοφαὶ
γνῶμαι, Φιλοκτῆτ', ἐμποδίζονται θαμά.
(vv. 431–32)

[He is a *clever wrestler* (*sophos palaistēs*), that man,
but even *clever ideas* (*sophai gnōmai*) can be tripped up.]

We are ourselves tripped up on the ellipsis here. Why has the mention of Nestor's "wise counsels" triggered the trope of Odysseus as a wrestler? Nothing has been said hitherto of Odysseus's wisdom. Rather, up to this point Neoptolemus has presented Odysseus as callous, coarse, even brutal.

The link here between the two names, Nestor and Odysseus, signified by the use of *sophos* in reference to the two of them, is "ideas." Before Plato added the word "idea" to the Greek language, the Greeks relied on other terms for those mental constructs, two of which are employed here. To speak of Nestor's ideas, Philoctetes uses first a verb that denotes deliberation (*bouleuōn*) and then adds *sopha* as its object: Nestor makes wise deliberations; he offers wise counsels. Neoptolemus in turn in shifting the conversation to Odysseus speaks of him as a wrestler but then adds that even good wrestlers can be tripped up, using *sophos* to refer first to Odysseus himself as the clever wrestler, and then to his ideas (*gnōmai*). He is a clever wrestler, and clever ideas are his skill. It is incongruous to have Neoptolemus, a conspirator in a plot that depends on cleverness, suddenly turn philosophical and suggest Odysseus's possible failure, but Sophocles needs to develop a thesis, which must be done through conversation and debate among the three characters of the play. Nestor is made here to represent the man whose wisdom considers the good of the whole, while Odysseus is the new man with a new kind of so-called wisdom, whose skill is in manipulating words and ideas. He is, in short, the fifth-century sophist. Odysseus wrestles with ideas and words as the athlete wrestles; he spars; he looks to knock his opponent to the ground; he fights only for his personal victory.[10] This brief discussion between Philoctetes and Neoptolemus comparing the wisdom of the good counselor with the skills of the wrestler is the poet's commentary on Odysseus's *sophisma* in verse 14, which is now to be seen as a wrestling match. In the larger context it is directly applicable to the political atmosphere in Athens.

LOGOS

Logos as used in this play is inextricably connected to *sophos*. Odysseus states his *sophisma* as follows:

Νε. τί δῆτ' ἄνωγας;
Οδ. τὴν Φιλοκτήτου σε δεῖ
ψυχὴν ὅπως λόγοισιν ἐκκλέψεις λέγων
(vv. 54–55)

[Ne. What then do you command?
Od. It is necessary for you—you must see how you using words will steal the soul of Philoctetes.]

The translation that I have given of Odysseus's instructions is not to be found in the commentaries. Instead, Richard Jebb translates: "Thou must beguile the mind of Philoctetes by a story told in thy converse with him," and Lloyd-Jones follows his lead: "You must beguile his mind in words." No one reading such translations would suspect that with this sentence Odysseus sets in motion one of the most powerful tragedies in the ancient repertoire. If we fail to feel the shock here, that is because we have only a small understanding of the value of the word *logos* in the heated atmosphere of fifth-century Athens.

The word is hardly used in Homer. The common word was *mythos*, signifying not myth in our sense but word or story, with no prejudice as to the story's veracity. In the sixth century, however, *logos* began to arise to a new prominence, in time replacing *mythos*.[11] The philosopher Heraclitus thrust this word into the limelight when he argued that everything was change but change itself was governed by Logos. In one of his pregnant aphorisms Heraclitus wrote: "Even if you travel by every path, you will never reach the boundaries of *psychē*, so deep is its *logos*."[12] This theorem is significant in three respects. First, *psychē*—the life force of the living person, but the person's bloodless and insubstantial ghost after his or her death—is now elevated to being the organizing principle of the living person. It is becoming synonymous with the person. Second, the *psychē* is organized according to the law of the *logos*, that same *logos* on which every other being, animate or inanimate, depends. Third, this *logos*, seen by Heraclitus as essential to every moment and event in nature, was Word, Reason, and Logic.

The link between *logos* and *psychē* comes to fruition in Gorgias's *Encomium to Helen*.[13] We can scarcely understand the full significance of what Odysseus means by his *sophisma* unless we bring Gorgias to bear on the text. His *Encomium* is a set speech putting forth arguments to exonerate Helen from any share of the responsibility for the calamity of the Trojan War. All the blame was to fall on Paris, whose *words* had an irresistible effect on Helen's *soul*. Given his style, which reveled in artful paradox, it is difficult to decide to what extent Gorgias expected the speech to be accepted at face value or whether it was intended simply as an exhibition piece to show the rhetorician's skill in making the lesser argument the stronger. Whatever the degree of sincerity in the argument, we can accept that the speech expresses the fundamental principle of Gorgias's philosophy, that *logos*—as language—is the most powerful tool of human consciousness; that it is a form of magic that works its influence chiefly on the *psychē*. This intimate connection between *logos* and *psychē* and the invincible effect of language on the *psychē* form the foundation of Sophocles' *Philoctetes*. "Beguilement" is a weak translation in such a context. The better word is "bewitched." Philoctetes must be bewitched, and Neoptolemus will be an effective wizard, first because his breeding gives him a stunning likeness to the handsome and heroic Achilles, and then because he will learn from Odysseus the magic of the *logos*. He will *seem* to be Achilles, but in practice he will be Odysseus.

Dysphemia and *logos*: the two poles of human communication. At one pole the sheer sound of pain, at the other its antidote, the Logos; and from the vortex of their vibrations this play emerges, Sophocles' meditation on the language of pain versus the rules of logic or political expediency. Because this is tragedy and not some graceful lyric, the victory must go to *dysphemia*, since the unembellished sound of pain is more convincing than the finest syllogism. The *dysphemia*, prohibited at Troy and banished to Lemnos, breaks in on our ears at the exact midpoint of this play, and with that scream the Logos is undone. How could cleverness outwit that scream?

SOPHIZOMAI

Odysseus, continuing to develop his word *sophisma*, turns the idea into a verb: *sophizomai*:

ἀλλ' αὐτὸ τοῦτο δεῖ σοφισθῆναι, κλοπεὺς
ὅπως γενήσῃ τῶν ἀνικήτων ὅπλων.

(vv. 77–78)

[But you must put your skill to this,
how you will become the thief of those invincible arms.]

Phillips translates the verb here (*sophizomai*) as "this is what we must devise" (his v. 86). Webster in his note at verse 77 has "we must plan this very thing." Lloyd-Jones gives us "scheme." But surely the unscrupulous and indeed cowardly *sophisma* that will drive the plot of this play calls for a stronger rendering than "plan," "device," or "scheme." Speaking to Neoptolemus, Odysseus can be understood to mean "you must use your intelligence on this project." As we hear the verb, however, Sophocles must expect us to be horrified, especially when it is immediately followed by the word *klopeus* (thief). Odysseus spells out the project in the plainest way: "This very thing must be ingeniously thought out—a thief—how you are to become a thief." Webster, in first weakening the verb *sophizomai* (in v. 77) to "plan," then would have us weaken the noun *klopeus* (thief), giving us for verses 77–78: "We must plan this very thing, how you shall become . . . the perpetrator of the stratagem." Thus both the thief and his theft have been deftly removed from our sight and the criminal action made almost respectable by being called a "stratagem."

Sophos and *sophizomai* are further glossed in one more passage late in the poem, in a debate between Neoptolemus and Odysseus on the meaning of the word *sophos*:

Νε. σοφὸς πεφυκὼς οὐδὲν ἐξαυδᾷς σοφόν.
Οδ. σὺ δ' οὔτε φωνεῖς οὔτε δρασείεις σοφά.
Νε. ἀλλ' εἰ δίκαια, τῶν σοφῶν κρείσσω τάδε.
Οδ. καὶ πῶς δίκαιον, ἅ γ' ἔλαβες βουλαῖς ἐμαῖς,
πάλιν μεθεῖναι ταῦτα;
Νε. τὴν ἁμαρτίαν
αἰσχρὰν ἁμαρτὼν ἀναλαβεῖν πειράσομαι.

(vv. 1244–49)

[Ne. You were born wise (*sophos*), but nothing you say is wise (*sophon*).
Od. But you are neither speaking nor are you about to do anything wise (*sopha*).
Ne. But if my actions are just, they are stronger than the wise (*sophon*, whether wise words or wise actions).

Od. But how would that would be just, to give back what you took through my plans?
Ne. The disgraceful error (*hamartia*) wherein I sinned (*hamartōn*), that I will now try to undo.]

At this point, almost at the end of the play, Odysseus and Neoptolemus have left the scene to return to their ship, since neither has been able to convince Philoctetes, whether by persuasion or threats, to forego his hatred of the Greeks and join them at Troy. Neoptolemus now holds the precious bow in his hand, which Philoctetes has passed to him at the midpoint in the play. He and Odysseus could leave Philoctetes on Lemnos and proceed themselves to Troy with their mission accomplished. So at least Odysseus would have Philoctetes believe. But Neoptolemus has a change of heart. He has come to see that he is a thief, that the bow in his hands is stolen property, and he must return it to its rightful owner. Odysseus is stupefied. To throw away victory and the mission at Troy for a mere scruple? The two men fall into an altercation once Odysseus understands Neoptolemus's intention to disobey him and ruin their mission, with *sophos* being the grounds of their contention.

Neoptolemus is generous to credit Odysseus here with a noble pedigree—"you were born intelligent"—since other passages in the play repeatedly undercut his heroic pretensions. But for the sake of the present argument, Sophocles has Neoptolemus fall back on one of the shibboleths of the tribal culture, when wisdom was one of the inherited virtues of the ruling class. Odysseus has betrayed that ethos, so Neoptolemus asserts. Odysseus may look the part of a hero, but his words are not those of a hero, if the true nature of a hero is to be wise. Odysseus replies in turn that Neoptolemus himself is neither speaking nor acting with intelligence if he continues with his present intention. The two men have a completely different understanding of the word *sophos*. As spoken by Odysseus in this passage, we may take it to mean "intelligent." When Neoptolemus uses the word, however, its meaning is closer to "wise." Neoptolemus accuses Odysseus of being unwise, but to Odysseus, Neoptolemus's "wisdom" is folly.

Now, shifting his ground, Neoptolemus introduces justice into the argument, making justice (*ta dikaia*) his gloss on *sophos*. Just acts are stronger than the wise, he claims, whether "wise" here is to be taken as meaning wise actions or the actions of wise people. Neoptolemus has now become thoroughly Platonic: only what is truly just can be wise. When he uses "wise" in verse 1246 (*sophōn*), we should italicize it to indicate his sarcasm. Just actions are stronger than the *so-called wisdom* of men like Odysseus whose skill is in knowing how to prove the weaker argument the stronger.

But if justice is at issue, then Odysseus must have his say too. How could it be just for Neoptolemus to give away something that he now possesses solely thanks to another man's wits? To which Neoptolemus responds with a single sentence that takes us to the heart of the problem: "I shall undo my *hamartia,* the *hamartia* that I committed [namely, when I stole a man's property]." True justice is to correct the *hamartia,* and in true justice lies true wisdom. This is where the *sophisma* of Odysseus comes to closure, now completely discredited as being neither clever nor wise.

GENNAIOS, SŌMA, KAINOS

Before he states his *sophisma* in its baldest terms, Odysseus prepares Neoptolemus for his assignment by speaking first of his noble birth and then reminding him that it also places a duty on him to serve the royal command:

Ἀχιλλέως παῖ, δεῖ σ᾽ ἐφ᾽ οἷς ἐλήλυθας
γενναῖον εἶναι, μὴ μόνον τῷ σώματι,
ἀλλ᾽ ἤν τι καινόν, ὧν πρὶν οὐκ ἀκήκοας,
κλύῃς, ὑπουργεῖν, ὡς ὑπηρέτης πάρει.
(vv. 50–53)

[Son of Achilles, in the task for which you have come here,
you must be true to your birth (*gennaion*) not only in the body (*sōma*) but . . .
if you hear something new (*kainon ti*), something you've never heard before,
you must serve me, since you are here to serve.]

The strategy depends on Neoptolemus's noble birth if it is to succeed. Only a man of such stature as the son of Achilles can hope to establish the credibility required to win Philoctetes' confidence. At the same time this lineage must be undermined. The two contradictory aspects of Neoptolemus's character, the noble and the ignoble, are brought together in a single sentence. Neoptolemus must look like Achilles and made to believe that he acts like Achilles, but underneath the facade must lurk an entirely different character. Neoptolemus, priding himself on his heritage as the honest son of the army's most honest man, must also consent to rob a cripple of his only means of sustenance. The argument must be made with care. But Odysseus is a practiced rhetorician.

The first word to be highlighted is *gennaios* (of good breeding), which, once stated, Odysseus explicates with the word *sōma* (body). Neoptolemus must be true to his noble lineage *in his body*. We understand *sōma* here as a reference to Neoptolemus's father, Achilles, the hero born of a goddess with the perfect physique and endowed with all the graces and virtues that are the natural inheritance of such a physique. His son, Neoptolemus, is now about to go up against a formidable foe who is armed with a lethal weapon, while Neoptolemus himself will engage the enemy with no weapon (but words). He must have the fortitude and daring that were once his father's glory. He must also have *physical* stamina to an unusual degree since he is to associate with a man whose physical presence was an offense to the noblest leaders of the entire Greek army. Neoptolemus must have the charity of a saint and the daring of a conquistador. *Gennaios* and *sōma* take us directly back to the Achilles of the *Iliad*.

Neoptolemus is to be noble both in the body but also . . . Here Odysseus swerves into a strange ellipsis. The Greeks loved antithesis, and the antithesis begs to be heard here, "both in body and mind." Jebb argues that Odysseus begins his sentence as if *gennaion* were to be explicated by both *sōma* (body) and an implicit *gnōmē* (thought).[14] The strongest word in this sentence should be "mind," or some equivalent, since mind is at issue in this whole prologos. But it is the word suppressed, and with good reason. Neoptolemus is about to be ordered to surrender his mind in return for a different kind of mind altogether. To bridge this lacuna, Odysseus continues, "Both in body *and if you hear something new* [*kainon ti*], something you've not heard before." This conveniently leads into the stern reminder that Neoptolemus is serving under his command and is to obey his commander, as was expected of every ephebe serving in the military in fifth-century Athens.[15] "Obedience" has replaced "mind" in this commander's advice. It is an elegant gambit since the ephebe in this adventure, while certainly he must keep his wits about him, must remember that they are to be put under his commander's control.

If it were not for Plato's *Apology* we could hardly guess that a simple word, *kainon*, as used in this context, was one of the most inflammatory words bruited about in fifth-century Athens. In that speech, which Plato offers as the verbatim record of Socrates' defense at his trial in 399 BCE, Socrates states that the indictment against him was that he was teaching the young to worship not the gods (*theoi*) that the city worshipped but other new spirits (*daimonia kaina*).[16] The "new"—that was the triumphant glory of the sophists; it was a word so powerful, so charged with numinous energy, that it became Socrates' death sentence. Sophocles has Odysseus become the spokesperson for this new kind of consciousness, and the "newness" here is made as terrible a reproach as it was to be in the indictment of Socrates ten years later. Instead of the expected parallelism between physique and thought, Odysseus veers sharply in the opposite direction, to join Achilles' superb physique with the deformation of thought that is now necessary for the success of this mission.

The Neoptolemus of this play is to be two persons, representing not only two different characters but also two very different epochs. He is to be the old hero in the Achilles mold, a Bronze Age warrior who would be at home in Homer's *Iliad*. But to this antique and almost obsolete character a second persona must be attached who is to be both the Athenian hoplite and also the progressive thinker of the fifth century, entirely liberated from obsolete Homeric ethos. To manage this dichotomy, he is to be the son with two fathers, to be an Achilles in his physique but to become an Odysseus in his mind.

PHYSIS

After Odysseus has spelled out his *sophisma* to Neoptolemus, he acknowledges that such an assignment runs contrary to Neoptolemus's true nature:

ἔξοιδα, παῖ, φύσει σε μὴ πεφυκότα
τοιαῦτα φωνεῖν μηδὲ τεχνᾶσθαι κακά·
(vv. 79–80)

[I know, boy, that you were not born with the *nature* (*physis*)
either to speak such things or to accomplish evil by cunning
(*technasthai*).]

Odysseus addresses the idea of nature with two words, first using the abstract noun *physis* and then a verb built on the same root to refer to Neoptolemus's birth. Neoptolemus is noble both in his birth and in his nature. Our English vocabulary makes it difficult to express so compactly the two concepts discussed in this passage in words derived from the same root, "nature" being of Latin origin, and "birth" Germanic. Neoptolemus in his response uses the same word for "birth" twice, once of himself and once of his father:

ἔφυν γὰρ οὐδὲν ἐκ τέχνης πράσσειν κακῆς
οὔτ' αὐτὸς οὔθ,' ὥς φασιν, οὐκφύσας ἐμέ.
(vv. 88–89)

[I was not born to do anything with an evil craft (*technē*)
Neither myself nor, from what they say, he from whom I am born.]

Lloyd-Jones gives "nature" its proper emphasis here by using the word three times in translating this single sentence: "It is my nature to do nothing by treacherous plotting; that is my nature, and it was also my father's nature." But even with this emphasis, our English word "nature" might not seem as charged a word as *physis* was in late fifth-century Athens. Nature is, of course, still a hotly debated topic, but for the Athenians *physis* represented a new concept in the process of definition.

In making a man's ethos dependent on his birth, Sophocles faced one of the liabilities of the fifth-century dramatist required to find his foundational texts in the obsolete ethos of the heroic tradition. In that tradition all heroes were wellborn, including Odysseus, but fifth-century Athens was far removed from Homer's heroic world. The citizen body of Athens was largely composed of yeomen—farmers, artisans, sailors. Sophocles, if he is to find his paradigm in the ancient myth but at the same time introduce a new concept of a man's nature, is brought up short against a challenging paradox. He needs his Neoptolemus to represent nature in the old sense, a man with nobility in his bloodline, a natural-born hero, while Odysseus, if the syllogism is to work, must be made the opposite, completely without "nature," therefore a man with a vacancy where ethos should be.[17] In various ways as the play progresses the point is made, that Odysseus, being ignoble, has a defective nature, hence is devoid of ethos, since to have an ignoble nature is to have no nature at all. Being unnatural, he must be all *fabrication*. But nature as Sophocles defines it in this play requires Neoptolemus also to represent a new person whose nature lies not in a blind automatism but in his own conscience. The ethos that will emerge in Neoptolemus is a quality that could never be discovered in Homer's Achilles, who was the paradigm of virtue in the old heroic tradition. If the Homeric situation of this play were to be relevant to the artisans watching it in fifth-century Athens, they must have been able to read themselves in its portrait of the noble Neoptolemus. The message for them would be what once was true only for the aristocrats, that virtue is innate. To follow Gadamer's suggestion, *physis*, once the native disposition of the nobly born, functioning now in this play as a philosophical concept, has come to signify that mystical inward essence of every individual.

TECHNĒ

In the two passages in the prologos where Neoptolemus's nature is under discussion, *physis* and *technē* are strongly contrasted, nature versus craft. In verses 79–80 Odysseus acknowledges that Neoptolemus was not born with the *nature* to *contrive* evils (see the preceding section, concerning *physis*), using the verb built on *technē*, but "fabricate" might be a better translation than "contrive." Neoptolemus neither has the nature to be a fabricator nor was he born with that kind of *unnatural* nature. Neoptolemus in his response brings the same three terms together again in a single sentence, *physis, technē, kakos*, when he says that neither he nor his father was born with the nature to work by means of an evil skill.

Technē signifies an acquired skill. The word need not be pejorative, but as used in this prologos it is entirely pejorative. Set in the broader context of fifth-century Athenian discourse, it serves as the antonym to *physis*: nature on one side and artifice on the other; something contrary to nature, *unnatural*, perverse. Achilles could not have fabricated anything, even if he had wanted to, such is the implication of these passages. In him was no faculty corresponding to the Odyssean *technē*.

The word has a long history in ancient Greek. We find it first in Homer, as the skill of the artisan, *homo faber*, the maker of things. For the most part it is used in a neutral sense, but the wonder that *technē* arouses in human hearts easily shades into fear, for *technē* is a dangerous kind of cunning.[18] A striking passage describing the uncanny power of *technē* is given in the *Odyssey*, when Odysseus sees the eidolon of Heracles among the ghosts of the dead (11.609–14). Odysseus, looking at Heracles' war belt, is horrified: "Awful was the belt about his breast, a baldric of gold, whereon wondrous things were fashioned, bears and wild boars, and lions with flashing eyes, and conflicts, and battles, and murders and slaying of men. May he never have designed, or hereafter design such another, even he who stored up in his craft the device of that belt."[19]

In the fifth century *technē* had become a common topic of debate as the sophists and rhetoricians undertook their analysis of the various human crafts, questioning whether they were inherited or could be taught. The craft of rhetoric (called in Plato *technē rhetorikē*) emerged as superior to all others in their arguments since its power was persuasion and all other crafts depended in the end on persuasion. Success in the court of law as in politics, everywhere success now depended on the skillful manipulation of humans through language. The clever speaker was king. "When I was young," Odysseus explains to Neoptolemus in the prologos, "I too had a slow tongue and a hand quick to action. But now, when I go forth to engage with other humans, I see that not deeds but the tongue governs everything" (vv. 96–99).

Here again Plato contributes to our understanding of this word as it is used in this play. In his *Phaedrus*, he uses some form of *technē* seventy-eight times; in his *Gorgias*, eighty-two times. Even with due allowances made that the Platonic dialogues are not verbatim transcripts of Socrates' conversations, they must represent to some degree Socrates' ideas, and certainly they employ some of the same terms that could be heard daily in the intellectual circles in which Plato grew up. The rhetorician Gorgias, who later was to lend his name to Plato's dialogue, the *Gorgias*, gives us evidence that *technē* was one of the primary terms in fifth-century intellectual discourse. The few surviving fragments of his writings give us twenty-seven instances of the word, most of them alluding to the uncanny craftiness of language, since Gorgias understood "the craft of rhetoric" (*technē rhetorikē*) to be a form of sorcery.

With the fragments from Gorgias, on one hand, and Plato's dialogues, on the other, we can deduce that Socrates was engaged in a war with Gorgias and other intellectuals of a similar persuasion, a war to the death as it turned out, over the meaning of this word. In the *Gorgias*, Plato has Socrates dueling with Gorgias himself and with other interlocutors to define the nature of *technē*. Our translations mostly give us "art" for Plato's *technē*, but "art" is misleading. The Greeks knew nothing of the arts. Even the greatest sculptor in Greece was not an artist but a *technician*. *Technē*, as craft, takes us back to the artisans. Rhetoric was a craft like carpentry, vase painting, or medicine. If rhetoric is a true *technē*, Plato insists, it must, like medicine, be oriented to a person's good health, whether of the body or the mind.

In Plato's *Gorgias*, Socrates divides the human being into two parts, *sōma* and *psychē*, body and soul, and then describes the crafts appropriate to each. The two genuine crafts (*technai*) that tend to the body are medicine and gymnastics. The craft that tends to the soul he calls "the craft of politics" (*technē politikē*), and it can be divided into two disciplines, "legislation" and "government." Each of the genuine crafts has its counterfeit, its eidolon as Socrates calls it, a mere semblance of the true craft. The crafts that counterfeit those tending to the body are cooking and cosmetology, and the counterfeit craft in politics is rhetoric. These spurious crafts Socrates calls "flattery," using a highly pejorative term, whether they are directed to the body or to the soul. "Pandering" might be a more appropriate translation.

In his use of *technē* in the *Philoctetes*, Sophocles invests the word with the pejorative senses that Plato was to ascribe to the false craft of rhetoric, the aim of which is neither wisdom nor truth but flattery. The *technē* that Odysseus intends to teach is, as Gorgias put it, "the incantatory power which by its witchery enchants, persuades and changes the souls of men."[20] In his body (*sōma*) Neoptolemus is to be the true son of Achilles, but mentally he must now become an adept in the witchcraft of word. This obligation calls for Neoptolemus to mimic the mind of Odysseus, who, being without a true nature, has no difficulty practicing perjury and theft.

Once we sense the passion invested in the word *technē* in the fifth-century debates, we comprehend why Sophocles would want to have his Odysseus *fabricate* a plot that depends on fabrication. Odysseus fabricates the plot for this play because he is himself a fabrication. All this is made plainer as the play progresses.

PSYCHĒ, EKKLEPTŌ

All the strong words in the prologos come to a focus in the one word that is the key to the whole play: *psychē* (soul or mind). Odysseus, after his careful preamble, is ready to spell out his *sophisma*, which is in turn to serve as the whole plot of this play:

Νε. τί δῆτ' ἄνωγας;
Οδ. τὴν Φιλοκτήτου σε δεῖ
ψυχὴν ὅπως λόγοισιν ἐκκλέψεις λέγων,
ὅταν σ' ἐρωτᾷ τίς τε καὶ πόθεν πάρει,
λέγειν, Ἀχιλλέως παῖς, τόδ' οὐχὶ κλεπτέον.
(vv. 54–57)

[Ne. What then do you command?
Od. It is necessary for you—you must see how you using words will
steal the soul (*psychē*) of Philoctetes.
When he asks you "Who are you?" And "whence have you come?"
say, "The son of Achilles." This need not be stolen.]

We would have to search hard to find a more provocative opening to a Greek tragedy. This drama, as we are shortly to learn from Neoptolemus himself, is to be a wrestling match, with a man's *psychē* as the prize. The key concepts in this passage are embroiled in the three words: *logos* (word), *ekkleptein* (to steal), and *psychē* (*soul*). These words, as the foundation blocks of the whole play, call for our strongest reading. Unfortunately, commentaries and translations gravitate to a weaker reading as if the trope were too bold for our ears, like Jebb's "Thou must beguile the mind of Philoctetes by a story told in thy converse with him." In his translation, the weapon to be used in this contest has been removed, *logos* being taken not in its broadest sense as language but more narrowly as story. The crime has been eliminated, with theft euphemized as "beguile"; and finally, *psychē* has been rendered down to the more innocuous "mind." Thus the crime that motivates this plot has been attenuated into the more pleasant entertainment of story-telling. Odysseus would be pleased to see how successful his *sophisma* has been in persuading even the most careful modern philologists.

The syntax of the sentence in verses 54–55 presents certain problems, as if it were a reflection of the awkwardness in the mind of Odysseus as he reaches for the best rhetorical varnish to brush over an odious project. The main verb of the sentence is the impersonal δεῖ, "it is necessary." Preceding the verb are three words, τὴν Φιλοκτήτου σε, and the word immediately following the verb is ψυχήν, leading us to expect a sentence that goes "the soul of Philoctetes—it is necessary that you (to be followed by an infinitive). . . ." After ψυχήν, however, the sentence breaks off with an anacoluthon and shifts into a different construction with ὅπως, which introduces the verb ἐκκλέψεις in the future indicative, as if the whole sentence ran: "See to it how you will steal the soul of Philoctetes." Jebb smooths away the anacoluthon and treats the sentence as a simple command: "Thou must beguile the mind of Philoctetes." In doing so, he fails to catch the hesitancy in diction of a live speaker casting about for the best way to make a crime seem no more than a political maneuver.

For the unusual construction of this sentence, Jebb points to two other examples, one in Sophocles' *Ajax* and the other in the *Nemesis* by the comic poet Cratinus.[21] He notes that in both these passages the construction "is used by an elder or superior giving a precept of conduct." We hear two sentences in one. Neoptolemus has asked Odysseus, "What is your command?" Odysseus begins his reply with a direct command: "It is necessary that you . . ." He then shifts into a different tone, from a command to admonishment: "The soul of Philoctetes—see how you will steal it."

The greater problem of the sentence, however, is in its semiotic content. The justification for downgrading the crime from theft to deception is provided by the lexicon, which informs us that the verb *ekkleptein* (to steal) and also the base verb *kleptein*, from which it is derived, when used in such a context means "to deceive." The lexicon offers only a few examples of these verbs used in this sense, and all are from Sophocles, as if to suggest that this is a Sophoclean trope. Even if the verb in this passage were understood by Sophocles' Athenian listeners as signifying deception, certainly they also heard "theft" as the first meaning of the word. As if to reinforce this idea, a few verses later Odysseus makes it even more transparent: "This is how you are to use your wits, to see how you will become the *thief* [*klopeus*] of those invincible arms" (v. 77). The adjective "invincible" (*anikētōn*) is significant here, built on the noun *nikē* (victory) with its suggestion of victory in a competitive event or even in a military context. Heracles' bow must be captured, but it can be captured only by theft.

To translate Odysseus's command to Neoptolemus as to practice deception rather than theft is made easier by Odysseus's second allusion to theft, when he explains that when Philoctetes asks Neoptolemus to identify himself, Neoptolemus is to answer with the truth, that he is the son of Achilles. "This is not to be stolen," Odysseus explains. Needless to say, theft is being used in two different senses here, and while theft may be acceptable in the first instance, since it refers to an actual entity (a man's *psychē*), we find it awkward to speak of stealing a fact from a story. Hence we are glad to accept the lexicon's guidance here and take both instances of theft in this sentence to mean deception. In this prologos, however, Odysseus three times specifies theft as the object of Neoptolemus's mission. Seldom has robbery been so well enhanced by rhetoric. Deception is certainly at the heart of the play, but deception is only the means. The act itself is robbery. Rendering ψυχήν here as "mind" weakens the force of the sentence and takes us further from the heated political environment in which this play was staged. The reason for preferring "mind" to "soul" here is that by general consent the word *psychē* had not come to mean "soul" as we might understand the word before Plato articulated his theory of the *psychē*. But if "soul" is anachronistic for late fifth-century Athens, "mind" is equally anachronistic. The evidence, fragmentary as it is, is strong enough to suggest that *psychē* as soul was by no means Plato's invention. It has a long history in the cosmological constructs of the sixth-century philosophers, such as Heraclitus and the Pythagoreans, in poets such as Pindar, in fifth-century rhetoricians like Gorgias, and in the Athenian dramatists, especially Sophocles and Euripides.[22] To translate the word as "soul" here at the beginning of the play better enables us to understand that the plan is not simply a mental exercise but is an attack on a man's very essence. Setting the word in its broader historical context allows us to hold before ourselves a wide range of significations.

In Homer, a man may be said to fight for his *psychē*, but the word is then to be understood to mean his life. In the *Iliad*, when Achilles and Hector are racing around the walls of Troy, they run not as men might run who compete for prizes; they run for "no festal beast, no ox-hide" (to quote Lattimore's translation); they run for "the life [*psychē*] of Hector, tamer of horses" (ἀλλὰ περὶ ψυχῆς θέον Ἕκτορος ἱπποδάμοιο).[23] The title given to *Iliad* 22 in antiquity was *Hectoris anairesis* ("The Slaying of Hector"). But an even more pointed title could have been *Hektoris psychē*, for *psychē* is the most commanding term in the whole book.

Many in Sophocles' audience would have known those verses by heart. They were probably earmarked by many a rhapsode as a purple passage worthy of a purple delivery. He would be a dullard indeed, the Athenian sitting in the Theater of Dionysus, who did not think of Homer's swift-footed Achilles racing to take Hector's *psychē* when he heard Sophocles' Odysseus instructing the son of Achilles to seize Philoctetes' *psychē* using a method that would have disgusted Achilles. The Homeric *psychē* had not lost any of its meanings when Sophocles came to use the word; it had only accumulated new meanings. It still signified the person's life, but "life" was more fully rendered now as more than biology; it was one's essence, one's very being.

If as moderns we are uncomfortable with the word "soul," with its long history of religious accretions, we can think of the *psychē* in this passage as comparable to the *Geist* of the German philosophers, that *Bildung* of which Gadamer writes. Odysseus's plan is Platonic but also thoroughly Homeric. When, later in the play, Neoptolemus rectifies his *hamartia* by returning the bow to Philoctetes, thus restoring to him the physical conditions requisite for his biological survival, even then Philoctetes will not surrender his will to those who have done him harm. He fights to the last for his *psychē*, exactly as any Homeric warrior would.

Homer, where our literary sources begin, has various words for cognition, but *psychē* is not one of them.[24] Thinking or emotional impulses originate in some part of the person's anatomy, an organ or quasi organ, like *nous* or the *phrenes*. The *psychē* was never an organ but always in some sense the whole person, even in death. In the living person it was the person's life force; as cognate with "breath," it was the breath of life. A warrior fighting for his *psychē* was fighting for his life. Upon the person's death it separated from the body (*sōma*) and fluttered into the underworld, where it continued as the person's image, an eidolon, but still a whole, albeit in the insubstantial form of the person's ghost.

The distinction between body and soul, *sōma* and *psychē*, often assumed to be Plato's invention, was first introduced into Greek poetry in Homer and remained a principle firmly established throughout the history of ancient Greek thought. In his *Gorgias*, Plato has Socrates say to Gorgias, "I suppose you call something the *sōma* and something the *psychē*," to which Gorgias replies, "I do."[25] They then proceed to distinguish the crafts as they tend to one or the other of these two entities. This dichotomy appears in the writings of Gorgias himself. He opens his *Encomium to Helen* with a bold and beautiful assertion: "A city's adornment is the valor of its men; for the body [*sōma*], it is beauty; for the soul [*psychē*], it is wisdom [*sophia*]; in action it is virtue; in speech, truth."[26] Later in the same speech Gorgias writes, "The power of speech over the disposition of the *psychē* is the same as the disposition of medicine with respect to the body [*sōma*]."[27]

Mind is a mystery, but the Greek *psychē* is even more mysterious, having two separate and apparently contradictory functions. In the living person it is the life force itself, but in death it becomes a kind of vacancy, still the outward form of the person, merely an image; yet in some indefinable way it still continues a life of its own. It persists. It is still the person's life though translated into the mysterious form as the semblance of the once-living person. This idea is more prominent in folk religions where a person's ghost continues to have a powerful demonic aspect. Latent in the word from the earliest times but emerging ever more plainly in the fifth century was the idea of *presence*. Even as a mere eidolon after a person's death, the *psychē* still expressed in some mysterious way a person's presence. It retained something of the living person's potency and also the person's continuity. "There is continuity, after all," Achilles exclaims in the *Iliad* after he has conversed with the *psychē* of Patroclus; "there is a spirit and an image, but the mind is not in it. All night long the ghost [*psychē*] of poor Patroclus stood beside me, mourning and lamenting, and it laid out for me everything I must do, and it was marvelous in its likeness to himself."[28]

This numinous ambiguity inherent in *psychē*, which is a presence even in its absence, engaged the best minds in Greece in the sixth and fifth centuries, among them Heraclitus and the Pythagoreans. Heraclitus has left us with one fragment that, however obliquely, has influenced the idea of *psychē* ever since (frag. 35, Kahn): "Traveling by every road you would not find the boundaries of soul [*psychē*], so deep is its measure [*logos*]."[29] In another fragment (frag. 101 Kahn), briefer and perhaps even more enigmatic, we find Heraclitus saying, "To the soul [*psychē*] belongs a report [*logos*] that increases itself" (Kahn's translation). These fragments and a few others attributed to Heraclitus mark the moment when *psychē* takes on its modern meaning of "soul." Exactly how the *logos* in its association with the *psychē* is to be defined is hard to say. Some take the *logos* in the *psychē* to be "measure."[30] In both these instances Charles Kahn translates it as "report," but "report" seems a weak translation for the *logos* of the *psychē*, which is the same Logos governing all the changing phenomena of the world. These are the first texts from antiquity that bring *logos* and *psychē* together. Bruno Snell notes the shift here from outwardness to inwardness, but equally important is the shift from the mere image, the eidolon, to the living essence and form.[31]

This shift in thought of the *psychē* from ghost to the soul endowed with *logos* became the ongoing project of all the philosophers, and we can see its effect in a rhetorician like Gorgias. If *logos* governs all things including the *psychē*, and if *logos* is, as it was for the sophists, language, then language emerges in Greek thought as the greatest power in the world. As Socrates puts it for his friend Phaedrus: "And so, in a word, the craft of rhetoric would be the power to lead the soul by means of language."[32] And again, in the same dialogue: "The power of the word [*logos*] is to lead the soul [*psychagogia*]."[33]

David Claus argues that in the pre-Platonic writers, including the tragic poets, where *psychē* is used to refer not to the ghost but to the living person, while its meaning can still be traced back to the root meaning of "life force," it can be used as a poetic trope, merely a periphrasis for the person's name.[34] In Euripides' *Hecuba*, when Hecuba wonders where she might find the "divine soul [*psychē*] of Helenus [the Trojan seer] or Cassandra" to read her dream, Claus can detect no distinction between Helenus or the *psychē* of Helenus.[35] All these instances in the post-Homeric poets Claus explains as still derived from the old Homeric concept of the *psychē* as the person's life force. His argument, however, holds true for Plato and also Aristotle. When in the *Phaedo* Socrates defines death as the separation of *sōma* and *psychē*, that dichotomy can be traced back to Homer.[36] It is the same dichotomy throughout Greek thought from the earliest poets to the most sophisticated philosophers: Throughout his essay on the soul (*De anima*), everything Aristotle writes about the *psychē* issues from his understanding that it is the life force or the very principle of life, which in humans includes nutrition, regeneration, locomotion, and intellect and emotions. For Aristotle life and *psychē* are virtually synonymous.

Claus's argument, while true to a certain extent, ignores the linkages between *psychē*, *technē*, and *logos* in authors such as Gorgias and Plato. It also fails to factor in the proliferation of the word in the works of the fifth-century dramatists. The *Thesaurus Linguae Graecae* (*TLG*) gives us some 50 instances of the word in Aeschylus, but most of them refer to a dead person's ghost. Sophocles provides around 40 instances, but now mostly referring to the living person. These are instances culled from only his 7 extant plays. Sophocles is said to have produced 123 plays. Extrapolating and projecting, we might hazard that the total for the whole Sophoclean corpus might be 500 occurrences of the word. The surviving plays of Euripides give us 187 instances. Following a similar projection for Euripides, we might have another 500 instances in his plays. The *TLG* gives us 1,268 instances of the word in Plato, most of them referring to the living person. But put the two dramatists together, Sophocles and Euripides, and we might have 1,000 instances. Such a practice begins to beg for comparison with Plato. The proportion of the word's usage in comparison to the author's total vocabulary is also instructive. The *TLG* gives us some 20,500 unique words in the entire surviving Sophoclean corpus (including plays and fragments). The proportion in the uses of *psychē* to the total usage of other words would be 1:500. In Euripides the proportion becomes 1:185; in Plato, 1:40. Clearly, in the dramatists of the fifth century the word was assuming a progressively greater significance. If Euripides had in fact used the word hundreds of times, we must assume that some motive is at work other than mere poetic embellishment.

In his *Oedipus Tyrannus* Sophocles has Oedipus refer to his *psychē* twice in the opening lines of the play; first when he tells the Thebans that his ψυχή grieves for them, for the city, and for himself; then, moments later, when he tells Creon that he suffers the *penthos* of the citizens as if it were for his own ψυχή.[37] It is easy for translators to gloss over the *psychē* in these instances; in some translations both instances vanish altogether. But surely Oedipus must intend his fellow citizens to understand that his *psychē* represents something more than his commonplace self. We hear in his use of the word its Homeric echo, as Sophocles would have us recall that passage in the *Iliad* where Achilles and Hector battle for Hector's soul. This play opens with Oedipus emphasizing twice over that the *penthos* that brings pain and sickness to the citizens of

Thebes is the same *penthos* at the very core of his own being. And indeed it is.

The thinkers of the fifth century, among whom we can include Gorgias and Sophocles, were reaching for a new global concept to signify the whole person, especially some term that would include both the cognitive functions and the emotions. The word certainly has a strong emotional aspect in Gorgias. *Psychē* was a good word for this purpose since it had always been something other than a cognitive organ and had a long-established history, both in literature and in popular culture, as signifying the whole person, in life and in death. From the beginning, the *psychē* was always in some way a person's doppelgänger, a person's invisible and other self.[38]

John Burnet argues that Plato represents Socrates in his last days as having no coherent philosophical concept of the soul.[39] In the *Apology* Plato has Socrates assert that even if the jurors at his trial were to acquit him, provided he promise to stop *philosophizing* (his word), he would not consent to the terms. He would continue as he had always done, exhorting citizens and residents alike to care for their soul. "Sir," he would say, "O best of men, you are an Athenian, a citizen of the greatest city, and the most renowned for wisdom and strength, and are you not ashamed to be concerned with wealth, how much you can accumulate, and with reputation and status, but care nothing for thought itself, for truth or for the soul [*psychē*], how it might be best?"[40] If these are indeed Socrates' words (and Burnet accepts them as such), Burnet takes them to represent a revolution in thought. The care of the soul becomes a common trope in the fourth-century philosophical texts, but the idea, as Socrates expressed it, "must have come as a shock to the Athenian of those days, and may have even seemed not a little ridiculous."[41] But if the Athenians had heard the word hundreds of times spoken from the stage in the plays of their dramatists and if it was constantly on the lips of such thinkers as Gorgias, Socrates' call for the care of the soul could hardly have seemed as outlandish as Burnet suggests. When Socrates devotes the last day of his life to meditating with his friends on the nature of the *psychē*, his interlocutors seem comfortable with the idea of the *psychē* as signifying a person's essence. Specifically, they are conversant with the Pythagorean definition of the *psychē* as harmony, and Socrates goes to some lengths to argue that this is an inadequate definition.

Burnet finds only two instances in the pre-Platonic literature where *psychē* can be taken to mean "character," and both are in this play. The first is in this instance, where Neoptolemus is to steal the *psychē* from

Philoctetes; and the second is in verse 1014, where Philoctetes accuses Odysseus of having an evil *psychē*, which lurks in hiding and peers through crevices seeking those whom it may corrupt. These instances, occurring in a play produced at the end of the century, in Burnet's view prefigure the usage that was to become commonplace a few decades later.[42]

Sophocles' *Oedipus Tyrannus*, and even more obviously his *Philoctetes*, are as much concerned with the care of the soul as any of the Platonic dialogues, though their dialectic must follow a different trajectory. In the *Minos*, a dialogue once attributed to Plato, Socrates describes tragedy as being a very ancient institution, which gives the greatest pleasure to the *demos* and has the *greatest power to lead the soul* (*psychagōgikotaton*).[43] The dialogue is generally considered spurious, but this sentiment conforms to Socrates' sentiments, at least as they are expressed in Plato's authentic dialogue, the *Gorgias*. When Sophocles introduces the *psychē* as the battleground of the tragic conflict in his *Philoctetes*, with Logos as the weapon, which Gorgias argues is the wizardry that overwhelms the *psychē*, why should we not call this wizardry "theft"?

Once Odysseus has given Neoptolemus the word *psychē* at verse 55, we understand the function of the ellipsis at verse 52, when Odysseus tells Neoptolemus that he must show his nobility not only in the body but also *if he hears something new, something he has never heard before*. The unspoken word here is *psychē*, but of course Odysseus could not instruct the youth to be noble in both body and soul. The rest of the prologos is his camouflage for the word so artfully suppressed.

SOPHOS AND *AGATHOS*

After Odysseus has laid out his plan and explained that the present necessity calls for a temporary abeyance of Neoptolemus's moral code, he clinches the case with one last argument:

Οδ. ὡς τοῦτό γ' ἔρξας δύο φέρῃ δωρήματα.
Νϵ. ποίω; μαθὼν γὰρ οὐκ ἂν ἀρνοίμην τὸ δρᾶν.
Οδ. σοφός τ' ἂν αὑτὸς κἀγαθὸς κεκλῇ' ἅμα.
Νϵ. ἴτω· ποήσω, πᾶσαν αἰσχύνην ἀφείς.

(vv. 117–20)

[Od. If you do this you would win two prizes.
Ne. Prizes? What sort of prizes? If I knew those, I would not shrink from doing the deed.

Od. You would be called at the same time both virtuous (*agathos*) and wise (*sophos*).
Ne. So be it. I will do it, putting aside all dishonor and disgrace.]

These two prizes held out to Neoptolemus again situate us in the intellectual milieu of fifth-century Athens. As this play opens, Neoptolemus as son of Achilles must be motivated by the heroic ethos of his father, which Odysseus sums up here in the word *agathos* (good), the word signifying the virtue and valor of an Achilles who would risk life itself if honor were the prize.[44] But a second prize is needed if Neoptolemus is to be a surrogate both for Achilles and for Odysseus. To the traditional prize, to be spoken of as valorous in the face of danger, Odysseus adds another that was never held out as an inducement to any Homeric hero: he must also be thought to be clever. The inducements that Odysseus offers to Neoptolemus constitute a revision of a commonplace formula of Athenian discourse. The conventional expression in Athens for a "gentleman" was *kalos k' agathos*, literally "beautiful and good," the two epithets together summing up the old ideal, the natural endowments of the aristocrat.[45] A "gentleman" was handsome by definition and as virtuous as he was handsome, beautiful and virtuous in all his acts. But Odysseus alters this formula, substituting *sophos* for *kalos*. *Kalos* was a given. Neoptolemus was the handsome son of the most handsome man who ever went to Troy. But now he must be schooled in the new curriculum.

Lloyd-Jones translates verse 119: "You would be called clever, and at the same time valiant." He draws here on the scholiast whom Webster quotes in his note on the verse: "The scholiast rightly says 'clever because of the deceit and valorous because of the sack [of Troy].'" True enough if we restrict our reading to the mythical context, but our reading must include the play's relevance to the sophistic climate of its time. Odysseus is teaching Neoptolemus to remake himself into a fifth-century sophist. He holds before Neoptolemus the prize that had young aristocrats flocking to the rhetoricians to study the new kind of magic called rhetoric. While Odysseus means Neoptolemus to hear in *sophos* a promise that he can become "wise," we hear also Sophocles himself putting an entirely different spin to the word. How could learning to be a thief be called wisdom? We might have Odysseus put the inducement this way: "Neoptolemus, you will receive two prizes: you will be called both valorous and *sophisticated*."

A passage from Plato's *Hippias Minor* comes apt to our argument, where Socrates uses this same phrase, speaking of an ideal geometrician as being both "good and wise" (ἀγαθὸς καὶ σοφός).[46] Such an expert, Socrates says, would have the greatest power both to tell lies and to tell the truth in his field of expertise. The dialogue is now almost universally regarded as spurious; nevertheless, its vocabulary seems of its time, and this particular phrase to describe an expert proficient in a certain skill as being both *agathos* and *sophos* suggests that the trope might have been passing into the vernacular in fifth-century Athens. This allusion to the expert geometrician adds resonance to the prizes Odysseus holds out for Neoptolemus. If Neoptolemus succeeds, he will be both good and clever exactly as Socrates means those terms in the *Hippias*: he would become an unparalleled expert, hence *an unparalleled expert in telling lies.*

Odysseus's words hit their mark. What Athenian ephebe would not want to be sophisticated? Even theft can be acceptable if it can be made to seem sophisticated. Who would not want such power? Neoptolemus consents to fabricate for himself a new self. He too will become a wizard in words: "I will put aside all shame."[47] "If you succeed," Odysseus says, "you will be worshipped with the greatest veneration as the most pious of men," concluding his argument with an allusion to the hero cult of Neoptolemus in the historical period. Shame was a shibboleth of another time, useful perhaps in its day, but it had no place in the modern curriculum.[48]

So ends the prologos. We are now ready to meet our protagonist, Philoctetes.

4

The Parodos

(Verses 135–218)

The Nature and Function of the Chorus

"Parodos" in Greek is a passageway or entrance. In the Theater of Dionysus it was the side entrance into the *orchēstra*. The word came to refer to the entrance of the chorus into the theater and also to the first choral ode sung by the chorus after it made its entrance, which preceded the formal agon of the play. In the parodos of this play, Neoptolemus is already on stage, though Odysseus has moved out of sight for reasons given in the prologos. The chorus now sings its first ode, and when it completes the ode, Philoctetes, the protagonist, arrives on the scene.

This choral ode is composed of two sets of strophes, each set composed of one strophe followed by another strophe of exactly the same metrical form, called the antistrophe. Each set, of strophe and antistrophe, follows its own metrical system. The names point to the origin of choral poetry in Greece, as dance: *strophē* is "turn" and *antistrophē* is "counter-turn." All choral poetry in ancient Greece was a dance performed in a public space for a public occasion, with the members of the chorus moving through turn and counter-turn as they sang the poet's song.

In our culture the dance company and the choir have become separate entities, but this was not so in ancient Greece. Those whom the Greeks called "poets" did not compose poems in lines to be read off the page by a silent reader. Their compositions are songs, marked by melody, rhythm, words, and dance. They were also the choreographers of the dance company, teaching the dancers to perform their songs. The

Greek word for the playwright was *didaskalos*, the "teacher." We think of the playwright as the composer of a text, but in Athens the emphasis was on his role as teacher since he was both the composer and the choreographer of the spectacle set forth in the theater. Ancient tragedy was a musical composition from beginning to end. Even the so-called spoken parts were musical roles, though the metrical schemes used for these parts were closer to the rhythms of ordinary speech than the more complex rhythms of the choral odes.

The chorus in Greek tragedy usually represents the protagonist's community, whether it be the elders of the city if the protagonist should be the king, or the female friends if the protagonist is the queen. The chorus watches the unfolding spectacle with a variety of emotions, sometimes expressing horror at the protagonist's hubris or its faith in the immutable laws of the gods, and often it retreats into the safe mediocrity of the passive spectator, keeping itself at a respectable distance from the violence and arrogance of the protagonist.

The role of the chorus in Greek tragedy has provoked much discussion. The choral component of Greek tragedy is so unlike anything in a modern drama that we have difficulty orienting ourselves as the Athenians might have oriented themselves to the choral odes, or to determine how the odes fit into the overall drama. No consensus is possible if we look for one single defining function of the chorus. Each poet had his choruses serve his particular ends, which might vary from play to play and even within the compass of a single play. Paradox and inconsistency are inevitable since the ancient chorus was used to express an emotional outpouring from the deepest levels of the communal psyche. One scholar has argued that we cannot expect consistency in a character's words or behavior in ancient tragedy since the idea of the fully formed individual had not yet been developed in ancient Greek thought.[1] If this argument holds true for the characters in the drama, it is equally true, perhaps even more so, for the chorus.

Some of the inconsistencies apparent in the chorus may be attributed to the individual playwright's creative genius, but others are the product of the long history in the evolution of the chorus. In its origins the chorus was not the spectator that it became in the later stages of ancient tragedy. Far from it. The chorus was once the actor, being the collective voice and conscience of the whole community.[2] According to Aristotle, both tragedy and comedy evolved from simple and even crude rustic festivals in honor of Dionysus, the god of wine.[3] Tragedy, he claims, grew out of the dithyramb, a choral ode first associated with Dionysus, which had a reputation for being a dance of orgiastic intoxication. In time these uncouth village dances evolved into a more serious form. First, a single individual was singled out from the collective dance. This person was not yet an actor in our sense of the word; he seems rather to have been the leader of the chorus, the *exarchon*, as he was called. The Greek word that came to be used for the actor, *hypocritēs*, meaning the "answerer" or "interpreter," indicates this individual's role to be at one time the leader of the dance who later became its interpreter.[4] A. W. Pickard-Cambridge suggests that this single performer was one of the singers who "separated himself from the rest and engaged in lyric 'question and answer' with his companions."[5] Aeschylus, so Aristotle informs us, added the second actor, and at this point we have what can be recognized as drama in our sense of the term, with two characters engaged in conflict with each other, and their conflict dominating the action and consequently reducing the part of the chorus. Sophocles introduced the third actor (that is, allowing for three speaking parts to be on the scene simultaneously). This alteration, as it multiplied the possibilities for more complex relations among the characters, led to further diminution of the choral part. We see the effectiveness of this development in Sophocles' *Philoctetes*, which gives us a sophisticated triangulation in the conflict among the play's three characters. The gain for the characters is a loss for the chorus; yet even so, this chorus is far from being only a spectator.

In antiquity a saying regarding tragedy became proverbial: "nothing to do with Dionysus." The atmosphere in which the plays were performed was saturated in the Dionysiac cult. The plays were presented in the Theater of Dionysus in Athens at the festival in honor of Dionysus called the Greater Dionysia. A cult image of the god was brought into the theater at the time of the performances and placed beside the priest of Dionysus. The priest himself sat in the place of honor, on a stone seat in a row of seats on the *orchēstra* floor, flanked by the officials of the polis. The god himself and his chief priest watched the spectacle ex cathedra, as it were, not only as spectators but as the spectacle's highest judges. Yet our extant plays show little preoccupation with Dionysiac themes. The myths of Dionysus figure no more conspicuously in the plots of the tragedies than do the myths of the other gods and heroes. So striking is the absence of Dionysus from the tragedies that one scholar, rejecting Aristotle's derivation of tragedy from a primitive cult of Dionysus, posits that tragedy was invented out of whole cloth at the command of Peisistratus (tyrant of Athens 560–527 BCE) and simply added in effect arbitrarily to the city's festival of Dionysus because of the festival's pan-Athenian popularity.[6]

The Altar

Certainly, it is problematic that tragedy as we find it in Aeschylus could have grown in a short time from a crude origin in simple peasant rituals. Yet it is difficult to accept the theory that tragedy was brought into existence at a single moment and by order of the tyrant casting about for ways to inculcate a new civic consciousness. Tragedy is replete with primitive elements, choral song being one of the most primitive of all. Even without Aristotle's authority we have scraps of testimony, which, taken together, sketch a picture that seems consistent with his thesis that tragedy arose in the cult of Dionysus. In the simple staging of the Athenian theater there were, it seems, two altars. One altar, placed on the stage, was used as a stage property as in the plays when a character uses it to claim sanctuary from some threatening enemy. But in the *orchēstra* stood another altar. No doubt this was the altar around which the chorus gathered after it had entered the theater. This altar was not so much a stage item as something symbolic signifying the original function common to altars in any religious ritual, as the table on which the animal was sacrificed. Its continuing presence in the theater signified the essential theological nature of the dramatic performance. One source informs us that this altar was called a "table" (*eleos*), and on this table, according to our source, "before Thespis a single man mounted and answered the choreuts."[7] The *Etymologicum Magnum* (*EM*) adds another clue as to the nature of this table before it became a dance floor. The *EM* dates from the Byzantine period; it was available for Eustathius, archbishop of Thessalonika, to consult in the thirteenth century CE, and its compilations go back to the ninth century CE. As a dictionary it is an invaluable source for meanings of words in use long before the Common Era. Under the entry *thymele*, the *EM* has this to say: "The *thymele* which still exists in the theater is named from the table, because the sacrifices were cut up on it, i.e., the victims being sacrificed. It was the table on which they stood and sang in the fields, when tragedy had not yet been organized."[8]

Here we have it: the butcher's block, the altar, and the dance floor, all in one. To think ourselves back before Aeschylus, back even earlier than the legendary Thespis, we must think of villagers killing the animal on a table and then leaping onto the same table to sing their song of lamentation and triumph. We can infer that the earliest chorus would have been composed of the young athletes of the village, who would have been the butcher boys. In Catholic churches today this sacred table is called the high altar; in nonconformist churches, where talk of altars and priests is taboo, it is the Lord's table. Of this altar Pickard-Cambridge writes that it was "the ritual altar of Dionysus, which belonged to the festival, not to the play, and was in the center of the orchestra."[9] This altar once had been the centerpiece of the ancient passion play.

The original festival from which tragedy arose centered on sacrifice of an animal. This was the first sacrament of organized religion, evolving from two human needs; first, the biological need to kill other living animals for food, and, second, the higher-level need to placate those invisible powers on whose goodwill food, health, and prosperity depend. The great sacrifice that gave birth to tragedy is contained in the myth of the death and rebirth of Dionysus, the god ritually killed in the harvesting of the grape but then reborn in the spring as the new grapes bud on the old vine. Once he is slain, whether as the grape pressed into wine or in his totem form as the goat, the god's worshippers drink of his blood (either literally or as the new fermented wine) and devour his flesh in the roasted meat, to satisfy the hunger that was both biological and spiritual. The dithyramb, from which Aristotle derives the tragic chorus, was the ecstatic dance with which the villagers celebrated their orgy of hubris in killing and eating their own god.

In those rustic dances celebrating the slaughter and resurrection of the god, the chorus was not a group of horrified bystanders but the members of the community who had first sanctified the animal and made it into their god, then commissioned their priest to kill the animal, and following the kill joined in the celebration, which was a dance of both lamentation and triumph. Freud conjectured that the original *mythos* from which tragedy evolved was the oedipal crime. He suggests that the men who formed the early chorus in Greek tragedy were the primal horde, the sons who rose up against their tyrannical father, slew him, and appropriated his powers and privileges.[10] The protagonist who suffers the tragic destiny was once, in Freud's view, the primal father, on whom was placed the burden of guilt to free the chorus of its collective guilt. It is worth noting that when Plato has Socrates condemn the pernicious influence of tragedy, he singles out as the most pathological myth of tragedy the cosmogonic oedipal myth as told by Hesiod, of the mother and son conspiring to castrate the father.

Tragedy began, then, in the crime of parricide. As that original father became deified, the original crime became deicide, and in time, as Athenian society developed into more sophisticated political forms, deicide was translated into tyrannicide. In Aeschylus's *Agamemnon*, Agamemnon, the protagonist, plays all parts; he is the sacrificial victim; he is the king who must be slain, the tyrant, and the god surrogate. Greek tragedy, if we dismiss Freud's theory and prefer, in Emerson's words, a "more commanding theory" of our own, certainly focuses on the most primitive crimes, with most of them being in-house crimes such as abound in Greek myth and in the histories, mythical or legendary, of the noble houses of ancient Greece—the father killing his daughter, the son castrating his father or killing his mother, the mother killing her children.

If we accept Freud's speculation about the original function of the tragic chorus, that function has been vastly transformed by the time we have the fully developed tragedies of the fifth century. Once the conspirators in the primeval crime have shed their guilt by projecting it onto the sacrificial host, the chorus becomes the impotent spectators watching the deadly combat among their rulers. "The scene upon the stage," Freud writes, "came into being through purposive distortion of the historical scene or, one is tempted to say, it was the result of refined hypocrisy."[11]

In the tragedies as we have them, the animal sacrifice has disappeared, replaced by the passion of the suffering hero. The butcher's table has divided and metamorphosed into two forms, into the stage where the actors perform their drama and the *orchēstra* below the stage where the chorus enacts the drama in dance and song. At this point in the evolution of the form, the chorus has passed its criminal propensities on to the protagonist, who, like the scapegoat in ancient religions, must be a blameless victim yet blameworthy at the same time. We can trace the dynamics of this contradiction both in our extant tragedies and in Aristotle's definition of the ideal tragedy. The catastrophe has the greatest emotional force, Aristotle argues, when the protagonist is better than we are, by which we understand him to mean that this doomed person must be of a higher rank, should be a ruler or a member of the great ruling houses of ancient myth. Such a person occupied a loftier station morally than the people simply by the divine right of kings. He is "blameless" in that the king in mythical times cannot be judged by ordinary human standards since his authority and privilege derive directly from the gods. Yet this person, all but divine himself, must be guilty of some moral infraction if he is to incur divine retribution and we are to experience the emotions proper to tragedy. Hence Aristotle's hamartia must also enter into the equation. A transgression is required if the drama is to engage our emotions. The protagonist must make some error, some miscalculation; he or she must transgress. A catastrophe befalling a completely innocent person would be anathema, Aristotle argues, and similarly with a catastrophe befalling a completely corrupt person. The tragic fate must be deserved and yet not deserved at the same time.

Aristotle has little to say about two of the most fundamental aspects of Greek tragedy: the role of the gods and the role of the chorus. On the chorus he has but one brief reference to its origin in the dithyrambic dance, and later in his discussion of the parts of a tragedy, he calls the lyric element (what Butcher translates as "song") the sweetest of the embellishments. Such casual remarks indicate that for him tragedy was primarily plot and character. Yet the chorus was once the heart of the drama. The true understanding of tragedy must begin with the chorus as the music of the play. As such, it will naturally express the flux of emotions as they may be generated in one episode after another. We should expect contradiction and paradox, the very qualities that Plato condemned as concessions to irrationalism.

At this late date in the development of tragedy, the chorus might seem almost superfluous to the action, and the plot of this play makes the old-fashioned chorus otiose. The chorus should represent the protagonist's community, but the protagonist of this play has no community. Both Aeschylus and Euripides found a compromise for their productions. Both of them had presented Lemnos as an inhabited island, and when a chorus is needed, behold! a chorus materializes out of nowhere, a group of Lemnian citizens who were apparently aware of Philoctetes' existence but tactfully minded their own business until they were needed in the drama. This is an unsatisfactory solution. The Lemnians dragooned into the drama in these earlier versions are not Philoctetes' community. His community was the Greek army at Troy, from which he had been expelled. From Dio's essay, we learn that Aeschylus had his chorus of Lemnian citizens appear without any apology or explanation, while Euripides had his Lemnians offer some tepid excuses for their improbable arrival on the scene, admitting that they had acted poorly in ignoring Philoctetes' suffering during the ten years of his residence on their island.

Sophocles will not settle for this awkward compromise. He makes his theatrical space even more resistant to compromise by having the island completely uninhabited except for Philoctetes himself. He then devises a solution dramatically more plausible and considerably more emotional. First, he adds Neoptolemus to the plot, and with him added, a chorus can now be justified and given a legitimate use. It will be composed of the Myrmidons who had served under Achilles (we are to infer) but are now serving under the son of Achilles. Just as Neoptolemus is in significant ways a compromise, so his chorus is a compromise. When it is needed to serve Odysseus's purpose, it fits neatly into that part. When, at the end of the play, Neoptolemus has changed from being Philoctetes' false friend to being his true friend, the chorus adapts accordingly, becoming the sages of Philoctetes' own community, scolding him, counseling him, expressing both sympathy and disapproval, as befits the elders visiting a sick member of their own community.

One effect of giving the chorus to Neoptolemus, while depriving Philoctetes of his, is to shift the center of gravity from Philoctetes to Neoptolemus, making Neoptolemus the virtual protagonist. The novelty of this play is that Sophocles is experimenting with two protagonists whose dramas interact with and influence each other until they synthesize into a single drama. The bipolar function of the chorus accentuates the polarity of the play as a whole. In working his way toward two protagonists, Sophocles brings into the foreground the point made in the myth itself, that the fall of Troy depended on two individuals who were both absent from the battlefield until the last days of the war, yet whose simultaneous presence is needed to turn the tide toward Greek victory. Each had his own separate destiny, but the two destinies are linked together in the prophecy given by the seer Helenus. Sophocles makes the linkage between the two destinies explicit; even more significant, however, he makes the linkage itself the subject of his drama. How did these two men, made by Sophocles to seem of utterly diverse character, unite into creating for themselves a single destiny? How the two heroic destinies come into conflict with each other, to unite finally in a single destiny, becomes the larger agon of the play. The shifting allegiances of the chorus help us to understand that this is a new kind of drama.

The Aporia

In this play, the chorus enters the theater in a state of aporia. This should not surprise us. Perplexity and vague forebodings are the normal state of a Greek chorus, which is by definition passive and dependent, aware but only vaguely so of the crisis at hand. But the aporia takes on added significance in this play in that it represents the emotional state not only of the chorus but also of its master, Neoptolemus. As the play unfolds, he is faced with one aporia after another and even collapses in total aporia at the end of the play when Philoctetes has won him to his point of view. This final irresolution, which passes itself off as manly resolution, is brought to its true resolution only when Heracles descends from heaven to intervene directly and correct the human mistake.

Normally in Greek tragedy, the chorus, regardless of the clouds gathering ominously on the horizon, is in its own domicile, or at least in its own milieu. Here, however, the chorus, to use its own words, is a stranger in a strange land. It knows not where it is or what it should do:

τί χρὴ τί χρή με, δέσποτ', ἐν ξένᾳ ξένον
στέγειν, ἢ τί λέγειν πρὸς ἄνδρ' ὑπόπταν;
φράζε μοι.

(vv. 135–37)

[What, oh what must I hide, my lord—
I, a stranger in this, a strange land?
Or what must I say to a suspicious man? Tell me.]

The chorus knows neither the place where it has arrived nor the protagonist since he has never been a member of its community. He is as much a stranger to it as is this island on which it now finds itself. This is new territory for the chorus, as indeed it is also for Neoptolemus. Lacking roots in this soil and any real kinship ties with the protagonist, the chorus clings to its lord, Neoptolemus. Danger lurks in this unfamiliar terrain, but its aporia springs from a deeper source. It is not the simple anxiety of men who have arrived on a foreign shore. Pretense is the real burden of the chorus's perplexity. What shall we *pretend* to know? What shall we *pretend* not to know?

The chorus, expressing first its aporia, turns to Neoptolemus for guidance, addressing him with the kind of flattery that a monarch could expect from his subjects:

τέχνα γὰρ τέχνας ἑτέρας
προὔχει καὶ γνώμα παρ' ὅτῳ τὸ θεῖον
Διὸς σκῆπτρον ἀνάσσεται.
σὲ δ' ὦ τέκνον, τόδ' ἐλήλυθεν

πᾶν κράτος ὠγύγιον· τό μοι ἔννεπε
τί σοι χρεὼν ὑπουγεῖν.
(vv. 137–42)

Phillips gives us (his vv. 152–56):

Tell me.
For his cunning surpasses that of others,
As does the wisdom of kings—those who wield the divine scepter of
Zeus.
All this ancient mastery has come to you, young man—
tell me then: what must I do to help you?

The syntax here is awkward, but the sense is clear. Lloyd-Jones translates: "Tell me, for his skill and judgment are better than another's, his in whose hand the scepter is wielded. And to you, my son, has come all this ancient power." Webster, in his note at verse 137, gives us two alternatives: "*Either* a paratactic simile 'one art surpasses another and the judgment of kings (surpasses other judgments) . . . *or* 'the art and judgment of the king surpasses other arts (and judgments).'" He prefers the latter.

The chorus, to acknowledge Neoptolemus's superior wisdom and craft, uses the two words, *technē* and *gnōmai*, soon to be used by Philoctetes and Neoptolemus in the first episode, when they contrast Odysseus's craft in wrestling with ideas with Nestor's wise counsels. Webster refers us to a passage in Sophocles' *Oedipus* (v. 380), where Oedipus speaks of "*technē* surpassing *technē*," and glosses that passage to mean "the art surpassing art in competitive life clearly is the royal art." Webster gets at the essential idea in this passage but fails to give their full weight to these terms as used in this play. Neither word is innocently used. The wisdom for which Neoptolemus is being praised is about to issue in theft, and his royal *technē* in this context is not art but fabrication. Stripping away its compliments, we read the chorus to mean: "Help us. You are our king, and kings are more clever at fabrication. Teach us how to fabricate a successful lie." The chorus steps winsomely across this bog by talking of its king's *ogygian* power, the primeval authority and wisdom that he has derived from Zeus. Phillips brings the covert message in this passage to the fore when he translates *technē* as "cunning," but whoever has praised a king's cunning as superior to other men's cunning? The message here must be thoroughly ethical and obnoxious at the same time. The chorus, for all its piety, is not as naive as it may sound. It knows whereof it speaks. Its reference is to the *sophisma* outlined by Odysseus in the prologos. In opening this ode with a sumptuous genuflection in honor of its king's divinely endowed wisdom, it smooths the way for him to become Machiavellian. Malfeasance is the subject of our song.

Neoptolemus responds prosaically enough. While Philoctetes is absent from his cave, the chorus may indulge its curiosity; it may look at that "place at the far extremity where he has his bed." But when Philoctetes appears, it must turn its attention back to Neoptolemus, to watch for his hand signals and give him its service, which Neoptolemus calls its *therapeia* (ministry). Neoptolemus identifies Philoctetes as "*deinos hoditēs* [the terrifying traveler]" (v. 147). Why "traveler" or "wayfarer"? And why is he terrifying (*deinos*)? *Hoditēs* alludes to his walking, to the wound that has made him a cripple. He is *deinos* both because of that wound, which was divinely afflicted, and because he is invested with Heracles' numen, which came to him when he received the bow. Philoctetes is marked both by the wound and by the bow, the incurable wound and the invincible bow, both given to him by divine dispensation. His is no ordinary wound, and his weapon is no ordinary weapon. Everything about him is awesome—his wound, his pain, his way of life, his solitude, his survival, his destiny. He has been set apart from humankind. He walks a different road.

The *Kairos*

Told to keep alert for its master's signals, the chorus opens the first antistrophe with the solemn assurance that its king's welfare has always been its greatest concern: "This, the care you speak of, has been my concern from days of old, to keep my eye on guard for your best interests [*kairos*], from moment to moment" (vv. 150–51). The challenging word here is *kairos*. The simplest translation would be "opportunity," but "opportunity" is the weakest of all translations for this august concept. Phillips gives us "your best interests" (his v. 163), which I have borrowed here, but adding the phrase "from moment to moment" to allude to the culture of meanings nested within the word *kairos*. Lloyd-Jones gives us "my eyes should ever be vigilant for what you most need." On the prosaic level, the chorus merely articulates the conventional duty of the king's subjects to keep watch over their lord's welfare. But these men are not merely the king's courtiers. They are *actors* in a play, and they are learning their parts from the man they call their king.

Kairos is a magnificent word. The lexicon gives as its primary meanings "due measure, proportion, fitness," and as its third broad meaning "exact or critical time, season, opportunity." The Greeks venerated the moment, not time in the abstract, but *timing*. *Kairos* is the moment of crisis. Out of a deep reverence, colored by a deep anxiety, for the significance of the moment in human life, they made Kairos a god. The *Oxford Classical Dictionary* calls this Kairos "personified Opportunity." Time for us may be stooped and old, but *timing* can never be old; it is always born anew in every new crisis.

Pausanias, in his topographical tour of Greek cities and sites (second century CE), saw two altars at the entrance to the Olympia stadium, one to Hermes Enagonios, the other to Kairos.[12] These two gods at Olympia were two sides of the same coin. Hermes Enagonios is Hermes of the contest, Hermes of the brilliant opportunity, of the unexpected good luck; as such, he is *puer aeternus*. Every moment is a golden opportunity. Kairos too is also ageless, and for the same reason. He too is the god of the moment, the moment itself personified. In every one of the athletic contests held at the sacred site, Kairos would shine on one youth, and one alone—the victor. Neoptolemus's talk of hand signals would emphasize for the Athenian audience that *kairos* here has the significance it would have for every young athlete at the Olympic games. Neoptolemus is about to make his entry into manhood with a wrestling match, and on its outcome will depend the whole of his future life, whether it be glorious or forever marked by shame. While the chorus is to keep its eyes on Neoptolemus, as if he were its *didaskalos*, Neoptolemus himself is following the instructions of his own *didaskalos*, Odysseus. The craft to which the chorus alludes, of course, at least as we understand the reference, is not the craft of the perfect king, but the craft in which Odysseus excels, the craft of fabrication.

The chorus, having assured Neoptolemus of its absolute dependability, continues in its mood of anxiety and ignorance. What is permissible? it asks. What kind of place has it come to? Where is the man? Is he inside his cave or wandering about outside? Its questions, while establishing its character as alien to this place, reinforce the terrible truth that the alien here is Philoctetes. He has been set apart. The chorus needs to know his habits, his usual circuits, lest he, that monstrous wayfarer, come on it unawares (vv. 154–55). Neoptolemus completes this antistrophe with his response, pointing out the cave where Philoctetes makes his bed and speaking of his nature being to hunt prey with his bow and arrows, a painful kind of action and a painful livelihood.

In its second strophe and antistrophe (vv. 169–90), the chorus makes an abrupt shift both in the context of its ode and in its tone. Neoptolemus had opened the way for this shift by speaking in the previous antistrophe of Philoctetes' arduous way of life and of his pain for which there is no healing. Even so, the shift is pronounced and surprising. Forgetting its role as conspirator, the chorus now sings a lamentation over the pathos of this unhappy man, so grievously sick, so destitute. How could he endure such a life? He is in no way inferior to other men; he comes from among the foremost families. Yet he is given a life worse than any other; he exists alone, cut off from others, living among the shaggy beasts, enduring a pain unendurable and undeserved.

"He cries out," the chorus sings, "but Echo mocks him, repeating his bitter sound in the far distance" (vv. 188–90). Echo is given two epithets: *telephanēs* (appearing at or from a distance) and *athyrostomos* (with babbling mouth). The lexicon gives us "babbling" as the meaning of this rare word and translators follow suit. Sophocles' *athyrostomos* is an epithet appropriate to a little girl; it conjures up the child's playful and meaningless chatter. But is "babbling" the best description of the Echo of this play? Echo in this play is no child but a demon, and cruel indeed is her sport in this desolate place. Since Echo is the only other living being who shares this island with Philoctetes, as its genius loci her genius is to echo back to him his own voice but drained of meaning, made inhuman. Even inhuman sounds can be tolerable when they are the sounds of nature. Echo is human sound dehumanized, made to be neither human sound nor the sound of nature.

If we are surprised by the change of theme in the choral strophe and antistrophe, we are even more surprised to find Neoptolemus, with not a word to mark the transition, now exchanging one persona for another:

Νε. οὐδὲν τούτων θαυμαστὸν ἐμοί·
θεῖα γάρ, εἴπερ κἀγώ τι φρονῶ,
καὶ τὰ παθήματα κεῖνα πρὸς αὐτὸν
τῆς ὠμόφρονος Χρύσης ἐπέβη,
καὶ νῦν ἃ πονεῖ δίχα κηδεμόνων,
οὐκ ἔσθ' ὡς οὐ θεῶν του μελέτη
τοῦ μὴ πρότερον τόνδ' ἐπι Τροίᾳ
τεῖναι τὰ θεῶν ἀμάχητα βέλη,
πρὶν ὅδ' ἐξήκοι χρόνος, ᾧ λέγεται
χρῆναι σφ' ὑπὸ τῶνδε δαμῆναι.

(vv. 191–200)

[Ne. None of this amazes me.
For these affairs are divine, if I am thinking aright,
both the sufferings (*pathēmata*)
that have come to him from the cruel-minded Chrysē
and his present labors here, separated from other people.
It is not possible that these events are not a concern to one of the gods—
that this man should not train the invincible weapons of the gods
on Troy until that time should come
when it is decreed
that the city should be vanquished by them.]

Moments earlier Neoptolemus was an ephebe, idealistic and naive, who had been persuaded to become a thief in the expectation that he will recover his ideals at a later time, and even augmented by a greater honor. In this new persona, Neoptolemus has become Miltonic, defending the ways of God to man. This passage is our first clear indication that the play itself is theological through and through.[13] Of the theology, Odysseus had nothing to say. From his words in the prologos, we would assume that we were engaged in a completely secular drama. Now we are given to understand that the essential nature of the drama is not political but spiritual.

As modern readers we are caught off guard because in the second half of this ode the chorus, into which Neoptolemus himself has now been assimilated, regresses to its most ancient functions. When the chorus in the second strophe sings a lamentation for Philoctetes' suffering, speaking of "the dark dealings of the gods" and "the hapless races of men, whose destiny exceeds due measure" (to borrow Jebb's translation), it has stepped outside its dramatic role and reverted to its primordial role as the collective congregation singing the passion hymn. Neoptolemus too has stepped out of his role as an actor in the political drama and reverts to the actor's earliest function in tragedy as the *exarchon*, the leader of the chorus; but he is also the *hypocritēs* in the oldest sense, interpreting the drama to the members of the chorus. In this shift, so unexpected for us if we are measuring ancient tragedy by modern criteria of realism, the politics are altogether put aside for the moment, and we are taken back to tragedy's roots in the passion play. The shift from politics to the passion hinges on one fact: suffering.[14] Of suffering Odysseus had not a word to say.

The sorrow expressed by the chorus, while it relates specifically to Philoctetes, is also the generic lamentation for a tragic hero's pathos. It strikes all the notes that we expect in such a hymn: this man is inferior to no one; no doubt he is the scion of a noble house. Yet he is cast out, cut off from humankind, made to live with the beasts, almost a beast himself, and made to suffer beyond human measure. The implication, that this is an innocent man visited with suffering far beyond any transgression, leads the chorus to raise the questions of theodicy that are inevitable in any tragic performance.

Neoptolemus speaking as the *hypocritēs* interprets for the chorus the collective wisdom that the passion is part of divine Necessity. Having the chorus assigned to Neoptolemus rather than to Philoctetes makes his transition easier from actor to spokesperson for the spiritual values of the drama. It may be confusing for us to have Neoptolemus move so abruptly from the trickster to the exarchon of the chorus, but Greek tragedy is a palimpsest. Old functions are not simply eliminated; they may be modified as the form evolved, but they can still be deciphered beneath the latest texts. Indeed, they are *expected*. Neoptolemus's function as the *exarchon* is as central to his role in this play as his other persona, as the duplicitous actor of the drama.

Neoptolemus's whole response to the choral lamentation is his gloss on the word *kairos*. The chorus uses the word in its blandest sense to mean its master's best interests, but Neoptolemus now elevates it to the cardinal principle of ancient tragedy. In tragedies where the protagonist is doomed, it would be tactless to dwell on the protagonist's *kairos*, but in this play the passion ends in triumph. This outcome gives Neoptolemus as the "interpreter" more room to celebrate even the hero's suffering as a paradigm of *kairos*. "It is not possible that this is happening except through the care of some god"—so Neoptolemus gives his priestly interpretation of the tragic hero's destiny.

At the heart of Greek tragedy is destiny, but destiny is a vortex of irreconcilable cross-purposes. The protagonist must be exalted and cast down, a victim of the supernatural powers yet also a person who makes a fatal mistake. There are no accidents in tragedy. Tragedy requires coincidence, and *kairos* is coincidence. Everything in the tragic cosmology is to be accepted as ordered according to *kairos*, even when this *kairos* includes seemingly ruthless deities. Troy must fall; that is decreed by the gods. It is also decreed that the bow of Heracles will be the instrument to bring about the fall of Troy. But this instrument must be kept in hiding for ten years until its *kairos* calls for it to emerge and bring the wicked city to the ground. Nothing here is not a concern for the gods.

This processional hymn, simple as it is, is layered with many antique functions of the chorus in Greek tragedy, especially if we understand Neoptolemus to be its principal singer. Beginning in absolute dependency, the chorus modulates into a different key when it speaks as the king's nobles, asserting that his welfare has always been their greatest concern. But then its focus shifts to Philoctetes, that stranger so horrifying in his disease, in his nature, and in his fate, estranged from human nature and from nature itself. At this point in the old village performance, we can assume that the chorus would have entered into the sacred space and grouped itself in a circle around the altar where a short time earlier the sacrifice was consummated, now to become the dance floor on which the tragic drama is to be told. Neoptolemus thereupon takes up his sacerdotal function to affirm the theology of this ancient festival, that the hero of this passion play has been sanctified for his role in this tragedy so that his destiny, which includes both his suffering and his victory, may declare the majesty of God, whom Philoctetes himself names in the final verses of the play as Δαίμων Πανδαμάτωρ, "the Spirit who conquers all."

But quiet! The play is about to begin. The final words of this parodos are the cue for Philoctetes to appear.

The Sound

"Hold your tongue, boy," the chorus breaks in on the priest's homily on the just and perfect destiny (v. 201). With these words the chorus exits from its primordial role as the communicant celebrating the ancient rite of sacrifice and reenters the political arena.

"What is it?" Neoptolemus asks, now no longer the *exarchon* but the actor caught up in the machinations of a plot imposed on him by that prince of actors, Odysseus.

"A sound rang out," the chorus replies. Here it sings what may be the longest ode in all of Greek poetry dedicated to a single sound, which is amplified through the final eighteen verses of the parodos (vv. 201–18). The chorus brings this extended moment of listening to a close with the word *deinon*. The sound is "awesome." It *strikes* the ear like a blow, the sound of a man in agony. It comes from this direction and from that; it *reverberates*. It is truly the voice of a man who treads his path by *necessity*. It is an unmistakable *sign*, the *sign* of a man in pain.

"What is it?" Neoptolemus continues. The chorus further amplifies the sound by describing it as what it is not. This is no shepherd piping pastoral ditties to his sheep on some upland meadow. It is the cry of a man who stumbles by *necessity*. Necessity strikes upon our ears a second time, and having just listened to Neoptolemus discourse on necessity as the essence of tragedy, we are now to understand that this man's necessity is both personal and cosmic. His is no ordinary movement. There is no freedom here, no joy in physical activity. Every step is forced labor. The noise he makes is stark, strange, *unmusical*. Neoptolemus has already spoken of this man as the *deinos hoditēs*, the terrible wayfarer, and now, hearing his noise, we understand why it too is called *deinos*. This is the man whose cry was so uncouth that ten years earlier it stopped religion altogether until it could be removed far from human ears. It breaks in now on the pieties of the choral ode. At the same time, it is the ode's concluding note, that one long note for which the whole ode is the overture. This cry, so human yet so inhuman, echoes throughout the theater as the first chord of the Via Dolorosa theme, which is to sound and resound throughout the rest of this play.

Enter Philoctetes.

5

The First Episode

(Verses 219–675)

We have taken the term "episode" (*epeisodion* in Greek) from Aristotle to refer to the dialogue sections in tragedy. *Epeisodion* is that which is "added onto, or inserted into" the song. The word, assuming that it was part of the traditional nomenclature, gives us further evidence of the primacy of the chorus. Other meanings for *epeisodion* include "adventitious," "addition to give pleasure" (as sugar might be added to coffee), or "parenthesis." How far we have come from the original idea, that the spoken conflicts between the characters on stage are the parenthesis in the drama: we take the dialogues to be the essence of the drama and consider the function of the chorus to be to provide musical interludes.

The Human Voice

The cry that concludes the parodos leads directly into the first sound of this episode.

"O strangers," the strange man calls out to Neoptolemus and his chorus, "who are you who have just put into this land that has neither good anchorage nor human habitation? Who are your fathers? Who are your people? Your dress is Greek, dearest of all apparel to me, but I need to hear your speech [*phonē*]."

Several words built on the same root are used to emphasize voice, speech, language. First, *phonē*, which Lloyd-Jones translates as "voice" (v. 225); then the verb *phonēo*, "to speak"; then the abstract noun *phonēma*, "utterance." Philoctetes has heard no human voice for ten years. The only voice to reach his ears has been his echo, which relentlessly accentuates his own voiceless condition. Philoctetes begs these strangers not to flee from him as if he were some creature gone wild, but to speak to him, to recognize in him a human being. When Neoptolemus pauses in silence, Philoctetes adds greater urgency to his appeal: "Answer me. It is not right that I should fail to receive this from you, or you from me" (vv. 230–31). "This" is language, not mere sound but human discourse. Communication is his greatest need, greater even, at this point at least, than his need to have his wound healed. Philoctetes' opening words give us to understand that communication, the true versus the false, is central to the play as a whole.

"Yes, stranger, we are Hellenes," Neoptolemus responds, "for this is what you need to know" (vv. 232–33).[1]

"O dearest sound!" Philoctetes responds. "To think that I would once again receive the human voice after so long a time, and from such a man." The words here are *phonēma* (simple "utterance") and *prosphthengmai*, the latter meaning "speech addressed to someone," a salutation. Philoctetes is overjoyed at the sound of his own language, but his joy is doubled when he hears himself *spoken to*. The first link between him and Neoptolemus is forged through *logos*. Now after ten years of solitude, speech has been restored to Philoctetes, and "with such a man"—a Greek, dressed as a Greek, speaking as a Greek, and, as he will now discover, the noble son of the noblest man in Greece. But this first and dearest human sound to fall on Philoctetes' ears is a false note, as false as the Echo named in the parodos but more devastating than Echo's blind mimesis. Echo is a trick of nature. Neoptolemus is a trick of human ingenuity.

Neoptolemus identifies himself: "My clan is from sea-girt Skyros. I claim to be the son of Achilles, and I am sailing for home" (vv. 239–41). So Neoptolemus begins, weaving a thread of truth into his tapestry of lies exactly as he has been instructed. Philoctetes is swept away by this news—the son of Achilles! And the trap is sprung: "O son of the dearest father and sprung from the soil dear to me" (v. 242). Philoctetes uses *philtatos* (most beloved) three times, first when speaking of the men's Greek dress, then of the speech that issues from Neoptolemus's mouth, and now of Neoptolemus's father. These superlatives tell us that the *sophisma* is about to fall on welcoming ears.

Philoctetes asks for more details, and now comes the story invented to forge the bond between the long-suffering Philoctetes and the son of

Achilles. Neoptolemus explains that he is sailing back to Skyros from Ilium. Ilium! Ilium? Philoctetes is perplexed. How could Neoptolemus be coming from Ilium? He was not a member of the original armada that had sailed to Troy. Philoctetes asks for clarification. Now it is Neoptolemus's turn to show surprise: "What? Did you too share in that labor?" (v. 248).

Philoctetes is stung to the quick, thrown from ecstasy into mortification. He is unknown: "Child, you do not know him whom you behold before you?" "How could I recognize a man whom I have never seen?" is the reply. "You mean," Philoctetes continues, "you know neither my name nor anything of the evil condition that is destroying me?" "I know nothing of all that," Neoptolemus replies, now as glib as his coach (vv. 249–53). Philoctetes is devastated. The man who had led the Greek commanders to the shrine of the goddess, he who holds the bow of Heracles—completely unknown? He has truly been cast out, robbed of name and story.[2] So much for the "dearest sound" that had come to Philoctetes' ears.

Philoctetes is now given the opportunity to share his story: communication from one side, miscommunication from the other. This man whom Neoptolemus now sees is Philoctetes, a great hero in his own right and exalted even higher by the privilege that came to him from Heracles when he received the bow. Furthermore, the tale of his woe is itself memorable. How could such a tale disappear? Neoptolemus learns now, or so he pretends, the story of the snakebite, of how Odysseus brought Philoctetes to Lemnos and left him on this desolate soil. Philoctetes goes on to describe his existence. The island has no anchorage; any ship that appears in its harbor is driven there by sheer necessity. The soil is destitute of water and vegetation. The physical conditions have reduced Philoctetes almost to the Stone Age. His only source of food is provided by the birds that his bow can bring down, and then he must drag his crippled body across the hard terrain to retrieve the prey. To accentuate his pathos, Philoctetes speaks of spending the past ten years "feeding his insatiable disease" (v. 313). He concludes his story with a prayer to the Olympian gods for vengeance: may the sons of Atreus and Odysseus suffer as he has suffered.

This gives Neoptolemus his cue. He now gives his story in exchange, which is remarkably similar to the story he has just heard from Philoctetes, the false story mimicking the true. Neoptolemus claims that he can bear witness to Philoctetes' story; he has his own testimony of the treachery of those leaders and their abuse. When pressed for details,

Neoptolemus begins his story with the death of his father, Achilles. Learning of the death of that great man leads Philoctetes to offer his condolences: "Wellborn was He who killed him [that is, Apollo] and wellborn was he who died" (v. 336). Neoptolemus accepts the condolences and continues the story. Two men, Odysseus and Phoenix, were sent from Troy to Skyros to bring him to Troy after his father's death at Troy. His fiction is woven from Homeric strands. The allusion here is to the embassy sent out by Agamemnon to Achilles' tent, when the same two men were sent to bring Neoptolemus's father back onto the battle line in the *Iliad*, book 9. Sophocles also works in here the traditional tale of how the armor of Achilles was awarded to Odysseus. Neoptolemus, so goes his masquerade, when he discovers that those famous weapons, which were his rightful inheritance, have been given to Odysseus, registers his vigorous protest. But the sons of Atreus refuse to rescind their decision, and to make matters worse, Odysseus heaps his own contempt on the magnificent son of Achilles, who had been comfortably absent for the previous ten years of the Trojan War. Neoptolemus, in full bloom as an actor, now appropriates the anger of Ajax when he was similarly treated in the Homeric tradition. Neoptolemus claims that he has forsaken the Greek army altogether, as his father had threatened to do in the Homeric story that he has borrowed for his own use on the present occasion.

Neoptolemus concludes his tale with an apology that appears to exonerate Odysseus of any responsibility for the supposed fiasco: "But I do not blame him so much as those in authority. For the city is wholly in the hands of those who are its leaders, and likewise the whole army. For the disorderly become evil through the words of their teachers" (vv. 385–88). The apology comes strangely on the heels of a verse in which Neoptolemus excoriates Odysseus as "the most evil of men and sprung from the most evil ancestors":

> τῶν ἐμῶν τητώμενος
> πρὸς τοῦ κακίστου κἀκ κακῶν Ὀδυσσέως.
> (vv. 383–84)

The disconnect between the two ideas is so marked that some editors have taken the apology for a later interpolation. If we accept the verses as authentic, we must assume that Sophocles felt the need to soften his stark critique of Odysseus.[3] At the same time, he may have wanted to have Neoptolemus express some misgivings about his own present role in the plot. After all, it is not easy to have this noble youth play the villain.

"There you have it," Neoptolemus concludes; "that is the whole story" (v. 389). Indeed not. But this gives the chorus its cue to sing its next ode, which is delivered in an "excited iambic-dochmaic strophe (instead of the normal two lines of iambic content after a major speech)."[4] The chorus here discovers its ancient voice as it sings to the Great Mother an intoxicated hymn such as Nietzsche posited as the original music of tragedy. In conventional hymnal style, the chorus begins the strophe with three verses of address to the Great Mother, whom they call Ga (we know her as Gē or Gaia): "O Ga, goddess of the mountains, who nourishes all, mother of Zeus himself, you who wield your power over the great Pactolus, rich in gold" (vv. 391–93). This is the great Asian goddess, known also as Cybele, worshipped throughout Anatolia with her center of worship in Sardis, the capital of Lydia, made rich from the gold flowing from the surrounding mountains into the Pactolus River. The chorus adds further details to the portrait of this goddess at the end of the strophe: "O blessed one, who hast thy seat on the bull-slaughtering lions, worthy of reverence sublime" (vv. 400–402).

Webster suggests that this hymn may be an allusion to the statue of Cybele in Athens carved by the great sculptor Phidias. That the Asian Cybele had been assimilated into the Athenian pantheon helps to justify the anomaly here that Neoptolemus's Myrmidons should claim to have poured our their hearts at Troy to the great Asiatic deity rather than to a goddess in their own pantheon. We cannot but suspect too that if Sophocles will have these sailors pretend to be calling upon a goddess, better she be a foreign deity rather than one of their own. This ode has the rich texture of a traditional choral hymn, but its piety is all hocus-pocus. This is the chorus responding as instructed to the signals given by Neoptolemus, playing its part in the plot as the horrified witness of its master's pretended pathos. Webster notes that the chorus treads a narrow path here, in implying but without stating in so many words that it has called on the Great Mother to take vengeance on the sons of Atreus: "Their words would sound to Philoctetes like an invocation to Cybele to punish the Atreidae, but they skillfully avoid committing themselves."[5]

Philoctetes is now entirely convinced of the truth of the story he has just heard. He speaks of a *symbolon* (v. 403), a token or tally. Two persons communicating to each other through a third party would each possess one end of the tally. If, when a message was delivered, the two parts of the tally fitted together, the fit would certify that the message received was authentic. The chorus, in calling on the great goddess herself to witness its lord's pathos, has done its share to authenticate his story. His story tallies with Philoctetes' experience. Story matches story; pathos matches pathos, thanks in part at least to the emotional resonance lent by the choral ode. This is not the usual function of the chorus, to use its liturgical powers to weave deception, but the nature of the chorus is changing here, as indeed the nature of tragedy itself.

Philoctetes responds to this choral ode first with vituperative hyperbole at the very thought of Odysseus:

ἔξοιδα γάρ νιν παντὸς ἂν λόγου κακοῦ
γλώσσῃ θιγόντα καὶ πανουργίας, ἀφ᾽ ἧς
μηδὲν δίκαιον ἐς τέλος μέλλοι ποεῖν.
(vv. 407–9)

[I know him, that he would give his tongue to evil speech
and to every kind of villainy from which he might make some injustice
come to fruition.]

These are strong words and, parenthetically, a misreading of Homer. The Homeric Odysseus was a trickster, loved by many though hated by others, but he was never the epitome of evil, nor would it be fair to claim that his every thought was bent on crime and injustice. This Odysseus is made satanic so that Philoctetes may be elevated almost to sainthood.[6]

Philoctetes then questions how the great Ajax could have stood by in silence as the son of Achilles was so insulted. But Ajax was dead, he is told. What Neoptolemus could not tell him, because he could not know it, is that he himself has just been given the story of Ajax for his own misuse. His appropriation of the old myth lends his story plausibility, not so much for Philoctetes' benefit as for us, who expect all fictions to be certified by Homer's authority.

A briefing now ensues between Neoptolemus, who has just entered the story, and Philoctetes, who has been kept outside the story for ten years, regarding the affairs at Troy, its main point being to have both men establish their credentials as authentic Homeric characters. We run through a list of the fallen heroes at Troy: Achilles, Patroclus, Ajax. Philoctetes fulminates at the apparent injustice of the gods, that the best men are carried off in death while the evildoers, Diomedes and Odysseus, live and prosper. The catalog of the fallen leads Philoctetes to muse on another man, whom he does not name at first but describes as "fearsome [*deinos*]" and "sophisticated [*sophos*] with the tongue" (v. 440). Neoptolemus assumes that such a description could signify only one person, Odysseus. But no, Thersites is his name. By having Neoptolemus innocently mistake Thersites for Odysseus leads us into the same confusion, to equate the foul-mouthed Thersites of the *Iliad* with Odysseus.

Philoctetes, as if recognizing that his interest in Thersites is inappropriate in this catalog of heroes, covers the incongruity by calling this same awesome speaker "a worthless fellow" (ἀναξίου φωτός, v. 339). Philoctetes invokes the name first to insinuate himself into the Homeric story. We can assume that Philoctetes, excluded from the Greek army ten years before the events told in the *Iliad*, could know nothing of Thersites as Homer portrays him. We are gratified to discover, however, that he has read our *Iliad*. We catch his reference to the scene in book 2, where Thersites, called by Homer the ugliest man who ever came to Troy, hurls abuse at Agamemnon, the commander in chief. The principal reason for these men to allude to Thersites, about whom they could know nothing, is to attach themselves to the great authorized text. We are intrigued to watch the same legerdemain at work in these two characters' reference to Ajax:

Φι. ἀλλ' οὔ τι τοῦτο θαῦμ' ἔμοιγ', ἀλλ' εἰ παρὼν
    Αἴας ὁ μείζων ταῦθ' ὁρῶν ἠνείχετο.
Nε. οὐκ ἦν ἔτι ζῶν, ὦ ξέν'· οὐ γὰρ ἄν ποτε
    ζῶντός γ' ἐκείνου ταῦτ' ἐσυλήθην ἐγώ.
Φι. πῶς εἶπας; ἀλλ' ἦ χοὖτος οἴχεται θανών;
Nε. ὡς μηκέτ' ὄντα κεῖνον ἐν φάει νόει.

(vv. 410–15)

[Phi. This is no great surprise for me. But rather, if
    Ajax the Greater had witnessed this and tolerated it.
Ne. He was no longer alive, my friend. Certainly I would not
    have suffered this while he was alive.
Phi. What are you saying? Was this man also dead?
Ne. Yes. Think of him as no longer living in the light.]

We know, but they do not, that Philoctetes and Neoptolemus are alluding to the most famous act in the life of Ajax, his suicide when the arms of Achilles were awarded to Odysseus rather than to him. Philoctetes has not been to Troy; hence he could not know that story. He must, however, be so familiar with the character of Ajax that he would assume that Ajax would never tolerate the abuse that Neoptolemus has now claimed has been meted out to himself. We can read the subtext of Philoctetes' surprise: Ajax, in such conditions, *would have committed suicide.*

Neoptolemus, on the other hand, has already been to Troy. He knows, therefore, that Ajax is dead, but he cannot know the cause, since he himself is the cause, so to speak; that is, Ajax must be dead so that Neoptolemus can step into his place and appropriate his story. Again, we can read the subtext. Philoctetes and Neoptolemus must be, quite unwittingly, discussing the suicide of Ajax, first to insert themselves into the story and then to have his suicide add its resonance to their story. The contest for the arms of Achilles has been rewritten in such a way as to eliminate Ajax while leaving his influence to add emotional force to Neoptolemus's pretended outrage. The death of Ajax, to which Neoptolemus alludes, thus references the suicide of the old epic tradition while at the same time marking the lacuna where Ajax has been removed from that story to make room for Neoptolemus.

In his second function Thersites is inserted into the list of heroes, where he does not belong, to demonize Odysseus, though this requires an egregious misreading of Homer.[7] No one, reading the *Iliad*, would call Homer's Thersites *deinos* or *sophos*. In the *Iliad* he is a sordid character, the antithesis of *sophos*, described as physically deformed, disorderly in mind, and disorderly in thought. But the Homeric Thersites has been loaned to this play so that he may be metamorphosed into a fifth-century sophist. Socrates, defending himself at his trial, held only ten years after this play was produced, argued that the true charge against him was that he was both *deinos* and *sophos*. He was in fact convicted and put to death for exactly these qualities that Philoctetes here attributes to Thersites.

Heavy indeed was Homer's hand on the whole of Greek tragedy, even at this late date in the form's evolution. Sophocles in borrowing from Homer reveals at every turn the constraints on his creative power. The plot of this play calls for a politician, or at least a man deeply imbued with sophistic arguments and principles, but such a character cannot be invented from whole cloth. Sophocles must find characters in Homer who, with a little revision, can be made to serve his purpose, blended together to form a composite photograph of the persona needed for this play. We look at this Odysseus and at first we might recognize him as we remember him from Homer's tales. But on second glance we discover that this modernized Odysseus has become a Thersites.

Introducing Thersites into the dialogue as the paradigm of the clever speaker makes Odysseus equally "worthless." Even more important, the juxtaposition of this Odysseus and the Homeric Thersites works to make Odysseus not only devious but also ugly and deformed.

The degradation of Odysseus's character is made explicit in Philoctetes' reference to Sisyphus as the true father of Odysseus. In the *Odyssey*, Odysseus has as one of his epithet formulas "Odysseus son of Laertes." But here he is the son of Laertes only in a manner of speaking. Philoctetes refers to him contemptuously as "fathered by Sisyphus and bought by Laertes" (οὑμπολητὸς Σισύφου Λαερτίῳ, v. 417). This is not Sophoclean invention. The story was part of the tradition but one that lurked far on the periphery. However, it serves Sophocles well as a means to impugn the man's pedigree. In the myth to which Philoctetes alludes, Laertes had paid a dowry for the hand of Anticleia, daughter of the arch-trickster Autolycus (who, in the *Odyssey*, gives Odysseus his name). As Philoctetes puts his spin on these negotiations, Anticleia was *bought* by Laertes, who was no doubt unaware that Sisyphus had already had his way with her and that she would bear his child. Thus Laertes had bought a wife, much as if he had acquired a slave, and unbeknown to him, we are to assume, he has also bought himself her bastard son, to be passed off as his legitimate son and heir. Odysseus is delegitimized twice over in a single insult. He is baseborn in being conceived outside marriage, and baseborn a second time in being the son of Sisyphus, not only a great trickster but also one of the great criminals of Greek mythology whom we see in the *Odyssey* enduring eternal punishment for his extraordinary hubris. In this drama, in which character is a central issue, character (*physis*) has various connotations; at times, however, it is to be understood in the most ancient, most traditional way, as woven into a man's being by his genetic stock. When it is meant in this sense, Philoctetes and Neoptolemus are by nature noble; Odysseus, being baseborn is by nature base.

Nietzsche, lamenting the death of tragedy, observes how the great protagonist of Greek tragedy becomes as the form declines the *graeculus* of Roman comedy, the clever Greek slave who manipulates the plot and the characters for various illicit ends. We can watch this process at work before our very eyes in this late tragedy, in the downfall of Odysseus from his status as hero in the Homeric epic to this bastard of the *Philoctetes*, who is both a trickster and by nature corrupt and as corrupting as he is corrupt. Nothing but evil can issue from a person so misbegotten.

Neoptolemus, completing the roster of the heroes fallen at Troy, now feigns impatience. In his rage he has separated himself from the Greek army, so his story goes, and is now sailing for home. It is time for him to get moving. He wishes Philoctetes well but must get back to his ship to be prepared for "whenever the god gives [them] the moment for sailing" (vv. 464–65). Philoctetes is astounded at this sudden turn in the conversation, but Neoptolemus persists, speaking now of *kairos*: "*Kairos* calls to post ourselves not at some point where we cannot see but at the place close [to the ship] where we can best keep watch" (vv. 467–68). Phillips translates *kairos* here as "chance"; Lloyd-Jones renders it as "to seize our opportunity" and also adds the word "chance" to suggest other shades of meaning in *kairos*.

If this were an ordinary moment in an ordinary day, we could be satisfied with the prosaic meaning of Neoptolemus's use of *kairos* to mean the best opportunity for sailing, but this is no ordinary day. Every tragedy is dominated by *kairos*, as Neoptolemus has already made clear in the parodos. The contrivance that set the plot in motion has almost run its course. Philoctetes has bonded with Neoptolemus exactly as the trick prescribes. Only one small step remains: Philoctetes must be got on board the ship. That *kairos* has arrived. But now Neoptolemus inserts a small trick of his own, pretending a sudden need for a quick departure and waving a spurious *kairos* as his flag. Philoctetes is thrown into a panic, fearing that his own *kairos* is lost. His desperation makes him all the more amenable to the trap being laid for him.

The trick works. Philoctetes begs Neoptolemus by his father, his mother, by whatever is dear to him at home, not to leave him in this desolate place. He makes a powerful appeal in the longest uninterrupted speech in the play (vv. 468–506). He admits that he is a loathsome cargo but pleads with Neoptolemus to endure his offensiveness "for to the wellborn what is disgraceful is odious, and to do good brings fair repute." The vocabulary here—*gennaios* (wellborn), *aischron* ("ugly" or "disgraceful, shameful"), *chreston* (useful, beneficial), and *euklees* ("of good reputation," from *kleos*, "fame")—is charged with moral significance. At the simplest level the message is clear: the wellborn shun what is disgraceful, and their good works bring them a good name. But the theological implications here are more complex. The ethos expressed here goes beyond the Homeric ethos. *Aischros* in Greek was both "ugly" in the physical sense and "disgraceful" in the moral sense. Thersites was both ugly and disgraceful; Achilles was both beautiful and honorable. But here the ugly is being separated from the disgraceful.

In the myth Philoctetes was both ugly and a disgrace, his suppurating wound an offense both physically and spiritually. When Odysseus had Philoctetes removed from human sight, he was benefiting the whole Greek army by expelling the ugliness from its midst.[8]

Now the time has come to reverse that decision, and for this reversal a new ethos is required. The social conscience underlying Philoctetes' appeal to Neoptolemus's noble nature was not highly developed either in Homeric times or even in the more enlightened culture of fifth-century Athens. The wellborn, although they could be persuaded to spend their capital on art, poetry, and monuments to their own magnificence, were not philanthropic. We see Sophocles moving toward a more compassionate ethos, which calls for the well-to-do to care for the pariahs of society.

Philoctetes concludes his appeal by reminding Neoptolemus of the hazards of life. No one's life is secure from moment to moment. His whole speech, and more explicitly the last lines of his appeal, are his commentary on *kairos*, the word spoken by Neoptolemus that has promoted this urgent response. Neoptolemus mentions *kairos* as if he were speaking of the weather, but when Philoctetes picks up the concept if not the word itself, it becomes a moral question.

The chorus now picks up the theme, singing the antistrophe that corresponds to the strophe sung earlier to the Great Mother (vv. 507–18). Still in its role as collaborator, it appeals to Neoptolemus to be merciful and pity the poor wretch, to take him on board the ship and give him safe passage home. This kindness would be, so the chorus argues, to turn the evil done to Philoctetes into his great good. At the same time, it emphasizes the morality by framing it in religious terms, arguing that in accepting Philoctetes as his suppliant, Neoptolemus would avoid nemesis from the gods (τὰν θεῶν/νέμεσιν ἐκφυγών, vv. 517–18). The chorus speaks in a curious mix of truth and falsehood. Its words are pious embroidery to add luster to the deception, but it also expresses a serious and more humane theology as it calls on Neoptolemus to return good for evil. Neoptolemus is being instructed into a new kind of vision of social justice. The choral ode achieves two antithetical aims simultaneously. The theatrical aim achieves its goal. Neoptolemus, at first feigning disgust at Philoctetes' condition, allows himself to be persuaded to sacrifice his personal comfort to the conscience of his sailors. But the theological aim also achieves its goal. Neoptolemus, beginning in pretended compassion, is moved to genuine compassion, though the full extent of that transformation will not be immediately manifest.

"O day most dear!" Philoctetes exclaims, returned from despair to ecstasy. "O sweetest man!" Salvation is at hand. He is ready to leave at once. But first he invites Neoptolemus to enter his cave so that the young man may kiss the very ground that witnessed such suffering:

ἴωμεν, ὦ παῖ, προσκύσαντε τήν ἔσω
ἄοικον ἐξοίκησιν, ὥς με καὶ μάθῃς
ἀφ' ὧν διέζων, ὥς τ' ἔφυν εὐκάρδιος.
οἶμαι γὰρ οὐδ' ἂν ὄμμασιν μόνον θέαν
ἄλλον λαβόντα πλὴν ἐμοῦ τλῆναι τάδε·
ἐγὼ δ' ἀνάγκῃ προὔμαθον στέργειν κακά.
(vv. 533–38)

[Let us go, my boy, and kiss the earth within
the home that is no home, that you may know the conditions in which
I have survived,
how I was born with the nature to have a strong heart.
I think no one but me seeing this sight with their eyes
could have endured as I did.
For from necessity I have learned to endure evils.]

This moment marks the point where the *Philoctetes* moves into its second plot, which will undo the first plot initiated by Odysseus in the prologos. The cave serves one function in the first half of the play, as the lair that Philoctetes calls his home that is no home. Now it serves a new function as the sanctuary from which the true spiritual drama of this play will emerge.

Why should Philoctetes need Neoptolemus to go into the cave with him? Philoctetes gives as his reason that he needs to make sure he has left no arrows lying about and to fetch the herb that alleviates his pain. But for this errand Neoptolemus is not needed, and time is pressing. Applying the criteria of plausibility and realism, we might suppose that Philoctetes has a good pragmatic reason to keep Neoptolemus in his sights. But pragmatism is not the reason given. The cave is made a significant fixture in the plot because it must be not only seen from the outside but also *experienced* from within. What Neoptolemus is asked to do is to enter the cave and *kiss* what Philoctetes calls the home that is no home. He is to witness what no other person could dare to witness. As becomes clearer as the play progresses, if Neoptolemus is to share in Philoctetes' *aretē*, he must also become one with Philoctetes in his suffering. The hero, in this paradigm, becomes a hero not only by performing some great deed but through his suffering. The verb Philoctetes uses is *proskyneō,* from which the noun *proskynesis* is derived. Lloyd-Jones translates verses 533–54 as: "Let us go, my son, when we have saluted the home that is no home inside." But why should a cave be saluted? The lexicon gives the verb's meanings as "to fall down and worship," to prostrate oneself, as to the king or to the god. Proskynesis in present-day Greek is to kiss the holy icon or to make a pilgrimage to a sacred site. Suffering has made the cave a sacred space. Philoctetes describes himself as *eremos* (v. 471), and in this context we cannot fail to hear in the word its modern derivative, *eremitos,* English "hermit." With this *proskynesis,* the winds shift in a new direction. We now understand that Philoctetes has been living in a sacred space. He has been sanctified. He is now a holy man. If Neoptolemus can be persuaded to perform this act of *proskynesis,* to worship the ground of the hermit's cave, the sophisma will be undone. Odysseus could not have foreseen this turn of events. A pilgrimage to a sacred place was never part of his calculations.

And behold! Here he comes posthaste to fend off this unforeseen complication, Odysseus himself, or rather his emissary, decked in the persona of a merchant. Odysseus had foreshadowed the arrival of this man back in the prologos (vv. 125–31), where he had told Neoptolemus that if Neoptolemus seemed to be making slow progress he would send the scout, in the dress of a merchant, to forward the action. Neoptolemus should take his cues from whatever this merchant might have to say. But why is this merchant needed now? Everything has proceeded exactly according to plan. Neoptolemus has played his part, and Philoctetes has fallen into the trap. He is in haste to put distance between him and this accursed site.

The merchant who now arrives on the scene is not Odysseus himself, or so we are to believe from the information given by Odysseus himself in the prologos. But the character playing this walk-on part (the third speaking part on stage) would have also been played by the same actor who played Odysseus. He speaks for Odysseus, delivering the script as given to him by Odysseus, and indeed he looks like Odysseus, at least the Odysseus whom we remember from the *Odyssey,* who when arriving at new locations was often taken for a seagoing merchant or worse, a pirate. This is Odysseus reflecting Odysseus reflecting Odysseus, a pretty piece of theater, albeit doomed to failure.

This old merchant, so-called, has arrived fortuitously at Lemnos, sailing from Troy to Peparethus. So he claims. O lucky day! Odysseus had alerted Neoptolemus in the prologos to expect to hear "embroidered words" from this merchant, and here they are. He proceeds to unfurl a new fiction, like a rug merchant showing his wares. At Troy, so his story goes, he had overheard the gossip that the Greeks, discovering Neoptolemus's departure, have sent out a ship to intercept him and bring him back to Troy. Neoptolemus, taking his cue, expresses astonishment at this hostile action against himself and surprise that Phoenix would head this mission rather than Odysseus. We watch Old Tragedy transforming itself into New Comedy. Here is Odysseus creating himself in a new persona and his youthful student Neoptolemus, improvising as he goes, chatting with the disguised Odysseus about the absent Odysseus. Odysseus is everywhere in this play, whether present or absent.[9] The merchant further explains that Odysseus could not be sent in pursuit of Neoptolemus because he and Diomedes (another vile man in Philoctetes' view) had been sent on another mission, to Lemnos, to fetch Philoctetes! We enjoy this embroidery on the old Homeric tale. Here is the new Odysseus, now dressed in a merchant's garb, telling Philoctetes the old Homeric story of the embassy sent out from Troy to dragoon him back to Troy, the true story worked into this play as if it were a fiction when it was the very truth. The merchant, having unburdened himself of his cunningly woven carpet of truths and half truths, exits back to the harbor, leaving Philoctetes in a paroxysm of rage. Jebb catches his amazement well:

> Now is this not wondrous, my son, that the offspring of Laertes should have hoped by means of soft words, to lead me forth from his ship and show me amidst the Greeks? No! Sooner would I hearken to the deadliest of my foes, the viper that made me the cripple that I am. (vv. 628–32)

If Philoctetes is amazed at the effrontery of Odysseus, we are not so much amazed as amused at this proliferation of missions sent out from Troy, plot laid upon plot, like a figure repeated endlessly down a hall of distorting mirrors. The number of missions now said to have been sent out from Troy boggles the mind. Here is the list in brief:

I. The Homeric tradition. The archetype.
   Two missions:
   1. Diomedes sent to Lemnos for Philoctetes.
   2. Odysseus sent to Skyros for Neoptolemus.

II. Aeschylus. The first revision.
   One mission:

1. Diomedes removed from the mission, replaced with Odysseus. Odysseus sent to Lemnos for Philoctetes.

III. Euripides. The second revision.

Two missions:

1. Diomedes returned to the story. Odysseus and Diomedes sent to Lemnos for Philoctetes.
2. A pretended Trojan mission added to the story. A Trojan embassy said to be en route from Troy to Lemnos to bribe and lure Philoctetes to join the Trojans.

IV. Sophocles.

Four missions:

1. True tale 1: Odysseus and Neoptolemus sent to Lemnos for Philoctetes.
2. False tale 1: Neoptolemus arrives alone at Lemnos en route for Greece.
3. False tale 2: Phoenix sent to fetch Neoptolemus back to Troy.
4. True tale 2: Odysseus sent to Lemnos for Philoctetes.

So much ingenuity expended to create a tiny fiction. If this play contains the germ of New Comedy, it signals also the birth of fiction. The *Philoctetes* must be one of the most *fictional* of the ancient tragedies, as if the form itself were straining under the weight of its own tradition and exerting itself to break free and express new thoughts. The famous Sophoclean irony here borders on the comic. If Odysseus is becoming the *graeculus* of comedy, Neoptolemus is on his way to becoming the *graeculus* too. Fortunately, amid this comedy of errors Sophocles never loses sight of the goal, the telos to which everything in the drama must move. But the brief carnival moment is almost done as we move into the second half of the play.

Weather

The merchant's tale has hit its mark. All alarms are sounded. Philoctetes must get off the island without a moment's delay. But wait. A new complication arises, a new aporia. What is the problem? The weather, Neoptolemus claims. With the merchant gone, Neoptolemus affects a sudden caution because the winds are now against them. But a few minutes earlier he had expressed impatience to be on his way and talked of the *kairos* of the prevailing winds. Has the wind really shifted direction? Of course not. The weather is but a trope. The weather that stalls him now is the condition of his own soul. The headwind that has arisen to impede his sailing is a spiritual force that threatens to prevent his execution of the scheme hatched by Odysseus. As if to make the point that the winds refer here to a state of mind, a discussion ensues between Neoptolemus and Philoctetes in which Neoptolemus feigns that he is talking about the physical conditions, while Philoctetes, in his every response, understands the weather to be a moral condition:

Neoptolemus: When the wind lets up against our prow, we can sail. Now it stands against us.

Philoctetes: There is always fair sailing when you flee evils.
Neoptolemus: I know. But the wind is against them too.
Philoctetes: There is never an adverse wind for pirates when they have the chance to rob and plunder by force.
Neoptolemus: Well, if that's your wish, let us proceed. Go inside and get whatever you need and most desire. (vv. 639–44)

Philoctetes' pleas and the chorus speaking of decency and compassion are making their influence felt. Neoptolemus is in a quandary. Should he continue in his theatrical persona as the false friend of Philoctetes, or should he shed the ill-fitting persona and become the authentic friend?

To this point we had no doubt that Philoctetes is the protagonist of this play. But when Neoptolemus temporizes and excuses himself by inventing a factitious headwind, the roles have changed, for the moment at least. Now he is emerging as the protagonist in his own right, and his pathos takes the center of our attention, while Philoctetes has become the supporting actor, the counselor urging the protagonist to accept his destiny.

The Bow

And now the scene for which we have all waited, if we are Greeks and know the story of Heracles and his bow. The time has come to present that famous bow. This bow was numinous in the hands of Heracles, and now its numen is about to pass from Philoctetes to the next man in the apostolic succession, young Neoptolemus. In Philoctetes' hands, it signifies the special relationship between him and Heracles, once a hero but now a god; when it is passed to Neoptolemus, it will signify both a new relationship between Neoptolemus and Philoctetes and the direct line of succession from Heracles to Neoptolemus.

Heracles, as the son of Zeus, was the greatest hero in Greece. Even Achilles, with a goddess for his mother, was hardly his equal. His feats were extraordinary; his death too was extraordinary. After completing the last of his labors, he returned to his home bringing the princess Iole to be his concubine. His wife, Deianeira, pained to think of this young woman taking her place in the matrimonial bed, dipped a ceremonial robe in a poison, which she mistakenly believed to be a love potion, and had Heracles offer his thanksgiving to the gods dressed in this robe. The toxins in the robe began to eat into the hero's flesh, and he would have died a hideous and shameful death, had he not chosen a more heroic mode of ending his human life. He had his own son construct for him a great pyre on the top of Mount Oeta. The son did as he ordered but balked at his father's final command, to set torch to the funeral pyre on which his father now awaited his own immolation. But Heracles' friend Philoctetes was willing to do his friend this final and most terrible favor. For his generosity he received from Heracles' hands the bow as the most precious gift that the dying hero could transmit to his successor.

This hero's death was more than monumental. When Philoctetes assisted at Heracles' immolation on the mountaintop, he became the celebrant officiating at a great mystery. Heracles' body was consumed in the flames, but Heracles himself ascended to Mount Olympus, where he was welcomed as a god and given Hebe (Eternal Youth) to be his wife forever. The bow is the direct conduit for the charisma of this remarkable hero to flow first toward Philoctetes and now from Philoctetes to Neoptolemus. Throughout the play it is treated as a sacred weapon. Though it remains on earth to function as an earthly weapon, the bow is also the signifier of Philoctetes' exalted status as a holy man. Odysseus in speaking of this bow in the prologos had said nothing of its religious nature.

Neoptolemus, speaking as the "interpreter" in the parodos, had informed us of the spiritual nature of this play, but his theological grasp of Philoctetes' suffering has entered the drama almost inadvertently, and somewhat implausibly, since the role given to him by Odysseus has been not to interpret the theology of Philoctetes' destiny but to act as the ringleader of a conspiracy against Philoctetes. But now in this episode the religious orientation of the play becomes explicit. The language and the attitudes expressed by both Neoptolemus and Philoctetes in respect to the bow and the cave are steeped in religious meaning.

The *Philoctetes* is two plays in one.[10] The first is the political play, engineered by Odysseus. Nothing in Odysseus's words in the prologos speaks of the numinous nature of Heracles' bow and certainly not of the numen that it has shed on Philoctetes and his destiny. Odysseus is completely oriented toward the political. By his calculation the bow is nothing more than an instrument, and Philoctetes himself is merely an impediment to the politics now driving the Greek commanders at Troy.

At this point in the play the mission is all but complete. In another moment we can expect the bow to be in Neoptolemus's hands, and Philoctetes will either be left to die on the island or he will be rendered helpless and completely docile. But then the bow itself comes into view, and its appearance we can describe only as an epiphany.[11] With its epiphany the political play is doomed, though its defeat takes several hundred more verses to be worked through. The bow translates the play from its political machinations into a spiritual pilgrimage. Its numen exposes the vacuum in Odysseus's arguments in the prologos, the shallowness of his ideology. The Odysseus of this play, unlike his prototype in Homer's *Odyssey*, knows nothing of the numen of the divine. He could in the prologos propose soul robbery as if it were no more than a trick of rhetoric. The bow leads us to talk of what Rudolf Otto calls the *mysterium tremendum*. When the bow is presented to us, we are on sacred ground. Once Neoptolemus is given to touch and take hold of the bow, he can never be Odysseus's man again.

Neoptolemus, seeing the bow, is overcome with religious awe:

ἆρ' ἔστιν ὥστε κἀγγύθεν θέαν λαβεῖν,
καὶ βαστάσαι με προσκύσαι θ' ὥσπερ θεόν;
(vv. 656–57)

[Is it possible for me to approach it closer and behold it,
and touch it and worship it as a god?]

Neoptolemus alludes to three aspects of the sacred here: to behold the sacred object, to touch it, and to worship it as a god.[12] Neoptolemus must be *sanctified* if he is to share in the sacred destiny of Philoctetes. Thus the education he has received from Odysseus must be completely undone. The verb he uses for "worship" is *proskyneō*, the same verb that Philoctetes had used moments before when he summoned Neoptolemus to worship the ground of his cave, signifying the act of prostrating oneself. Webster softens the religious intent here by having Neoptolemus ask if he may "salute" the bow, as if saluting a god were the normal protocol. This is not a salute but religious veneration. The ground of the cave must also be venerated because it has been sanctified by Philoctetes' suffering and also by the bow, which has been permeating the cave for several years with its sacred aura. With this realization we have a better comprehension of the merchant's interference in the action when no interference was needed. A mystery is about to be celebrated unless Odysseus can head it off by recalling for Neoptolemus his political mission.[13]

"This is permissible, my boy," Philoctetes replies; "this and whatever else is mine that might serve your interests" (vv. 658–59). To which Neoptolemus replies:

καὶ μὴν ἐρῶ γε· τὸν δ' ἔρωθ' οὕτως ἔχω.
εἴ μοι θέμις, θέλοιμ' ἄν· εἰ δὲ μή, πάρες.
(vv. 660–61)

[Indeed, I long for it. Yes, that is my longing.
I would want to touch it, if that is lawful. But if not, let it go.]

Neoptolemus lusts for the bow; he confesses his eros twice in a single verse, using first the verb (*erō*) and then the noun (*erōs*). He shields his audacious desire from possible nemesis by circumscribing it in religious terms: he would touch the bow only if doing so would be religiously lawful (*themis*). This is the lust that any ephebe might have to touch a weapon, and especially this fabled weapon.[14] But mixed with that erotic emotion is also the longing of a pious pilgrim to behold and venerate a sacred object. Neoptolemus longs to touch the bow but will not presume to do so if his touch infringes on the sanctity of the venerated object.

Who is to say what Neoptolemus is thinking at this point?[15] For those who consider him fraudulent from start to finish, this scene is one more example of his duplicity, and if his emotion seems genuine, that would be a credit to his acting skills. But certainly Sophocles seems to emphasize the boy's genuine emotion in the presence of a sacred object. If we grant no sincerity to Neoptolemus at this point, then we must add to the indictment that Neoptolemus is not only a fraud but also a blasphemer, being devoid of religious scruples and willing to use religion itself to serve his political advantage. The subtext here is that the bow, radiating its religious numen, can be handled only by those whose hands are pure. If this bow is passed to Neoptolemus, it will be a sacrament, which by my definition is a sacred transaction between the human and the divine, whereby the human partner in the transaction is transformed to a higher level of consciousness. Either the gift of the bow will pass into hands that are pure, or if not, its possession spells unspeakable catastrophe.

Philoctetes continues the religious language:

ὅσιά τε φωνεῖς ἔστι τ', ὦ τέκνον, θέμις,
ὅς γ' ἡλίου τόδ' εἰσορᾶν ἐμοὶ φάος
μόνος δέδωκας, ὃς χθόν' Οἰταίαν ἰδεῖν,
ὃς πατέρα πρέσβυν, ὃς φίλους, ὃς τῶν ἐμῶν
ἐχθρῶν μ' ἔνερθεν ὄντ' ἀνέστησας πέρα.
θάρσει, παρέσται ταῦτά σοι καὶ θιγγάνειν
καὶ δόντι δοῦναι κἀξεπεύξασθαι βρότων
ἀρετῆς ἕκατι τῶνδ' ἐπιψαῦσαι μόνῳ·
εὐεργετῶν γὰρ καὐτὸς αὔτ' ἐκτησάμην.
(vv. 662–70)

[You speak holy things, my child, and it is lawful for you
who have given me to look upon this light of the sun, to behold
the land of Oeta, you who have given me to see my aged father,
my beloved family, and have raised me above my enemies,
beyond their reach, when I lay under their foot.
Be of good courage! It will be possible for you to touch this bow,
and when I have given it to you, you will be able to give
it back to me in turn and boast that to you alone
it has been given to touch it because of your virtue (*aretē*).
For I too gained it through my good deeds.]

The overtly religious terms here are *hosia* (holy things) and *themis* (religiously lawful), but the speech is steeped in religious sensibility. Neoptolemus has given Philoctetes to see the light of the sun; to leave the light of the sun was a common trope for death. Neoptolemus has given Philoctetes back his life, the idea further explicated by Philoctetes' gratitude for the favor Neoptolemus has rendered in giving him to behold his father, his family, his ancestral soil, and in raising him above his enemies. In behaving thus toward Philoctetes, Neoptolemus has proven himself as virtuous as Philoctetes had been toward Heracles, and virtue here is certainly religious in its connotation. Neoptolemus alone will be allowed to hold and to receive the bow and then to give it back since he alone, of all human beings, will have done what Philoctetes himself once did for Heracles: raise him above his enemies. How different is this bow from the bow that occupied Odysseus's attention. There it was a signifier of political and military power. Here it signifies virtue and the relation of virtue with the divine.

The word that Philoctetes uses for virtue is *aretē*. Lloyd-Jones translates it as "your nobility"; Phillips gives us "kindness." Both meanings are contained in this present context, but something more even than nobility and kindness is needed here. In the epic *aretē* was "excellence," whether pertaining to a man or a woman, but it was used primarily of the manly virtues—courage in battle, boldness in action, and a profound fear of dishonor. But when Philoctetes speaks the word in this play produced at the end of the fifth century, the meanings have shifted more toward the virtue of the soul. Philoctetes indicates the nature of this sacred service by his use of liturgical language: "You speak what is holy."

Philoctetes speaks of the principle of reciprocity in doing good works. Neoptolemus will be able boast of his privilege, to hold the bow, because in his virtue he has given good for good. As Philoctetes received the bow from Heracles, so Neoptolemus will receive the bow in the same way, kindness given in return for kindness. So the god's virtue passes from god to man and from one man to another.

Neoptolemus picks up the theme of the true friend: "I am not in pain that I have seen you and taken you as my friend. Whoever knows to repay good when he has received good, that friend is stronger than any possession" (vv. 671–74). When Neoptolemus says it does not give him pain to look on Philoctetes and receive him as a friend, his language is strong, and translators balk and look for some lesser feeling. Lloyd-Jones has "I am not sorry," but something more than "sorry" is needed here. With the emphasis in the heroic aesthetic on the beauty of the manly body, Philoctetes was an ugly sight with his running sore, a cripple made uglier by desperation and anger. But Neoptolemus has dared to overcome his disgust and to make this *alien* his friend. To touch the bow, to hold it in his hand, will be his reward.

The Cave

The pilgrimage along the Sacred Way into the sanctuary of the cave has been interrupted by the profane voice of the merchant, arriving on stage to call Neoptolemus back into the original plot. With that profanity removed, the procession can continue to its fulfillment. With the adoration of the bow now completed, nothing remains but the sacrament within the cave, which Philoctetes has already described as the veneration of the ground of his suffering. Philoctetes and Neoptolemus now enter the cave, leaving only the chorus still standing in the *orchēstra*. A cave in myth is always a signifier of ambivalence and ambiguity, dangerous and at the same time alluring, threatening death or promising rebirth. This cave is the holy of holies.

But why the dithering at the mouth of the cave when all plans for departure have been put in place? And what is the urgent moral necessity for Neoptolemus to join Philoctetes inside the cave? "The disease makes me need your support," Philoctetes gives as his explanation for this pressing obligation (vv. 674–75). "My sick estate craves the comfort of your presence" is Jebb's translation. But why is this comfort needed in the cave, which Philoctetes plans to enter only to retrieve his arrows and his analgesic herb? Lloyd-Jones translates Philoctetes' words as "my sickness requires you to stand by me" in his attempt to accommodate the Greek noun *symparastatēs*. The simpler noun *parastatēs* (someone who stands at one's side) has a military connotation; spoken of a man's comrade in arms, it denotes the virtues of such a friend in battle—loyalty, courage, dependability. Philoctetes needs his ally. But Sophocles adds a second prefix, *sym-* (with), to give us that person who stands beside us and with us, giving a mystical overtone to the military word, taking the military word and using it to coin a new word for a new emotion, compassion.

Philoctetes certainly needs Neoptolemus as a soldier needs his comrade on the front line of battle, and his use of this word points forward to that time at Troy when, as Heracles is to inform him, Philoctetes and Neoptolemus will fight together as two lions in the field. But this need is hardly reason enough for the compulsion now laid on Neoptolemus like a divine command to join Philoctetes and prostrate himself within the cave. The long passage that occupies the space between Philoctetes' first call for Neoptolemus to enter the cave and his second, more insistent invitation (vv. 533–675) seems on the surface like a mere interruption. But it functions in this pilgrim's progress along his Sacred Way as a temptation that lies on the path of the initiate to distract him from his initiation by one last reminder of the worldly fame and glory now in jeopardy. With that distraction removed, Philoctetes now leads his initiate into the secret place. In his cave Neoptolemus is initiated into the great mystery. We are not given to know the vision vouchsafed to

Neoptolemus within the cave except that it centers on the act of *proskynesis,* but we can read it from its effects. Once he emerges from the cave, Neoptolemus has become one with Philoctetes, truly his *symparastatēs,* initiated into the mystery of suffering. And no better teacher could he find than Philoctetes, who has suffered more than any other human could bear. Neoptolemus enters the cave a political man; he emerges a spiritual being.

6

The Stasimon

(Verses 676–729)

Stasimon was the name given in antiquity to any choral ode in a tragedy sung between the entrance of the chorus into the *orchēstra* (the parodos) and its exit from the theater at the end of the play (the exodos). A play could have more than one stasimon. The *Philoctetes* has only one (vv. 676–729), which separates the first episode from the second. It is composed in the strophic form, with one strophe followed by its antistrophe in the same metrical form, followed in turn by a second set of strophe and antistrophe in a different metrical form. In this stasimon we have two sets: strophe alpha, antistrophe alpha; strophe beta, antistrophe beta.

Like strophe and antistrophe, stasimon refers us back to the time when an ode was a dance; the adjective *stasimos* means "brought to a stand, standing, stationary." When used of a choral ode, *stasimon* indicated that the ode was delivered when the members of the chorus were in place in the *orchēstra*, though they were not necessarily stationary during the singing of the ode. This stasimon marks the end of the first episode and is sung by the chorus while Philoctetes and Neoptolemus are inside the cave. Philoctetes and Neoptolemus would emerge from the cave just as the chorus brings the stasimon to a close. The ode is intended to hold our attention while the actors are off the stage, serving as a musical interlude in which the poet can meditate on the issues already presented and build the emotional intensity that a tragedy requires. If we look for Aristotle's "pity and terror" as the requisite emotions of a tragedy, we need look no further than this ode, which asks us to imagine Philoctetes suffering almost beyond imagining.

In his response to the chorus in the parodos (vv. 191–200), Neoptolemus surprises us when he speaks with a wisdom and an authority hardly to be expected from the youth who is presented to us in the prologos. The chorus in this ode presents us with a similar incongruity. In the first three strophes of the ode (strophe alpha, antistrophe alpha, strophe beta), the chorus dwells on the terrible suffering of the protagonist, but in the final strophe (antistrophe beta) it changes its tone and celebrates the good news that the suffering man has found a savior who will take him back to his home in Malis. Nothing is said of the intended destination, which is Troy, and nothing has been said to inform the chorus that Neoptolemus plans to deliver Philoctetes back to Greece at some future date.

Jebb offers the simplest explanation: "Down to the end of the second strophe (717) they are simply uttering what they feel. Then at 718 Philoctetes and Neoptolemus reappear from the cave; and in the second antistrophe the Chorus once more seek to help their master's design."[1] This is a reasonable interpretation but hardly adequate to account for the majesty with which the ode concludes. A deeper explanation lies in the transformation in the nature of the play itself when Neoptolemus accompanies Philoctetes into the cave. If we were to think of Neoptolemus as the protagonist, we would see his agon staged for him by two characters contesting for his soul: on one side, Odysseus, the man of words and ideas, and on the other side, Philoctetes, the man of suffering. Odysseus uses the language of the political arena, but Philoctetes uses a different language altogether. His is the language of suffering, the difference between praxis and pathos: on one side action, whether in words or deeds; on the other side, only pathos itself, which has no weapon, no tool, not even words, but has only compassion as its ally.[2] When Neoptolemus enters Philoctetes' cave, he gives his consent to take his stand for compassion. While Philoctetes initiates Neoptolemus inside the cave, the chorus standing outside sings the passion as if it were an oratorio.

If this ode were lifted out of this play, we would see more clearly the purity of its form. Disconnected from this specific plot, which depends on subterfuge and deceit, the ode is a paradigm of the passion hymn, beginning with the hero's suffering and ending in his triumph. Such a hymn would ill-suit a tragedy that ends in the protagonist's death, but in the religious cults the hero's death was not the end of his story. In Greek religion the hero was a human being of extraordinary achievements who after death was given a different kind of existence in the cult established in his own city, where he would be venerated first as a great hero and then even worshipped as a god, as a human immortalized. Gods were immortal; heroes were humans *immortalized*.[3] They were human beings whose immortality grew through the devotions of their worshippers.

The myth of Heracles exemplified this trajectory. He was born a human, although as the son of Zeus he was endowed with superhuman strength and courage. He lived his whole life in suffering, sinning again and again, dying the martyr's death, to be burned alive, but transcending the flames that consumed his body and ascending to heaven to be welcomed into the company of the gods. That is the framework of this stasimon, albeit with circumstances altered as appropriate to the passion of Philoctetes. The ode holds Philoctetes before us as the classic archetype of the hero who suffers and in his suffering reaches transcendence.

Jebb describes the chorus as expressing its own feelings in the first three strophes of this ode, but this is to think of it as composed of persons of flesh and blood, endowed with human thoughts and feelings. In this ode the chorus may still have its role as a participant in the drama, but it speaks also as the voice of the tradition, given the function to dwell in the sublimest way on the nature of suffering. With the actors inside the cave, the chorus, freed from the trammels of the plot, can sing the generic hymn celebrating the hero's suffering, his sanctification, and his transcendence. The chorus opens in a conventional way for such a hymn, searching through myth for some parallel to the present pathos and groping to comprehend the nature and scale of this hero's pain. The chorus comes upon the myth of Ixion, a name scarcely known today but in its time a byword for criminality beyond ordinary crime. To link Philoctetes' name with one of the great sinners of ancient myth might seem to us a far-fetched allusion, but Greek thought worked through strong polarities, and Ixion's relevance lies precisely in the disparity between the two cases. Ixion was an arch-criminal who suffered an extraordinary punishment as befitted his crimes. The *Oxford Classical Dictionary* has only a short entry on him, but it is pregnant with significance for this play. "The Greek Cain," the *Dictionary* calls him, a man who was "the first to kill his kin." The story goes that he murdered his father-in-law, and when no human was found willing to perform the rituals to purify him of this crime, Zeus himself undertook the task. But in return for this extraordinary benefaction, Ixion attempted to rape Hera, the wife of Zeus and queen of the gods. As the punishment for this hubris, Zeus had Ixion bound to a wheel of fire, always revolving, eternal torture of the first degree. This punishment is one of the earliest images in Greek myth of what would develop into the fire and brimstone of hell in Christian cosmology.

But why bring Ixion into the argument here? First, we need to feel that the chorus must hark far back "in the dark backward and abysm of time" to find some instance of suffering comparable to the pain endured by Philoctetes. But more important, suffering presumes a punishment, and punishment presumes a crime. Ixion's crime was not in question. In his assault on heaven Ixion was a pagan Lucifer, but Philoctetes, by contrast suffering in his own hell, is a man without sin, truly the man of sorrows.[4] The chorus emphasizes his purity: he has done no one wrong; he has taken no life; he has lived peaceably with his neighbors. "He was an equal among equals" is Sophocles' phrase (the democratic ideal), which Jebb translates as "a fair man to those who treat him fairly" (his note at v. 684). Philoctetes was not only innocent; he was virtuous in all his social relations, whereas Ixion's crimes were crimes against both humanity and the gods. Yet Philoctetes, the righteous man, is cast into the depths. The incomprehensibility of suffering is one of tragedy's constant themes. Sometimes it is sent as a punishment, but at other times, not. How are we to justify the cosmic order? The sentiment is generic, but it has a special reference to Philoctetes' case because in this ode he is the hero being singled out for beatification. Such a hymn would be the first step in this process. Students of Aristotle will look here for hamartia, that necessary flaw in the hero's character that would explain his tragedy. Hamartia will work its way into this drama in its own time, but the emphasis now is entirely on the hero's virtue, not his crime. Tragedy never entirely satisfies the two contradictory demands placed on it, to find the hero innocent and at the same time to determine his guilt.[5]

The ode continues to dwell on the suffering endured by this man, such as the chorus has never seen inflicted on any other human. Philoctetes has no neighbor to share his pain, to respond with sympathy to his wound, to apply healing herbs to assuage the pain from the reptile's bite. He crawls awkwardly across the ground this way and that like a child without its nurse. He gathers no food from the soil; he grows no crops, such as other humans grow; his only sustenance is from the birds of the air such as his arrows might happen to bring down.[6]

"O wretched soul," the chorus continues, as if singing to the man himself. David Claus would argue that the word *psychē* as used here would be no more than a poetic periphrasis for the name Philoctetes.[7]

But given the significance of the word for the play as a whole, we would do well to give the word its fullest religious and philosophical meaning. Webster writes that "the sense construction shows how near ψυχή is to meaning the whole personality."[8]

This ode itemizes the hero's physical deprivations, but they are seen in their religious context. Philoctetes does not gather the fruit of "holy Earth" as other humans do. For ten years he has not had the pleasure of wine, but has always had to find his water by crawling to some brackish pool. He is alienated from the Earth, which nourishes all humans, and with no wine to drink he is alienated from both gods and humans, wine being the signifier of the communion of humans with their gods and with their fellows. The chorus emphasizes the spiritual nature of Philoctetes' condition when it speaks of his wound as "the *atē* that gnaws at his spirit" (v. 705). Jebb is satisfied to call this a "devouring anguish," but *atē* in ancient Greek was always more than anguish. The word is steeped in religious associations, among the weightiest words to describe the tragic hero's fate. It is monumental ruin. Often it is treated as a blindness in a person's vision and judgment, but here it is seen less as a moral flaw in Philoctetes than as a curse that eats at his heart. Whatever its source, it is demonic. Philoctetes, deprived of proper human food or drink, is orphaned, reduced not only to the most primitive human condition but to the infantile state:

εἶρπε δ' ἄλλοτ' ἀλλ‹αχ›ᾷ
τότ' ἂν εἰλυόμενος,
παῖς ἄτερ ὡς φίλας τιθήνας,
ὅθεν εὐμάρει' ὑπάρχοι
πόρου, ἁνίκ' ἐξανείη
δακέθυμος ἄτα

(vv. 701–6)

[He would move now this way
now that, crawling,
like a child without his dear nurse,
wherever he might come upon some sustenance
when the spirit-consuming curse
would abate.]

This is the ultimate alienation of the tragic hero, cut off from health, from family and community, and reduced to the helplessness of the child not yet even able to walk.

In the second antistrophe, the chorus raises its voice in jubilation as if this were a victory ode. Such a hymn of triumph would be out of place in the conventional tragedy, but it would not be inappropriate in the context of the hero cults out of which Athenian tragedy developed. Herodotus writes of the people of Sicyon giving honor to the hero Adrastus and celebrating his sufferings with tragic choruses.[9] A hymn such as this could be sung by the people of Sicyon at the tomb of Adrastus during their festivals in honor of the hero, and we could imagine this choral ode itself being used later and being sung in the festivals honoring Philoctetes' tomb in his homeland in Malis.

This stasimon is a religious hymn from its opening notes of bewilderment to its final trumpet sound. It finds its paradigms of suffering in two heroes of the past, Ixion and Heracles. It begins with Ixion's crime but ends with Heracles, who transcended suffering to become one with the gods. The one paradigm presents a hero suffering eternal torment; the other shows the hero working through suffering to reach a state of bliss. Heracles was a lusty warrior, mighty in his deeds and mighty in his transgressions. Although he brought benefactions to many kings and cities, he was also guilty of great crimes, including, like Lucifer, an assault on the very gods themselves. When he had himself immolated on Mount Oeta, his fiery death was both the ultimate punishment for his transgressions and the catalyst for his transformation from his human status to the divine.[10] Archaeological evidence points to a cult of Heracles on Mount Oeta in historical times, where his apotheosis would figure largely in the celebration. In this last strophe of the stasimon, Philoctetes is so closely associated with Heracles that they almost merge into a single figure. Sophocles could not promise for Philoctetes the apotheosis vouchsafed to Heracles, but in celebrating Heracles' glory, he brings Philoctetes within the circle of that glory. We may infer that this ode looks forward to the cult of Philoctetes when he will share in Heracles' honor on Mount Oeta. He will be healed at Troy and given great honor for being the savior of Greece, and back in his own home after his death he will receive his hero's shrine and be worshipped in perpetuity as a hero in his own right and as the friend who stood by Heracles as his *symparastatēs* and assisted him in his death and resurrection.[11]

Transcendence is the theme of the final words of this ode, which speak of Heracles, "the hero of the brazen shield, ablaze in divine fire, who drew near to the gods beyond the slopes of Mount Oeta" (vv. 727–29). The funeral pyre on Mount Oeta was physical, but the fire in which Heracles approaches the gods above and beyond the heights of Mount

Oeta is metaphysical.[12] The final strophe of the stasimon celebrates much more than the success of a military mission. Philoctetes has found in the son of noble people a person who will make him *great* (*megas*) and he will become *blessed* (*eudaimōn*). When he is brought back to his own land, he will be returned to his own Spercheios River, the nymphs of Malis, the tutelary daimones of his own home, and to Mount Oeta, where Heracles, haloed in fire, drew near to the gods. Heracles' transcendence intimates that Philoctetes will find his own transcendence. The ode delicately avoids an outright assertion that Heracles himself became a god; instead, "he approached the gods." And Philoctetes will do likewise. Having been cut off from his gods by his own people, one day back in his own home he will join both his people and his gods. He will become blessed.

This stasimon begins and ends in fire. Fire is the element through which the transformation of the physical into the spiritual takes place. The ode begins with Ixion damned forever on his fiery wheel but comes at the end to the fire on Mount Oeta, now called "a godly fire," where Heracles becomes one with the gods. In Ixion's story, the fire is eternal punishment, but for Heracles, the fire purges him of his human state and reveals him in his true and everlasting self. That purifying fire reaches out now to include his friend Philoctetes. The ode ends in joy to celebrate the sacrament whereby suffering is made spiritual.

Except for one complication: The political plot has not run its course. It is only half done. For the rest of the play, the two plots must contend with each other. But while the chorus sings this ode, Neoptolemus has entered into a spiritual covenant. To violate it would be to put both his life and his soul at risk, as he is about to discover in the next episode.

7

The Second Episode

(Verses 730–826)

The stasimon comes to a close as Philoctetes and Neoptolemus emerge from the cave. Everything is ready at last for departure. But a new aporia emerges. Philoctetes stops. He stands transfixed. Sophocles uses the word *apoplectos*, "struck out of his wits," a word that the medical writers used for "paralysis" (v. 731). What troubles him, Neoptolemus asks. Nothing. Philoctetes urges Neoptolemus to keep walking, but something is seriously amiss. It is, of course, the serpent's venom, which is making an attack on his system. So far we have seen the disease in its secondary effects, in Philoctetes' labored movements and in the effect of the disease on his livelihood, but now we are to witness the disease in its more dire manifestation.

Philoctetes lets out an involuntary cry. He does his best to reassure Neoptolemus that all is well. But the serpent's venom overwhelms his self-control. He cries out: "O Gods!" "Why are you groaning?" Neoptolemus asks. "Why are you calling upon the gods?" "That they may come near and vouchsafe to be our kindly saviors." Another cry breaks from Philoctetes' lips. "What is it?" Neoptolemus asks again.

Now the disease itself explodes:

ἀπόλωλα, τέκνον, κοὐ δυνήσομαι κακὸν
κρύψαι παρ' ὑμῖν, ἀτταταῖ· διέρχεται,
διέρχεται. δύστηνος, ὢ τάλας ἐγώ.
ἀπόλωλα, τέκνον· βρύχομαι, τέκνον· παπαῖ,
ἀπαππαπαῖ, παπᾶ, παπᾶ, παπᾶ, παπαῖ.

(vv. 742–46)

[I am undone, my boy, and I will not be able to hide
my evil from you. Ah, ah ah! It comes upon me.
Oh, wretch that I am,
I am destroyed.
Ah! Ah! Ah! Ah! Ah!]

Neoptolemus is about to hear that cry that caused Philoctetes to be expelled from human society. The friendship between Philoctetes and Neoptolemus will surely be shattered once the loathsome nature of this disease is revealed to the young man who is as yet unpracticed in witnessing such horrors. Philoctetes' scream begins in words, but then the words are shredded by the pain. At the very center of the play, verse 745, Philoctetes abandons language altogether and lets the pain speak for itself, a sheer inhuman noise.[1]

papai!
apappapai! papa! papa! papa papai!

Sophocles, obliged to represent a sound that transcends human language, indicates its force by making Philoctetes shout in a continuous stream of explosive syllables—PA PA PA and AI mimicking a scream, repeated several times. At this point in the play it is as necessary for Neoptolemus to hear this sound at full volume as it was deemed necessary to have it suppressed in the Greek army ten years earlier. Neoptolemus must see and hear exactly the person to whom he has offered his friendship. So appalling is this involuntary sound that not one person in the whole Greek army, hearing it, could accept Philoctetes as his friend. This is the *dysphemia* with which the plot begins.

The rest of the episode deals with the consequences of this scream, which can be seen as framed by two questions. First, will Neoptolemus, exposed to this *dysphemia*, do what his elders had done ten years earlier when they ejected Philoctetes from their midst? Will his horror and disgust undo the whole scheme? The other question concerns the bow. What is to be done with the bow? The two questions are but the obverse and reverse of the same coin, and both depend on the character of Neoptolemus.[2]

When Philoctetes regains the power of speech, he hands his bow over to Neoptolemus because he knows that he will fall asleep after the attack of the disease abates. He must be allowed to sleep, and Neoptolemus must consent to hold the bow and to yield it to no one, whatever the inducements or provocations. At every juncture now the two contradictory plays are in motion. Philoctetes passes his bow to the man whom he takes for his true friend, but when Neoptolemus receives the bow and gives his word that he will surrender it to no one, he speaks with a forked tongue. In his one persona he speaks as Odysseus's agent. The bow, the object of their mission, is now in his hands. But in his other persona Neoptolemus is a youth who has just been through a profound religious initiation. For the moment the two personas speak as if in synchronicity, but in fact, they are about to break asunder.

In giving his bow to Neoptolemus, Philoctetes adds that Neoptolemus should accept it with the apotropaic prayer that it may not bring him misfortune as it had brought misfortune first to Heracles and then to Philoctetes. He expresses this prayer in an idiom alien to our ears: "Prostrate yourself to Phthonos [Jealousy], that the bow be not a source of woe to you" (v. 776). Jebb softens the trope to give us "Pray the jealous gods that it not bring you troubles." But the jealous gods are a polite euphemism for the more terrible religion encoded here. Lloyd-Jones gets closer to the primitive meaning with his "There, take it, boy, and kiss it to avert the curse." For "kiss" Philoctetes uses the same verb, *proskyneō* (prostrate oneself), that has already been used twice, first when Philoctetes all but commands Neoptolemus to prostrate himself within the cave (v. 533) and then when Neoptolemus asks if he might venerate the bow as a god (v. 657). Having prostrated himself to the bow and then to the Earth, Neoptolemus must prostrate himself a third time, now to that majestic and terrifying power Phthonos, Jealousy itself. The idea is primitive. Lloyd-Jones would have Neoptolemus kiss the bow, but Sophocles puts it more bluntly. Neoptolemus must kiss the curse itself.[3] In receiving the bow, he is to take on himself its curse, if that is the consequence.

Phthonos is the malevolent aura that human anxiety casts around any taboo. The gods, to lean on Schopenhauer here, are all will, wills embodied in divine forms. *Phthonos* is the jealousy that guards the exercise and privileges of that will. Every human act exposes that human to *phthonos* from another human, and divine Jealousy is this *phthonos* magnified. The bow of Heracles is as much a danger to its possessor as to its enemy. Its potential malevolence is now uppermost in Philoctetes' words. As Philoctetes traces the arc of his own life, he questions whether the bow has been his savior or his enemy. The bow in the end was no friend to Heracles, or so it must seem now. Perhaps it is in its very nature a curse. This *phthonos* links us directly with the *sophisma* with which

Odysseus instigated the political play. Philoctetes has taken Neoptolemus into a drama where divine Phthonos interferes with any simple and direct political expedience. For Neoptolemus to accept the bow and continue to play the part Odysseus has given him would certainly be to court Phthonos. After what we have heard about this bow and after Neoptolemus's acts of veneration, we know the bow will never allow itself to be passed into unclean hands.

Neoptolemus takes the bow and adds his own prayer: "O gods, grant that this be so. And grant us a fair sailing where you gods think it right and where our mission leads" (vv. 779–81). He speaks again with two voices, with one message to be understood by Philoctetes and another by us, with Philoctetes assuming the destination to be Greece while we understand it to be Troy.

With the bow transferred, Philoctetes suffers a renewed attack, which leads him to curse his enemies. But his anger is misdirected. The sons of Atreus are not responsible for this sickness. The etiology must be sought elsewhere, a point to be developed in the final choral ode. He begs Neoptolemus to throw him into the Lemnian volcano (which was still active in historical times), thus doing for him the favor that he had once done for the hapless Heracles.[4] But Neoptolemus stands silent. Yet another aporia has emerged. Perplexed, Philoctetes asks him an extraordinary question, which by delicate nuance suggests an inner life:

τί φής; τί σιγᾷς; ποῦ ποτ' ὤν, τεκνον, κυρεῖς;
(v. 805)

[Why are you silent? *Where are you,* boy?]

Neoptolemus continues to stand as if paralyzed; at length he gives an equally extraordinary reply:

ἀλγῶ πάλαι δὴ τἀπὶ σοὶ στένων κακά.
(v. 806)

[For a long time now I have been in pain suffering at your disaster.]

The verb he uses is *algō*, which signifies not just distress but real pain. He uses it in the present tense, which can be used in Greek to represent an action begun in the past but still continuing in the present: "I have been in pain for some time and am even now still in pain." The adverb *palai* (long since) is an important cue that Neoptolemus is speaking of a state of mind that now has a history.

Philoctetes assumes that Neoptolemus's distress is that same disgust that Philoctetes' disease provoked among the Greek warriors ten years earlier. When Philoctetes had suffered his attack, while he was still trying to control his voice, his great fear was that he could no longer hide from Neoptolemus his hideous condition. With the sound bursting from Philoctetes against his control, Neoptolemus is made to witness the full horror of his new friend's condition.

Philoctetes reassures the boy that the attack will pass and begs Neoptolemus not to abandon him. Neoptolemus gives his word that he will stay with him. Philoctetes adds that he would not think it right to put Neoptolemus under oath (since Neoptolemus has already proved himself a true friend). To this Neoptolemus replies: "It is not *lawful* [*themis*] for me to leave without you" (v. 812). Again we hear his two personas speaking as one. In his one persona he uses the word *themis* in its mundane, legal sense, meaning that Neoptolemus is serving under military orders, which require that he not leave the island without taking Philoctetes. But the word is also charged with religious significance. It signifies what is *ordained by the gods*. To violate this *themis* is sacrilege. In this persona Neoptolemus speaks as the man who has entered into a sacrament, which he dare not violate.[5]

Some scholars warn us against reading "character" in anything like our modern sense in ancient tragedy. For such scholars, even if Neoptolemus speaks of being in pain *for some time*, we are to accept that these are words relevant simply to this moment in the drama, and we should not insist that they might represent anything like our idea of character development. The question of character in any literary work, ancient or modern, is complex, and certainly we can accept that individuality in the modern sense is hardly to be found in pre-Renaissance literature. Even so, in his Neoptolemus we recognize that Sophocles is moving toward a new concept of character.[6] Earlier in the play Neoptolemus had expressed to Philoctetes his hesitation by speaking of the winds as being adverse to their sailing (vv. 639–40). Since nowhere in the play is the weather an actual issue, the winds to which he referred can mean only his own moral scruples. Now Neoptolemus hesitates a second time, but now he admits to an inner conflict more directly and without metaphor, speaking not of the winds but openly of his own pain.

In the agon of Neoptolemus, Odysseus and Philoctetes are presented as two fixed poles, and Neoptolemus is a character who wavers, veering now to one pole, now to the other. In Philoctetes Sophocles has given us one of his traditional protagonists, a character of inflexible will, but

Neoptolemus is a different kind of protagonist. Odysseus and Philoctetes remain the same character from beginning to end. Neoptolemus begins with one persona as the warrior son of a warrior father, then is persuaded by Odysseus to become someone else; then, as his friendship with Philoctetes evolves, he forsakes that political persona to take on yet another persona, which is nothing less than to stand with Philoctetes as his second self. Carol Gould considers this evidence that Neoptolemus is shown as having no fixed moral character, but I would argue rather for a character in confusion, cogitating, deliberating, developing an inward self.[7] We watch him going through a process, and this is certainly character development. Odysseus had dealt with the boy's moral scruples in the prologos, but a larger crisis now emerges, which takes him to a deeper level of his ethos. The crisis lies now in his conscience. He is becoming conscious.[8] Political expediency requires Neoptolemus to treat Philoctetes as an object, but Philoctetes is for him no longer an object. The awful sound that in other men's calculations had made Philoctetes an object to be discarded has the opposite effect on Neoptolemus. He begins to see that Philoctetes is, like himself, a subject.

When Odysseus in the prologos outlines for Neoptolemus the strategy for capturing the bow, he does not foresee the effect of suffering on a young man's conscience, nor the religious event that would undo his scheme, nor has he any understanding of the apostolic succession embedded in the bow, whereby the charisma of Heracles would pass through Philoctetes to Neoptolemus. In short, Odysseus had not reckoned with the power of *agapē*. It would be several centuries before the word *agapē* would enter the religious vocabulary of ancient Greece, but here we see the idea germinating. The affection that Neoptolemus is beginning to form for Philoctetes is what Buber calls the I-Thou relationship. This affection interferes with Odysseus's scheme because it defies all the conventional attitudes. For his fellow warriors, Philoctetes' disease had called not for compassion but for ostracism.

Aristotle gives us our first definition of *agapē* as spiritual love. He uses the verb *agapaō* (from the noun *agapē*) as a gloss on the more common verb for "love" (*phileō*, from the simple adjective *philos*, "dear"). "To be loved [*phileisthai*]," Aristotle writes, "is *to be cherished* [*agapaasthai*] in and for oneself."[9] This is the kind of love at work in Neoptolemus's crisis of conscience. Neoptolemus is beginning to experience compassion for a man so repulsive that he stands outside religion altogether. While Neoptolemus in promising to stay by Philoctetes may still be acting in obedience to the orders Odysseus has given him, another element enters into his deliberation. In the prologos Odysseus had said nothing about the healing awaiting Philoctetes if he consents to go to Troy with Neoptolemus. He had told Neoptolemus that Neoptolemus himself and Heracles' bow were essential for the Greek success. The bow itself was merely an object, as was Philoctetes. But the simulated friendship has blossomed into a genuine friendship. The feeling that Neoptolemus experiences now for Philoctetes cannot be the love that he might feel for the man that Philoctetes might become at Troy. Compassion for the man's pain as he is now, in his present repulsive condition—this is the new element that Sophocles brings to the old myth This kind of sympathy, for the diseased and repulsive, was not a heroic virtue. Neoptolemus is learning to be what Philoctetes had needed, truly his *symparastatēs*, the man who stands beside him and becomes one with him.

When Neoptolemus expresses his inward pain, we are to understand that he is coming face-to-face with the spiritual nature of the drama into which Philoctetes has initiated him. Odysseus had made it seem that it was a simple issue in which honesty must occasionally be sacrificed for political necessity. But the issue is more profound. It is the battle for the soul. Neoptolemus by his experience with Philoctetes and with his bow has been transformed. Whether or not this is called character development, it is certainly conversion in the religious sense. In the drama in which Neoptolemus now finds himself, he has bound himself to Philoctetes and his destiny by bonds stronger than any law. Having received the bow and with it taken upon himself the bow's divine Phthonos, Neoptolemus has entered a space where oaths are superfluous. When he assures Philoctetes that the law (*themis*) will not allow him to leave the island without Philoctetes, while he may be speaking as a man on a military mission, he also speaks proleptically, as the character he is to become, one who has discovered a higher law than the military code.

The second episode ends with Philoctetes passing first into delirium and then sinking to the ground in a deep sleep, with all his defenses gone but for his will, which dominates the rest of the play.

8

The First Kommos

(Verses 827–864)

The second episode comes to an end as Philoctetes sinks down into sleep. We are now given the next choral ode, but instead of a second stasimon the chorus sings this ode in the form known as a *kommos*. Jebb defines kommos as "properly a lyric lamentation (θρῆνος [*thrēnos*]) in which one of the actors took part with the Chorus. But the name can be used in a larger sense to describe any lyric dialogue between actor and Chorus, even when the character of lamentation is not present."[1] An ode jointly sung by the actor and the chorus takes us back to that earlier time when tragedy was all choral song and its nature was all, or almost all, pure lamentation.[2] This kommos, sung by the chorus and Neoptolemus, is composed of four parts: first, the strophe (vv. 827–38) and antistrophe (vv. 843–54). But between strophe and antistrophe is inserted the *mesodos* (the song in-between), the four verses in which Neoptolemus responds to the chorus (vv. 839–42). The kommos is then brought to a close with what was known in choral lyric as the *epode* (vv. 855–64). In this kommos, Neoptolemus is given only four verses, but the focus of the whole ode is to be found in those four verses.

The Strophe (Verses 827–838)

Ὕπν' ὀδύνας ἀδαής, Ὕπνε δ' ἀλγέων,
εὐαὴς ἡμῖν ἔλθοις, εὐαίων,
εὐαίων, ὦναξ· ὄμμασι δ' ἀντίσχοις
τάνδ' αἴγλαν, ἃ τέταται τανῦν.

ἴθι ἴθι μοι, Παιών.
ὦ τέκνον, ὅρα ποῦ στάσῃ,
ποῖ δὲ βάσῃ,
πῶς δέ σοι τἀντεῦθεν
φροντίδος. ὁρᾷς ἤδη.
πρὸς τί μένομεν πράσσειν;
καιρός τοι πάντων γνώμαν ἴσχων
‹πολύ τι› πολὺ παρὰ πόδα κράτος ἄρνυται.

The chorus opens the strophe with an ode to sleep, here personified as Hypnos and credited with the attributes of a divinity. We think of Sophocles the physician as we listen to his chorus sing this gentle song to the healing powers of Hypnos:

O Hypnos, thou that knowest nothing of pain,
nothing of grief, with gentle breath,
be now among us,
O Lord, our blessed Lord.
Keep now this radiance stretched before his eyes.
Come, oh come, our Healer.

(vv. 827–32)

"Radiance" is the word that calls for our attention. Sleep as darkness or night is a commonplace, but here we are to think of sleep as radiant light. The word used here is *aiglē*, an uncommon word in ancient Greek, rarely used after Homer and sparingly even in Homer. It is the *ethereal* light, the luminosity in the highest ether, where the gods abide. What has this light to do with sleep and especially with the sleep of this sick man? The lexicon, in searching for the appropriate meaning of *aiglē* in this passage, gives us "dream light as in sleep." The lexicon's authority might lead us to suppose that it was a commonplace of Greek thought that our dreams are lit by some kind of inner light. But we do not find this word used in such a way to refer to dreams elsewhere in Greek. This is Sophocles' own trope. This is the light where the gods dwell, the light of healing and wholeness.[3] Healing now is our theme.

The metaphor suggests that sleep is a state not of unconsciousness but of a different kind of consciousness, one more in touch with heaven, since it connects us to the good, the healthy, and the beautiful. With his eyes closed in sleep, so the chorus prays, may Philoctetes behold the inner light whence healing comes. Here the chorus speaks in a new role.

While still supporting the conspiracy, unwittingly, we might say, it has changed its theme and sings now not of deceit but of healing. For the moment, like Neoptolemus himself, the chorus is forced to wear two masks, the political and the spiritual. As the play progresses, once the deception has been exposed and therefore rendered useless, healing emerges as the real agon of the play, and the chorus will have to drop its conspiratorial role entirely to become, as best it can, the sick man's therapist.

Now, however, having in its persona as nurse sung the patient to sleep, the chorus turns to the more serious business at hand, which is of course the bow. The chorus has waved its magic wand and behold, Philoctetes is anesthetized. But not Neoptolemus. For him, quite the opposite; it is time for action. The decisive moment opens up before him. Could serendipity do better than this, Philoctetes comatose and his bow secured and grasped in Neoptolemus's hand? He has but to take advantage of this blessed coincidence and make a quick exit with the prize in hand, leaving Philoctetes to his unconsciousness:

> Consider, my son, where you stand,
> where you should go,
> what should be your next thought. Surely, you see it already.
> Why do we wait to act?
> Kairos, which holds the decision in everything,
> wins a great victory when it is right at our feet.
>
> (vv. 833–38)

The words here are deceptively simple, but they encode large domains of religious thought, which resist translation and even paraphrase. *Kairos* is the term around which this passage is built; it is the underlying theme of the ode. In the parodos the chorus has assured Neoptolemus that it would always keep its sight focused on its master's *kairos*, and here it is, the *kairos* that he and the chorus have been waiting for. Jebb gives somewhat blandly "occasion" as the meaning of the word in this passage, though the information in his note makes the word *kairos* far more important than mere "occasion."[4] Neoptolemus has already informed the chorus in the parodos that Philoctetes is living in sacred time. *Kairos* is that conjunction of sacred and secular time.

Kairos here puts us into the milieu of the athletic competitions. Neoptolemus is our athlete—young, beautiful, the very image of his father, with the chorus, who is his townsfolk, spurring him on to victory. But Sophocles surely intends us to hear a reference to something more profound that simply the good luck of an athletic victory. This Kairos is endowed with an extraordinary power: *"He holds the decision in everything."* The word for "decision" is *gnōmē* (from the verb *gignoskō*, "to know"). Webster informs us that the official meaning of the verb when used in the past tense (someone *had come to know*, hence *knew*) was "decided." However, the noun used here (*gnōmē*) is not simply "decision" but the whole mental process leading to decision; it speaks of mind and intelligence. This Kairos holds the intention and intelligence of everything. He is pure Intention. When all intentions, the greater and the smaller, are in alignment, victory is the result. In meditating on the *kairos* of this ode, we cannot forget the light that the chorus had introduced at the beginning of the strophe. Hypnos is also a kind of *kairos* with blessed properties, bringing closure to the sick man's seizure and then healing after his pain. But now the light has shifted to Neoptolemus. Philoctetes, so the chorus now advises, is to be left in the dark. Here again, at a moment's notice, we have shifted from the spiritual play to the political play. If Neoptolemus will but use his intelligence (*phrontis*), he must see that the darkness in which Philoctetes is enclosed is for Neoptolemus a golden *kairos*. But we who grasp that a new and different drama has begun know that the light here is all with Philoctetes. Should Neoptolemus hearken to his chorus, he will be as a blind man led by the blind.

The Mesodos (Verses 839–842)

ἀλλ' ὅδε μὲν κλύει οὐδέν, ἐγὼ δ' ὁρῶ οὕνεκα θήραν
τήνδ' ἁλίως ἔχομεν τόξων, δίχα τοῦδε πλέοντες.
τοῦδε γὰρ ὁ στέφανος, τοῦτον θεὸς εἶπε κομίζειν.
κομπεῖν δ' ἔργ' ἀτελῆ σὺν ψεύδεσσιν αἰσχρὸν ὄνειδος.

[Yes, he hears nothing, but I see that we have made our hunt
for these weapons in vain if we sail without him.
For his is the crown. The god said to bring him.
Disgraceful indeed would be the reproach if we boasted that we had
used lies and yet had failed to accomplish our task.]

If Kairos in this play is a trope of universal Mind, then the chorus, it now transpires, is so far from Mind as to be called mindless. This Neoptolemus makes clear in his short but value-laden response to the chorus's well-meaning advice. It has been noted that Neoptolemus sings the mesodos here in dactylic hexameters, the meter used in the responses delivered by the priests at Delphi to those who had come to consult the god. The unexpected meter clothes Neoptolemus's words in gravity. As Jebb puts it, "The stately hexameters—in contrast with the lighter rhythm of the Chorus—suit the authoritative tone in which Neoptolemus declares the purport of the oracle" (that is, the oracle spoken by Helenus regarding Philoctetes and his bow).[5] Neoptolemus now speaks with oracular authority.

Here certainly is an instance that might lend support to the argument that the tragic poets could give their characters words appropriate to the moment with an apparent disregard for realistic character portrayal. In this mesodos Neoptolemus is given to know things that he was never told by Odysseus, nor could he have discovered this information in the interval between the prologos and this choral ode, but the reason for the incongruity lies not so much in the poet's indifference to realism as in the nature of the chorus. It moves from its one function to another without giving any signal of the shift. At one moment the chorus is one of the characters within the play. At other moments it reverts to its more primitive function as the commentator on the action.

This formal oscillation between persona and commentator has a direct bearing on the portrayal of Neoptolemus. He too is both a person in the play and the leader of a chorus.[6] The same practice governs the function of Neoptolemus in this kommos. While the chorus here plays the part assigned to it at the beginning of the play, to be itself the person, the agent protecting and furthering its king's interests, Neoptolemus, breaking in on its sage counsels, assumes his other function as the exarchon of the chorus and hence becomes again the *prophet*. The dactylic hexameters, the meter used for oracular responses from Apollo's shrine at Delphi, signify that here, for the moment, Neoptolemus speaks for the god.

In his response to the chorus, Neoptolemus continues the theme of the contest but stages an altogether different contest: "Our hunt is in vain if we take the weapons but sail without him" (vv. 839–40). Now we are to understand that if Neoptolemus escapes with the bow but leaves Philoctetes on the island, the darkness will be his own. This is a new development in the plot. Sophocles had a sound dramatic intuition to leave it vague until this point, but now it must be clarified, that the mission requires not merely the bow but Philoctetes himself in person. Philoctetes is not the means to an end. He has become an end in himself.

Neoptolemus is even more oracular as he continues: "For his is the crown [*stephanos*]" (v. 841). Here we reach the keystone of the play. The reference again is to the athlete; *stephanos* is the garland with which the victor was crowned at any of the great athletic festivals. Neoptolemus begins this mesodos by using the image of a hunt only to dismiss that image altogether. The hunted animal does not compete for a crown. Only the athlete, the human contestant, can win a crown. The notion that tragedy was a contest like the athletic competition was familiar territory. In the old tragic form, the protagonist completed in this agon for his life, *and lost*, but in this new paradigm the protagonist must emerge from the trial as the undisputed victor.

What then is the contest? And who are the contestants? The larger context is the Trojan War, the contest of Greeks against Trojans, where Philoctetes will be acclaimed the victor when his arrow brings Paris down and so initiates the fall of Troy. But the Trojan War is no more than the backdrop to the real contest, between Odysseus and Philoctetes. If the bow is taken now, while Philoctetes lies asleep, the winner will be Odysseus, and the loser, Philoctetes. But this cannot be. Philoctetes must emerge as the winner, however that can be accomplished.

Neoptolemus concludes his justification for disregarding the counsel of his chorus by saying: "It would be a disgrace and a reproach to boast of success that is no success when we have used lies" (v. 842). Two thoughts are intertwined here. First, if Neoptolemus were to appear at Troy with Philoctetes' bow in hand but without Philoctetes, it would be a hollow victory; even worse, it would be no victory at all but a failure. How could a man boast of an action when the action itself was in fact a failure, and a failure that depended on lies? But the more important issue is that the real contest is for the soul. There can be no victory in stealing from an unconscious man. In this agon the victory must go to consciousness. If Philoctetes is to win the crown, he must act in full consciousness. He must go to Troy of his own free will. We have reached a serious aporia, which opens the field to a new kind of tragedy.[7]

Plato gives us the gloss we need for this Sophoclean contest. In the *Republic*, as Socrates is winding down his long discourse on justice, Plato has him offer an image comparing the just and the unjust to runners on a race course.[8] The unjust, Socrates says, may be formidable and clever, but they are like runners who make a good showing in the first half of the course, up to the marker at the end of the stadium, but make a dismal showing as they round the marker and come back down to the finish line. They spring sharply off the starting line, but on the homestretch they are a laughingstock. They are booed off the field, their ears down to their shoulders (in Socrates' picturesque language), *uncrowned*. The just, on the other hand, are like the runners who complete the course. They reach the *telos*, they carry off the prizes, and they *are crowned*. "Is this not the case with the just?" Socrates asks. "They are well esteemed in respect to the *telos* of every action, of every association, indeed in respect to the *telos* of life itself." This is the race in which Neoptolemus now finds himself.

On the surface, we might read the Neoptolemus of this play as a second Achilles. But for all the obvious correspondences between Sophocles' Neoptolemus and the *Iliad*'s Achilles, this Sophoclean character is far removed from the Homeric paradigm. We applaud Achilles in the first book of the *Iliad* when he dares to confront Agamemnon when Agamemnon's arrogance has put the whole Greek army at risk. But that confrontation, altruistic as it may be in its beginning, quickly degenerates into a colossal personal vendetta. The ethos of the Bronze Age is dramatically at odds with the ethos that we see Neoptolemus shaping before us on the Athenian stage. This Neoptolemus certainly fights for his integrity as Achilles does in the *Iliad*, but his integrity will soon force him to choose between his own ego and the ego of Philoctetes, and the ego of Philoctetes wins. *His must be the crown.*

The Antistrophe and the Epode (Verses 843–864)

ἀλλά, τέκνον, τάδε μὲν θεὸς ὄψεται·
ὧν δ' ἂν κἀμείβῃ μ' αὖθις, βαιάν μοι,
βαιάν, ὦ τέκνον, πέμπε λόγων φήμαν·
ὡς πάντων ἐν νόσῳ εὐδρακὴς
ὕπνος ἄυπνος λεύσσειν.
ἀλλ' ὅ τι δύνᾳ μάκιστον,
κεῖνο ‹δή› μοι,
κεῖνο ‹μοι› λαθραίως
ἐξιδοῦ ὅπως πράξεις.
οἶσθα γὰρ ὃν αὐδῶμαι·
εἰ ταὐτᾷ τούτῳ γνώμαν ἴσχεις,
μάλα τοι ἄπορα πυκινοῖς ἐνιδεῖν πάθη.

οὖρός τοι, τέκνον, οὖρος· ἀ-
νὴρ δ' ἀνόμματος, οὐδ' ἔχων ἀρωγάν,
ἐκτέταται νύχιος—
ἀδεὴς ὕπνος ἐσθλός—

οὐ χερός, οὐ ποδός, οὔτινος ἄρχων,
ἀλλά τις ὡς Ἀίδᾳ πάρα κείμενος.
ὅρα, βλέπ' εἰ καίρια
φθέγγῃ· τὸ δ' ἁλώσιμον
ἐμᾷ φροντίδι, παῖ, πόνος
ὁ μὴ φοβῶν κράτιστος.

[But my boy, the god will see to that.
But you, my boy, give me in reply a message
in words,
quick, quick.
The sleepless sleep of the sick
is always quick to see.
But whatever you do, do that—
see that you do that in secret.
You know of what I speak.
If your decision is the same as his,
then for those with their wits about them,
it is possible to foresee countless troubles for which there is no solution.

Look, child, a wind! A wind!
The man is without his eyes, he has no helper;
he is stretched on the ground, a thing of the night—
a good sleep is without cares—
he has neither hand nor foot, he has no control of any faculty,
but his sight is as the sight of one
who lies in the house of Hades.
See if your speech fits the *kairos* of this moment.
This, my son, is the principle my mind can grasp:
strongest is the deed attended by no fear.]

In the antistrophe (vv. 843–54) the chorus presses with even greater urgency, continuing in the function assigned to it by Neoptolemus at the beginning of the play to serve as his accomplice. The chorus still understands itself to be speaking to that political youth who brought it to this island when the play began.[9] As for his religious scruples, that the god insists that Philoctetes himself must come to Troy, "leave that," the chorus says, "to the god." It continues to argue for taking advantage of this felicitous moment: "Whatever you do, see that you do that in secret" (vv. 848–52). In the epode, the chorus concludes its appeal with one more expression of its own anxiety (vv. 863–64): "Strongest is the deed attended by no fear." But Neoptolemus is a changed man, as the mesodos reveals, and consequently the mission has changed. Pragmatism is not now his principal concern. The chorus continues to think of the mission as a hunt; its emphasis is on capture, not so much the capture of the man as the capture of his weapons. It is exactly aligned with Odysseus's instructions to Neoptolemus in the prologos as if it had overheard that conversation, that he must *steal* the weapon. There could be no better moment for the theft. But Neoptolemus, now overriding Odysseus, and hence his own chorus, has changed the nature of the contest into one where words suggesting the hunt and capture are completely out of place. His hesitation does not spring from fear. Lack of courage is not the issue. In fact, a bolder kind of courage is now the necessity.

The chorus continues its specious wisdom in the epode (vv. 855–64), representing a group of people completely ignorant of the true crisis at hand. It makes one final attempt to press Neoptolemus to act decisively, to take the bow and leave Philoctetes in his unconscious state, which it describes in vivid detail. Its language pointedly contrasts Neoptolemus's sight and Philoctetes' momentary blindness: "See, look," it says, using two different verbs, "he is blind; he has no eyes; his is the darkness of night; he is all but dead."

Why squander the advantage? When victory is at hand, the chorus foresees that scruples (that is, *moral scruples*) would open up a whole field of complications, which could be so easily avoided: "If you hold to your present intention, you can expect a host of problems from which there will be no escape" (vv. 853–54). Truer words were never spoken. In a few moments Neoptolemus will confess his error and put himself indeed in an impasse from which there is no escape. But were he to be obedient to the anxieties of his chorus, he would find himself in a worse impasse, being crowned for a victory for stealing his means of livelihood from a cripple at his moment of greatest vulnerability. *Kairos* is opportunity, but it is also crisis. This *kairos* now compels Neoptolemus to repudiate the victory that is already in his very hands. The kommos comes to an end as Philoctetes awakes. The third episode begins, and the crisis, which has been building for some time, comes to a head.

9

The Third Episode

(Verses 865–1080)

The third episode begins as Philoctetes awakes, beholds the light, and to his great joy sees his friend still waiting for him. Neoptolemus has endured to witness the degradation that the Greek commanders could not tolerate, good military men as they were, Philoctetes notes contemptuously (v. 873). Neoptolemus is made of a different mettle:

ἀλλ' εὐγενὴς γὰρ ἡ φύσις κἀξ εὐγενῶν
ὦ τέκνον, ἡ σή, πάντα ταῦτ' ἐν εὐχερεῖ
ἔθου, βοῆς τε καὶ δυσοσμίας γέμων.
(vv. 874–76)

[Your nature (*physis*) is wellborn, my boy,
and you are of the stock of the wellborn.
All this you made light of, my screams and my foul stench.]

Now that Odysseus's plan is about to be exposed, all the significant terms that Odysseus deployed in the prologos come to their fruition, no longer merely ideas but ideas translated into action. Philoctetes opens this episode with "nature" (*physis*), and by now we know that whenever he compliments Neoptolemus on his nature, his compliments are at the same time an attack on or a strong criticism of Odysseus's nature. He has earlier called Odysseus an evil person born of evil stock. He has also called him a bastard and a slave, bought by Laertes and falsely passed off as the legitimate son of Laertes when his real ancestor was the arch-criminal and arch-trickster Sisyphus. Being a bastard, having a bastard's nature, Odysseus is a priori incapable of a moral position. Having no ethos, he is all masquerade.

But the issue of character and breeding is not as simple as it might appear at first.[1] What of the two sons of Atreus, Agamemnon and Menelaus? Again and again Philoctetes vents his rage at these two as the primary culprits in his mistreatment. But in Homer no man was more royal than they. Their noble birth, however, was no guarantee of character. In the traditional myth Agamemnon and Menelaus acted as they did not because of some flaw in their character or in their breeding but precisely because they were the leaders of the nobility. The fault lay not in the sons of Atreus but in Philoctetes himself, whose contagion threatened the success of the entire mission. Compassion played a small part in the making of the Bronze Age warrior. Ruthlessness was more highly prized, and Achilles, held up in this play as the paradigm of moral rectitude, was as ruthless as any.[2] To endure a man's screams and his stench in a compassionate manner—this is a new kind of virtue and hence called for a new kind of breeding. Even so, Neoptolemus's appearance of constancy here is itself a fraud. In the ironic situation of the *Philoctetes*, Philoctetes may believe that Neoptolemus has remained at his side because of the youth's noble nature, but his action is in fact inaction, the result of two natures at war in him. The person whom Philoctetes takes to be a noble man is a trickster, still behaving as his part in the conspiracy demands.[3]

Philoctetes, now awake and in full possession of his faculties, is ready at last to quit the island. He rises to his feet to begin walking with Neoptolemus down the path to the harbor. But a new *aporia* opens. Both the noun *aporia* (the state of being at a loss) and the adjective *aporos* (being at a loss) are used in this episode. The *aporia* has shifted from Philoctetes back to Neoptolemus, but this is a much greater crisis than his hesitation earlier in the play when Neoptolemus had spoken of the need to wait for a more favorable wind. It truly establishes Neoptolemus as the protagonist in his own tragic agon. His agon is marked by five crises. The first is in the prologos, when Neoptolemus must be persuaded to cast aside his shame. His second dominates the kommos just concluded, when his sailors urge him to escape while he has the bow and Philoctetes lies unconscious, and Neoptolemus resists their pleas. We are now at the third crisis, when Neoptolemus's sense of shame undermines all the previous arguments and agreements. The fourth and fifth are yet to emerge as the play continues. The fourth crisis leads him to return the bow to Philoctetes, and his fifth is developed when

Philoctetes insists that Neoptolemus had given his word to take Philoctetes back to Greece.

"Ah! Ah! Woe! Woe! What am I to do now?" Neoptolemus exclaims (v. 895). His earlier crisis was a mere misgiving, but hesitation has now become paralysis. Webster notes that Neoptolemus uses the exclamation *papai!*—the same sound use earlier to represent Philoctetes' cry—to reinforce the parallel between Neoptolemus's mental agony and Philoctetes' physical seizure.[4] The whole play builds an indissoluble bond between Philoctetes and Neoptolemus, and pain is one of the elements in that bond.

Philoctetes is perplexed. What can be the problem now? "Where are you going with your words?" he asks:

τί δ' ἔστιν, ὦ παῖ; ποῖ ποτ' ἐξέβης λόγῳ;
(v. 896)

To this Neoptolemus replies:

οὐκ οἶδ' ὅπῃ χρὴ τἄπορον τρέπειν ἔπος.
(v. 897)

[I know not where I should turn my word. It is at a loss (*aporos*).]

Language itself is at a loss. Odysseus would never be at a loss for words. Aporia is not part of the sophistic repertoire, except as a trope. This newest aporia is the clue that Neoptolemus has failed as a rhetorician.

"You? You in a state of aporia?" Philoctetes replies in astonishment. "From what? Say it is not so." To this Neoptolemus replies in words that should provoke even greater astonishment:

ἀλλ' ἐνθάδ' ἤδη τοῦδε τοῦ πάθους κυρῶ.
(v. 899)

[But that is exactly where I am in my present *pathos*.]

Pathology in this play has shifted from the physical disease to become a matter of language.[5] Webster gives us "mental state" for *pathos* here; Jebb is satisfied with something even more pedestrian: "Indeed perplexity has brought me to this pass." Perplexity is a mild word for the moral crisis that now dominates this scene. While *pathos* can mean any condition affecting a person, mental or physical, the strong reading is "suffering," and suffering is certainly the meaning here. Every tragedy has its beginning in *pathos*. It is the word above all others that defines the protagonist of tragedy.[6] By his confession that he is suffering a *pathos* from which he can see no escape, Neoptolemus establishes that he too is a suffering hero.[7]

Philoctetes reverts to his own anxiety, assuming that Neoptolemus's talk of *pathos* and *aporia* issues from his disgust at Philoctetes' loathsome condition. But this *pathos* is the pain Neoptolemus experiences in and with himself. He himself is the offense:

ἅπαντα δυσχέρεια, τὴν αὑτοῦ φύσιν
ὅταν λιπών τις δρᾷ τὰ μὴ προσεικότα.
(vv. 902–3)

[Everything is discomfort when a person abandons his own nature (*physis*)
and does what is not seemly.]

Praised by others for his noble nature, Neoptolemus begins to shape a new idea, that character is something more than a reflex of his heroic ancestry; it imposes on him a moral choice moment by moment. Neoptolemus has discovered his conscience.[8]

Neoptolemus's crisis, as it unfolds through this play, contains the elements that Aristotle considered essential for the ideal tragedy. First, it is a *pathos* of such depth as to inflict acute suffering. Also, this pain is not physical but spiritual. Then we are given "recognition" (*anagnorisis*) and finally the dramatic "reversal" (*peripeteia*). Everything has been on course for the successful completion of Odysseus's plan, but now in this third episode everything is thrown awry and the cause for this *peripeteia* is the *proskynesis* in the cave. The two dramas, the political and the spiritual, have reached their point of irreconcilable difference.

Philoctetes, still misunderstanding the source of Neoptolemus's distress, appeals again to Neoptolemus's good nature, but speaking of it now as the nature of his father, Achilles: "You are not acting or speaking contrary to the nature of the man who sired you when you help a good man" (vv. 904–5). In invoking Achilles, Philoctetes speaks from within the old heroic paradigm, in which nobility is passed from father to son in unbroken succession. But the concept of nobility is moving into new territory. Neoptolemus is now caught in a dilemma: the only way he can be true to the nature that Philoctetes ascribes to him is to betray his word when he had consented to follow Odysseus's orders. Whatever action he takes, it will be a betrayal, either of Odysseus or of Philoctetes, and possibly even of both. Homer's Achilles was never faced with such a decision. In the *Iliad* Achilles' nobility rises to its heights only when his own honor is at stake. But Neoptolemus's crisis in this play is less about honor than about conscience. "I will be manifested as a disgrace," Neoptolemus replies to Philoctetes; "this for some time now has been my pain" (v. 809). The language is still that of the shame culture—Sophocles hardly has the vocabulary yet to articulate this intuitive idea of the private conscience—but an element other than public disgrace enters into this pain.[9] The ugliness of which he speaks is complex and has multiple facets. If he continues to follows orders, he will betray Philoctetes through his deception. But at the same time he will betray himself, his own ethos, because, in simulating friendship he has become a friend in fact. Neoptolemus plainly acknowledges this double duplicity in verses 908–9: "Am I to be found an evil man twice over, first by hiding what should not have been hidden and then by saying the ugliest thing that I could say?" The word he uses for "evil" (*kakos*) specifies wickedness, but it also signifies someone whose behavior is at odds with the heroic values of courage and decency. Having chosen inauthenticity, how is he now to become authentic?

Neoptolemus's word for "shame" here (*aischros*, lit. both "ugly" and "shameful") takes us back to the prologos, where Odysseus had argued that if Neoptolemus would give himself to shamelessness for one short part of one day, for the rest of time he would be revered as the most pious of all human beings. But that definition of wisdom exerts an uncomfortable pressure on Neoptolemus from the moment when he first begins to talk with Philoctetes, and his discomfort has been growing steadily during the play, as Sophocles indicates by the language he gives Neoptolemus to express his condition.[10]

The crisis comes to a head when Neoptolemus confesses that his pain is not at the thought of leaving Philoctetes behind but quite the opposite; the problem would be in taking Philoctetes aboard his ship: "My pain is not that I might abandon you but that I might in fact give you the escort you desire; this for some time has been the source of my pain" (vv. 912–13). If Neoptolemus were to take Philoctetes on board his ship, while Philoctetes might believe that his dearest wish had been granted, the victory would belong to Odysseus. Neoptolemus now recognizes that his shame would be twofold. He would be ashamed if he were to continue his present course of action, but he would suffer a different shame if he disclosed the conspiracy to Philoctetes and so proved himself disobedient to the military high command.[11]

There is no exit now but the truth. The fact is simple: their destination is not Greece but Troy. But the full truth, if Philoctetes will but listen, is that in acting thus Neoptolemus will be saving Philoctetes from his present evil, and together they will sack the city of Troy. "What is your intention?" Philoctetes asks, to which Neoptolemus replies:

σῶσαι κακοῦ μὲν πρῶτα τοῦδ', ἔπειτα δὲ
ξὺν σοὶ τὰ Τροίας πεδία πορθῆσαι μολών.
(vv. 919–20)

[First, to save you from this evil, and then
to go with you and ravage the land of Troy.]

How could Neoptolemus think of such a thing? the astonished Philoctetes asks. "Great Necessity governs these things," Neoptolemus replies. "Do not be angry when you hear this."[12]

πολλὴ κρατεῖ
τούτων ἀνάγκη· καὶ σὺ μὴ θυμοῦ κλύων.
(vv. 921–22)

Philoctetes now grasps the fact of his betrayal. He demands his bow back since it is stolen property, but Neoptolemus refuses:

ἀλλ' οὐχ οἷόν τε· τῶν γὰρ ἐν τέλει κλύειν
τό τ' ἔνδικόν με καὶ τὸ συμφέρον ποεῖ.
(vv. 925–26)

[But that is not possible. It is right for me to obey
those in command, and it is to (our) advantage.]

Neoptolemus cites three factors as the grounds of his refusal: justice, expediency, and his obedience to those in command. Rarely has robbery of a cripple's life-support system been defended in such lofty terms. His word for expediency (*sympheron*) would not perhaps sound as crass as our English word. It signifies advantage or benefit, and in the present situation, without further explanation, the advantage might extend to include Philoctetes. But the waters have been so muddied that Philoctetes could not be expected to hear anything in the word but some kind of sanctimonious varnish laid over ugly behavior. Whatever Neoptolemus may say, his actions are clearly determined by those whom Philoctetes considers his enemies. The advantage could only be theirs. How dare Neoptolemus speak now of justice? Philoctetes was betrayed once by Odysseus and the sons of Atreus, but this is a greater betrayal since it is a crime executed on the basis of a supposedly genuine friendship.

Philoctetes, now that the treachery is fully revealed, bursts into a diatribe of unmitigated fury, one of the great declamations of the ancient Greek theater (vv. 926–62). Our Philoctetes must be volcanic. He must storm, shout, bellow, roar. He must move through a large register of passions—hatred, wounded vanity, self-pity, suicidal desperation. The abusive language that Odysseus had encouraged Neoptolemus to hurl at Odysseus while playing the part of Odysseus's enemy is now hurled against Neoptolemus. Once praised for his nobility, Neoptolemus now hears himself excoriated as he had pretended to excoriate Odysseus. Philoctetes begins in an explosion of insults:

ὦ πῦρ σὺ καὶ πᾶν δεῖμα καὶ πανουργίας
δεινῆς τέχνημ' ἔχθιστον.

(vv. 927–28)

[Thou burning fire! Thou perfect monstrosity!
Thou most hateful *fabrication* of terrible and total wickedness.]

This is an Othello, a Lear at his most sublime. Philoctetes' words can hardly have for us the inflammatory effect that they were expected to have on the ancient Athenian audience. To be called a blazing fire might not seem to us the consummate insult and to be called a "fabrication" of wickedness (*technēma*) might also fail to raise our hackles as it might raise those of certain persons in late fifth-century Athens. "Fabrication" is admittedly a weak word for the Greek *technēma*. Phillips gives us "stratagem." Lloyd-Jones gives us a fine Shakespearean iambic with his "you hateful masterpiece of perfect villainy," borrowing "masterpiece" from Jebb's translation. But the word carries a sharper insult than either "stratagem" or "masterpiece" can convey. It takes us back to the prologos, where Odysseus had said to Neoptolemus, "I know that you were not born with the nature *to fabricate* evils." Goodness is not *manufactured*; goodness is innate, spontaneous; it is in the blood—that was the old thinking. But as Odysseus develops his line of argument in the prologos, *technē* can improve on nature, especially the technique of language, *rhetoric*. Now that the *technēma* has been exposed. Neoptolemus, whom Philoctetes had assumed to be good by nature, has turned out to be a facade, a total fabrication. Like Pandora in Hesiod's *Theogony*, who was an artificial woman fabricated by the gods to deceive humans, this Neoptolemus who stands before Philoctetes now is not a person; he is all artifice.[13] The underlying insult here is inauthenticity. As Odysseus was inauthentic to his very core in Philoctetes' eyes, so he has taught inauthenticity to this student in his academy.

Neoptolemus stands silent. Philoctetes, receiving no answer from Neoptolemus, addresses the landscape that for the past ten years has returned nothing to him but empty echoes. In words of deep *pathos* Philoctetes calls on the headlands, the harbor, the rocky cliffs, the beasts that were his only living company, to witness the treachery committed against him by the son of Achilles. Discovering that Neoptolemus is a person without a self, Philoctetes is thrown back into the company of the inhuman landscape, to which he pours forth the litany of his betrayal:

οἷ' ἔργ' ὁ παῖς μ' ἔδρασεν οὑξ' Ἀχιλλέως·
ὀμόσας ἀπάξειν οἴκαδ', ἐς Τροίαν μ' ἄγει·
προσθείς τε χεῖρα δεξιάν, τὰ τόξα μου
ἱερὰ λαβὼν τοῦ Ζηνὸς Ἡρακλέους ἔχει,
καὶ τοῖσιν Ἀργείοισι φήνασθαι θέλει,
ὡς ἄνδρ' ἑλὼν ἰσχυρὸν ἐκ βίας μ' ἄγει,
κοὐκ οἶδ' ἐναίρων νεκρὸν ἢ καπνοῦ σκιάν,
εἴδωλον ἄλλως.

(vv. 940–47)

[What acts he has done to me, this son of Achilles.
He gave me his promise that he would take me home;
instead he takes me to Troy. Having given me his right hand,
he has taken from me and now holds the sacred bow of Heracles
son of Zeus. He wants to display it before the Argives as if he had
captured a man in his strength and takes me by force.
He knows not that he is killing a corpse, the mere shadow of smoke,
nothing more than a phantom.]

In speaking of himself as now no more than an *eidolon*, he employs the traditional language used in Homer to describe the *psychē* of a dead person. Neoptolemus has indeed captured his soul. He has taken the man's life. Philoctetes also emphasizes the sacrilegious nature of this hubristic act, alluding first to the promise made by Neoptolemus and then to the covenant confirmed by the right hand. And last, and most important, the bow is a *sacred* weapon. Neoptolemus has already embraced the *phthonos* with which this weapon is impregnated. Philoctetes turns back to Neoptolemus to make one more appeal, speaking in words of great moral force:

‹ἀλλ'› ἀπόδος. ἀλλὰ νῦν ἔτ' ἐν σαυτοῦ γενοῦ.
(v. 950)

[Give it to me, and be once again in your own power.]

"Be in your own power" is Webster's translation for the unusual idiom here. Power is certainly implicit, but also implicit is the idea of self. Neoptolemus should take his power back from those to whom he surrendered it; in that way, he would also come back to himself. Jebb gives more emphasis to the self here with his translation: "Return, even now, to thy true self."

Neoptolemus continues his silence, and Philoctetes turns to the cave, which he will now enter as his tomb. The birds of the air, the beasts on the mountains will never again be his prey. Instead, the hunter will become the hunted: "I will become the slaughter in return for slaughter, and this I will experience at the hands of someone who seemed to know nothing of evil" (vv. 959–60). Ideas are broached here that are relevant for the entire history of Greek tragedy, among them the question of the fate of the tragic hero, whether he deserves the catastrophe that befalls him or is fate's innocent victim. This question, barely hinted at here, is raised and debated at some length in the choral ode that follows this episode.

Philoctetes makes yet another appeal to Neoptolemus. and the chorus interjects its own commentary, looking to Neoptolemus for guidance: "What are we to do? To sail or to accede to this man's words—the decision rests with you" (vv. 963–64). At last Neoptolemus finds his voice and explains the turmoil that has kept him speechless:

ἐμοὶ μὲν οἶκτος δεινὸς ἐμπέπτωκέ τις
τοῦδ' ἀνδρὸς οὐ νῦν πρῶτον, ἀλλὰ καὶ πάλαι.
(vv. 965–66)

[A terrible pity has come upon me for this man.
It did not begin now; it has been with me for some time.]

This is the third occasion on which Neoptolemus has spoken of this inward condition, and on each occasion he gives us to understand that it is not momentary but has been of some duration. What stronger evidence could we find that Sophocles intends us to see Neoptolemus as a character developing an inner life? In the way that Neoptolemus has progressed in this play, we are made to see the limitations in Odysseus's arguments. The element missing from his calculus has been compassion.

"By the gods, have pity on me and do not let yourself become a reproach among humans that you *deceived* me." So Philoctetes warns Neoptolemus, at least in our English translations:

ἐλέησον, ὦ παῖ, πρὸς θεῶν, καὶ μὴ παρῇς
σαυτὸν βροτοῖς ὄνειδος, ἐκκλέψας ἐμέ.
(vv. 967–68)

Jebb gives us "do not give men cause to reproach thee for having ensnared me." Ah, if only "ensnaring" were the worst of his misdemeanors. The verb that Philoctetes uses, which we translate as "deceive," is the same verb that Odysseus had used in the prologos for theft (*ekkleptein*). What the Athenians sitting in the Theater of Dionysus would have heard is "do not be a reproach for *having stolen* me." "Having stolen me" is certainly awkward in English; however, it is significant that this is the third occasion in the play when Neoptolemus's trick is represented as a theft: first the theft of the bow, a sacred weapon, which is also what sustains the man's life; then the theft of a man's *psychē*; and now the theft of the man himself. When Philoctetes talks of himself as now smoke, a shadow, an *eidolon*, we are taken back to the original sense of *psychē* in Homer, where to take a man's *psychē* is to take his life and all that is left of that man is his *eidolon*. These words are surely to be heard as a gloss on the word *psychē* as it first appears in the play in the prologos.

When Philoctetes accuses Neoptolemus of theft, he speaks as a character in the play, but he speaks also for Sophocles, who insists first that theft be understood as the foundation of this plot and then that this is the theft of the soul, which is indeed murder, both physical and spiritual. Theft played no part in the original myth. Nothing in Dio's account of the versions produced by Aeschylus and Euripides hints that theft figured in their plots. Both those poets have Philoctetes brought around to voluntary compliance. But in Sophocles' plot, since persuasion would be futile, Neoptolemus is given only one option: "You must steal the bow." Sophocles has taken advantage of the resources of his language, that a single verb, *ekkleptein*, can mean both "to steal" and "to deceive," and that the noun *psychē* still retains its Homeric meanings as both "life" and "ghost," to which have been added all those meanings gathered from the writers of the sixth and fifth centuries and tending in the direction of "soul." Surely, too, Sophocles would have us recall that *bios* in Greek signifies both "life" and "bow." The lexicon informs us that *bios* means not so much "life" (as in animal life) as manner or mode of life. This resonance arising from these words in conjunction makes for an obvious equation: bow = life = livelihood = *psychē* = soul.

As the theft was twofold, so the restitution must be twofold. Neoptolemus must return to Philoctetes not only the stolen bow but also his identity. From Dio's discussion of Aeschylus and Euripides, we do not sense that either of them treated the ethical problem in such a profound way. In Sophocles the focus is not on some riveting forensic debate such as Euripides may have staged in his production but rather on a crime, an offense against human custom and divine law. Though the dialogue between Neoptolemus and Philoctetes, and later between Philoctetes and Odysseus, reverberates with the language of debate—insult and accusation, argument and counterargument—the debate itself becomes a discourse on the soul.

Neoptolemus stands immobile. He has revealed the truth, not the whole truth but enough, though worse is yet to come. But the truth is no solution. His words express one persona, but the stolen property in his hand bespeaks another. Philoctetes appeals again to Neoptolemus's true self:

οὐκ εἶ κακὸς σύ· πρὸς κακῶν δ' ἀνδρῶν μαθὼν
ἔοικας ἥκειν αἰσχρά.

(vv. 971–72)

[You are not an evil person. You seem to have come here
having learned ugly things from evil men.]

This is only surmise; Philoctetes has yet to learn the name of Neoptolemus's tutor, but he has evidence enough of what seems like genuine compassion to believe that the boy is not by nature depraved. "Give to others their due and sail away," Philoctetes pleads, "but give me back my bow" (vv. 972–73), which we might paraphrase as: "Keep your persona if you must, but at least give me back what is mine."

This present crisis calls for a desperate solution. The moral force being exerted by Philoctetes threatens to throw the whole plot askew. With the deception exposed, a new plot is in the making. The time for disguise is past. Odysseus must emerge from his hiding place and assert his full authority if he is to undo the failure of his apprentice. He now storms onto the stage. Neoptolemus has shown himself an idiot. Odysseus demands that Neoptolemus give him the bow, but the Neoptolemus in this third episode is not the compliant youth of the prologos. He has, unfortunately for Odysseus, taken Philoctetes rather than Odysseus as his trainer. Sophocles is credited with adding the third actor in Athenian tragedy, and here we see his invention at its finest. While much of Greek tragedy is a set of debates between two characters, we have here three actors, all on stage simultaneously, each with his own point of view, or even, in the case of Neoptolemus, several points of view, and each of them compelling in his own way. For the moment, however, as Odysseus works to save the situation, Neoptolemus fades into the background as the scene is set for the violent altercation between Philoctetes and Odysseus. Philoctetes realizes now the worst, that his worst enemy is worse than he had imagined. He has been doubly betrayed by this man, first when he was dropped on Lemnos ten years earlier and now by the noble youth who has been corrupted by Odysseus. Philoctetes turns to Neoptolemus to make yet another appeal to the "boy," as he consistently calls him, to return his bow, but instead Odysseus answers for him, having taken command: "This he will not do, not even if that were his wish. You must come with these men or they will take you by force" (vv. 981–83). By force? Philoctetes asks, incredulous. "Yes," Odysseus replies, "if you will not come of your own volition" (v. 985). In his outrage Philoctetes calls on the very soil of Lemnos and the fire of the island's volcano to witness this abuse. Moments earlier Philoctetes had been eager to leave the island, but now he seems to cling to it as his only sanctuary, certainly his only court of appeal.

Odysseus only fuels the fire by responding with smooth pieties:

Ζεύς ἐσθ', ἵν' εἰδῇς, Ζεύς, ὁ τῆσδε γῆς κρατῶν,
Ζεύς, ᾧ δέδοκται ταῦθ'· ὑπηρετῶ δ' ἐγώ.

(vv. 989–92)

[It is Zeus, you should know; it is Zeus, I say, He who wields the power over this land—
Zeus has decided these things. I am but his servant.]

"O hateful man!" Philoctetes replies. "The things you find to say! Holding the gods before you, you make them liars." Unfortunately for

Philoctetes, Odysseus, though a master of deceit, here speaks the truth. On the human level he is the agent working on behalf of the army's high command, and on the divine level he is the agent of destiny. But how can Philoctetes hear his words as anything but blasphemy? "What pleas thou canst invent!" is Jebb's eloquent translation here (v. 991).

Philoctetes moves to hurl himself from the cliff where he has been standing, but even in attempting suicide his power is taken from him. Odysseus has the men physically restrain Philoctetes, and Philoctetes finds himself robbed yet again, now of the power over his own body. "You think nothing healthy or free," Philoctetes hurls the insult at Odysseus:

ὢ μηδὲν ὑγιὲς μηδ' ἐλεύθερον φρονῶν
(v. 1006)

This surely is the most cutting of all the arrows shot at Odysseus in this play. Jebb renders it: "O thou who canst not think one honest or one generous thought," and Lloyd-Jones gives a similar translation: "You who have no wholesome or generous thought." But the insult goes beyond honesty or generosity. We are taken back to Philoctetes' contemptuous accusation (at v. 417) that Odysseus was the bastard son of Sisyphus, bought by Laertes when he bought Odysseus's mother and born into his household as in fact his slave passed off as his son. That insult is here given its full significance. Being illegitimate, Odysseus is incapable of healthy thinking nor can he think the thoughts that befit a free man. Throughout the play, nature and breeding (*physis*) have been essential terms in the argument, and here the contrast is brought to its sharpest focus, that this is a contest between a free man and a slave, between Neoptolemus's noble nature and Odysseus's slavish nature. "You have hunted me down," Philoctetes continues (vv. 1007–12), parsing the meaning of his insults, "using that boy, who is more worthy of me than of you, as your screen [*problēma*], who now clearly feels grief at his own error and at my suffering." Philoctetes uses two words here without which we would not have Greek tragedy: the verb *hamartanō* (whence the noun *hamartia*) and *pathos*, attributing the *hamartia* to Neoptolemus and the *pathos* to himself, thus subtly binding Neoptolemus and himself into a single tragedy. Odysseus, planning a swift and clever military coup, finds that he has created a tragedy instead.

Philoctetes continues his diatribe on Odysseus's meanness of spirit, now speaking directly of Odysseus's *psychē*:

ἀλλ' ἡ κακὴ σὴ διὰ μυχῶν βλέπουσ' ἀεὶ
ψυχή νιν ἀφυᾶ τ' ὄντα κοὐ θέλονθ' ὅμως
εὖ προὐδίδαξεν ἐν κακοῖς εἶναι σοφόν.
(vv. 1013–15)

[That evil soul of yours, always peering through the crevices, has
taken this boy, against his nature and even against his will,
and taught him to be clever in evil.]

Again, the language, especially the words *psychē* and *sophos*, takes us back to the prologos, where Odysseus had explained to Neoptolemus that he could by stealing a man's soul be acclaimed as "clever." The verb *proudidaxen* (previously taught) also alludes to the prologos, where Odysseus had been the teacher and Neoptolemus his pupil. The image of Odysseus's soul peering through recesses or crevices is ambiguous: is he peering out from within his own internal shadows, or peering into the soul of Neoptolemus? In the end we can settle for both. We can also see it as an allusion to Odysseus, peering into Philoctetes' *psychē* to discover that weak point where language would have the magical effect that Gorgias speaks of. "Steal his soul," Odysseus had instructed Neoptolemus in the prologos, "and you will be called for all time both good and wise, *agathos* and *sophos*." We now see the fruit of the wisdom that he professed to teach. Neoptolemus can be truly *agathos* and *sophos*, good and wise, only if he disobeys Odysseus and suffers through the *pathos* that leads him to discover his own conscience.[14]

Philoctetes continues his insults:

καίτοι σὺ μὲν κλοπῇ τε κἀνάγκῃ ζυγεὶς
ἔπλεις ἅμ' αὐτοῖς, ἐμὲ δὲ τὸν πανάθλιον
ἑκόντα πλεύσανθ' ἑπτὰ ναυσὶ ναυβάτην
ἄτιμον ἔβαλον, ὡς σὺ φῄς, κεῖνοι δὲ σέ.
(vv. 1025–28)

[You, however, sailed with them yoked by necessity and deceit,
while I, wretch that I am, who sailed them of my own accord with my
seven ships—
they threw me out, as you say, stripped of my honor,
but they say it was you who did it.]

Here Philoctetes alludes to the story that Odysseus, to avoid service in the Greek expedition to Troy, had pretended madness and had to be tricked into revealing his sanity; he uses the story to reinforce his contrast between the ethos of the trickster and the ethos of the free man. Philoctetes himself went to the war as a free agent, while Odysseus, on the other hand, was coerced and served as an unwilling conscript.[15] Philoctetes has found another moment in the tradition that can serve to invalidate Odysseus. The word that Philoctetes uses for "deceit" here is yet another word that signifies theft (*klopē*). The lexicon gives as its first meaning "theft," but then adds that it can mean a fraudulent act. Certainly, it would hardly be intelligible to translate the word as "theft" in this present context. Yet it is significant that Sophocles has found another way to emphasize theft as the principal theme of this play.

Philoctetes finds another argument: "For ten years now I have been dead to you. O most loathsome to the gods, how is it that I am, in your eyes, no longer lame, no longer a stench? How will it be possible, if I sail with you, for you to make your sacrifices, to pour your libations to the gods?" (vv. 1030–33). Where has that piety gone? We are again taken back to the prologos, where Odysseus makes the argument in the strongest possible terms, that Philoctetes' very presence in the army camp was a blasphemy. Is he now to become a blessing? Has religion changed its catechism?

"Bitter is the stranger, and bitter his speech, Odysseus, and one that does not give way before his troubles." So the chorus responds to Philoctetes' long diatribe (in Lloyd-Jones's translation at vv. 1045–46). Here the chorus marks that inflexibility that, as B. M. W. Knox has so well discussed, is the chief characteristic of the Sophoclean hero.[16] Philoctetes is inflexible, to be sure, but a chorus with different perspective might see some force in his astonishment that he who was expelled from the camp as a leper is now to be the cornerstone of its military strategy. But the chorus is not at this point in the play given to act as a facilitator, only as a commentator. If the chorus is obliged to overlook the etiology of Philoctetes' pain, we might expect Odysseus with his intelligence to do a little better. But Sophocles has no intention of ascribing sympathy to this most unsympathetic character. In Philoctetes' rage Odysseus can hear only aspersions on his own character.

Odysseus defends himself in language appropriate to the law court:

πόλλ' ἂν λέγειν ἔχοιμι πρὸς τὰ τοῦδ' ἔπη,
εἴ μοι παρείκοι· νῦν δ' ἑνὸς κρατῶ λόγου.
οὗ γὰρ τοιούτων δεῖ, τοιοῦτός εἰμ' ἐγώ·
χὤπου δικαίων κἀγαθῶν ἀνδρῶν κρίσις,
οὐκ ἂν λάβοις μου μᾶλλον οὐδέν' εὐσεβῆ.

(vv. 1047–51)

[I could say many things in response to his words, if that were appropriate.
But now I hold to one argument (*logos*):
whatever kind of person is needed, that kind of person am I.
Whenever the trial (*krisis*) concerns good and just men,
you would not find anyone more reverent than I (*eusebē*).]

It is a biting irony that this man who had persuaded Neoptolemus in the prologos to give himself over to shame is now defending his own piety. To Philoctetes this must sound like casuistry of the worst kind. But armies need their Odysseus as much as they need their Philoctetes. Odysseus pulls us from our ruminations: "But I was born with this nature, always to desire victory. Except," he adds cleverly, as if it were an afterthought, "except in competing with you. In your case, I gladly concede defeat" (vv. 1052–53). This piety to which Odysseus lays claim sees not an iota of *justice* in Philoctetes' claims; Odysseus has not an ounce of compassion.

Sophocles has given Odysseus two lines of argument here, neither of them attractive. Odysseus begins with the necessity for political expediency and a reminder that piety can never be monochromatic; it must be situational. But then he shifts his ground to the idea of victory. Of course victory is a monumental concern in this play, but Philoctetes needs more than a political victory. What he needs is far beyond Odysseus's grasp. When Odysseus pretends to accept defeat, this is the last gambit available to him in his trickster role. He orders the men to release Philoctetes: "Let him stay. We do not need him. We have Teukros with us. He is an expert with the bow. And I too, I believe I am no worse than you in handling the bow. Let us be moving. And perhaps they will give me the honor that should have been yours" (vv. 1054–62).

Here again we watch Sophocles attaching his plot to Homer's larger epic to legitimize Philoctetes and to validate himself. In alluding to Teukros, Odysseus takes us to the *Iliad*, where Teukros is called "the best of the Achaeans in archery" (13.313) and also to the *Odyssey*, to a specific passage, in fact, where Odysseus links the three great archers who dominate this very play: Heracles, Philoctetes, and Odysseus himself. The occasion is the athletic contest in the *Odyssey*, book 8, when Odysseus, challenged by a young Phaeacian to prove himself in athletic contests, throws the weight well beyond the mark of the Phaeacian's best competitor. This success gives him an opportunity to boast of his skills, especially in archery. He was the best archer at Troy, he says, with the exception only of Philoctetes; he would not presume, he adds, to compare himself with the great archers of a previous generation, Heracles, for example, "who contended even with the immortals in archery."[17] How cleverly Sophocles works with the master text. Space must be opened, and why not by Odysseus himself, to have this updated Odysseus reference himself in the *Odyssey* acknowledging, as he had done in the *Odyssey,* that Philoctetes was the greatest archer at Troy, while at the same time reminding us that the archery contest of the *Odyssey* (books 21–22) has had the effect since Homer of making all other archers seem distinctly inferior to himself. This Sophoclean Odysseus, stitching himself into the Homeric fabric, makes two distinct and simultaneous insinuations. To this Philoctetes he insinuates that he might prove as fine an archer as Homer's Philoctetes had been. For us another insinuation hangs in the air, that Odysseus is indeed the greatest archer in ancient Greek mythology. Who remembers the archery skills of his greatest rivals, either Teukros or Philoctetes? Who indeed remembers even Heracles as an archer? But who can forget that most amazing archery contest in all of Greek mythology, which is still to be found in a thousand schoolbooks?

But if the anxiety of influence has Sophocles referring us back to the Homeric text, Odysseus has his own anxiety. Victory is still his objective. If Philoctetes is left on the island but deprived now of his bow, surely he can be expected to capitulate in short order. The final, most powerful persuasion would be the stinging threat that Odysseus, the second-rate archer and monstrous pretender, would wield the bow of Heracles and win the glory that should go to Philoctetes.[18] But even this last trick turns out to be a failure. Heroic braggadocio only adds to Philoctetes' anger and drives him to thoughts of suicide. Insult is the wrong protocol here. For all his cleverness, this Odysseus is useless where trust is the overriding issue.[19] Philoctetes is a case that calls for a different therapeutic.

Philoctetes turns again to Neoptolemus, but Neoptolemus remains silent. He then appeals to the chorus, but the chorus can act only in the role assigned to it: "This boy is our captain. Whatever he says, that say we also" (vv. 1072–73). Neoptolemus finds his voice at last, but it is not the voice of authority that the deferential chorus would lead us to expect:

ἀκούσομαι μὲν ὡς ἔφυν οἴκτου πλέως
πρὸς τοῦδ'· ὅμως δὲ μείνατ', εἰ τούτῳ δοκεῖ,
χρόνον τοσοῦτον, εἰς ὅσον τά τ' ἐκ νεὼς

στείλωσι ναῦται καὶ θεοῖς εὐξώμεθα.
χοὖτος τάχ' ἂν φρόνησιν ἐν τούτῳ λάβοι
λῴω τιν' ἡμῖν. νὼ μὲν οὖν ὁρμώμεθον,
ὑμεῖς δ', ὅταν καλῶμεν, ὁρμᾶσθαι ταχεῖς.
(vv. 1074–80)

[I will hear myself spoken of (by Odysseus) as having a nature full of
compassion. Nevertheless, remain with him, if he agrees,
for so long a time as it takes for the sailors to prepare the ship
and for us to raise our prayers to the gods.
And this man, perhaps, in the meantime will come to a better way
of thinking with regard to us. So let us set off, the two of us,
and you, whenever we call, be quick to set off also.]

Neoptolemus strikes an attitude of tentative authority, and his words betray his ambivalence. They are in fact an admission of defeat, though they appear to be another foray in the strategy to win over Philoctetes. Neoptolemus will go with Odysseus as Odysseus commands, and together they will return to the ship. By this action he will satisfy the military code that calls for his obedience, but at the same time, in allowing the sailors to linger with Philoctetes while he and Odysseus are offstage, he will satisfy his other agenda, which is to take more time to establish his credentials with Philoctetes as his friend: " I will hear myself spoken of as having a nature full of compassion."

Neoptolemus still struggles to accommodate his two personas: to be clever, as Odysseus had instructed him, and to obey orders; and to be compassionate, as Philoctetes calls him to be. This is a deft dramatic strategy, to have Neoptolemus and his chorus, who had been working the field as a team, now split from each other with their separation revealing Neoptolemus's split personality. The dutiful ephebe will follow his commander to the ship, while he leaves his kinder self with Philoctetes in the persons of the chorus, so that he himself can continue to speak and act, in Jacques Lacan's memorable phrase, "in the name of the father" (*le nom du père*).[20]

Neoptolemus leaves the chorus with no specific instructions. In his obedience to Odysseus, he cannot implicate himself too overtly in the business that will occupy the chorus when he is absent from the scene. In the parodos Neoptolemus had instructed the chorus to look to him for cues to guide its words and behavior. Now he plays, as it were, a second Odysseus, taking himself off the stage and leaving the chorus to execute his will as best it can without his direction.

We are impressed with the oddity here that Neoptolemus, who has been so conspicuously the leader of the chorus, should remove himself from the scene at this critical moment, leaving his chorus leaderless while assigning to it the sole responsibility to bring events to a satisfactory conclusion. The chorus is now to continue the dialogue with Philoctetes as if it were Neoptolemus himself. Perhaps it, although hitherto completely dependent on Neoptolemus, can develop its dormant rhetorical powers and win success where both Odysseus and Neoptolemus have failed. Perhaps with some adroit negotiation, the chorus can achieve a rapprochement with the bitter man. If so, every man would win his crown, and Neoptolemus would have satisfied both his teachers, Odysseus and Philoctetes.

The episode ends with Odysseus and Neoptolemus leaving the stage, headed for the harbor, and Philoctetes standing on the cliff above the stage with the chorus standing below him in the *orchēstra*, ready to step into its new role.

10

The Second Kommos

(Verses 1081–1217)

> You are what your deep, driving desire is.
> As your desire is, so is your will.
> As your will is, so is your deed.
> As your deed is, so is your destiny.
>
> Brihadaranyaka Upanishad 4.4.5

The third episode comes to a close with Odysseus and Neoptolemus exiting the theater, leaving Philoctetes standing at the entrance of his cave and the chorus standing in the *orchēstra* below. Their departure marks the moment for the next choral ode. Instead of a second stasimon, an ode sung entirely by the chorus, Sophocles gives us a second kommos, an ode to be sung by both the chorus and the protagonist. In the first kommos the actor (Neoptolemus) was given only four verses in the entire ode; the burden of the ode fell largely on the chorus. In this kommos the principal role has been given to Philoctetes. He is truly here the leader of the chorus.[1]

This kommos follows the conventional form of the choral ode: a strophe followed by an antistrophe in the same metrical form. Here we are given two sets of strophe and antistrophe. In each strophe Philoctetes leads off the song and sings the larger part, and the chorus makes a brief response. The same format is followed in the antistrophe. This is a dialogue but different from the dialogue of the so-called spoken parts, being more in the nature of an oratorio, with Philoctetes more singer than speaker. Webster, in giving A. M. Dale's metrical analysis of this ode, writes of the passion and despair conveyed by the ode's complex metrical schemes.[2] Though the kommos had become a form that could be used in a variety of contexts, its original function was lamentation, and here Sophocles returns the form to its origin. This is the protagonist's death song, its *pathos* made more intense because the dying man is both the subject of the song and its singer.[3]

The First Strophe (Verses 1081–1101)

THE TOMB

Philoctetes begins this strophe with one extended musical phrase. With the other actors gone from the theater, he sings as if this were his soliloquy. Even when the chorus makes its response, Philoctetes can barely hear it, so fixated is he on his own despair. Philoctetes has already poured forth his heart to Neoptolemus and Odysseus in the third episode. He is done with pleading his case with those who will not answer. His last tragic anthem is addressed to no one but himself. Solipsism is its ultimate theme. Philoctetes begins the strophe by addressing the cave, his only home for so many years, but now to become his tomb. There is no mistaking the meaning here. "This chamber in the hollow rock," as he calls it, which he was destined never to leave, is now readied for his burial.

THE DAIMON

The chorus completes this first strophe with its six-verse response. Stepping into the vacancy opened up when Neoptolemus abdicated his role as the leader, the chorus has become the counselor. Alas for Philoctetes, the best that the chorus can do is to act less as the counselor than as the judge. Judgment is what Philoctetes least needs now. His real need is for healing, of the serpent's wound but even more so of the wound inflicted on his self-esteem by his own comrades when they ostracized him from their community. Here is the chorus:

σύ τοι κατηξίωσας, ὦ βαρύποτμε, κοὐκ
ἄλλοθεν ἁ τύχα ἅδ' ἀπὸ μείζονος·
εὖτέ γε παρὸν φρονῆσαι
λωίονος δαίμονος εἵλου τὸ κάκιον αἰνεῖν

(vv. 1095–1100)

[O thou of heavy destiny,
this burden—thou hast deemed it right to inflict it upon thyself.
No external power holds thee in its grip,

This fate comes not to you from elsewhere,
from some greater source. When it was in thy power to use thy mind,
thou didst approve thine own worse *daimon*.]

In leaving the chorus in the theater with Philoctetes, thus detaching it from himself and attaching it to Philoctetes, Neoptolemus has now given the protagonist's role back to Philoctetes. Most significantly, gone completely is the chorus of the parodos, the assistant in the deception. The chorus here reverts to its primitive character as Hegel understood it, to speak as "a substantive and more enlightened intelligence, which warns us from irrelevant oppositions, and reflects upon the genuine issue."[4] Hegel amplifies on this point: the chorus is not merely a spectator, "a wholly disinterested person, at leisure to entertain such thoughts and ethical judgments as it likes, which, uninteresting and tedious on its own account, could only be attached for the sake of such reflections. The chorus is the actual substance of the heroic life and action itself."[5] The chorus is now the interpreter of this tragedy and the commentator on the nature of tragedy itself.

Daimon is the strong word in this first strophe. The easy translation is "fate," but fate is a colorless abstraction. "Fate," Hegel writes, "is what is devoid of thought."[6] It is not some notion in which "justice and injustice disappear in some abstraction," he continues; in tragedy "necessity is not a blind justice; on the contrary, it is recognized as the true justice." *Daimon* could be used in antiquity of any god, but in one of its specialized senses, *he* (*daimon* being a person) is often associated with fate, leading to the lexicon's definition of this *daimon* as "the *good* or *evil* genius of a family or person." The lexicon hazards the etymology that the noun derives from the verb *daiō*, "to distribute," though this etymology is in dispute.[7] If we accept this etymology, the *daimon* (masc. noun) is "he who divides and assigns the portions." Whatever the etymology, this *daimon* of popular belief, assigned to a person at birth, remains with that person throughout the person's lifetime, in some mysterious and opaque way governing and directing every moment in the person's life. Happiness is to have a good *daimon* (*eudaimonia*); unhappiness is to be cursed with an evil *daimon* (*kakodaimonia*). Until this point in the play, Philoctetes might consider himself to be the prime example of a man cursed with an evil *daimon*.[8] Not so, says the chorus; it is time to find a new way of thought.

The idea of a *daimon* allotted to one at birth who governs every moment of one's life might seem a primitive determinism. But Heraclitus, in his cryptic fragment DK 119, opens up another perspective: "*Ethos* for a human [is] *daimon*."[9] Since the verb is left implicit, the equation can be read in either direction: our ethos is our *daimon*; our *daimon* is our ethos. Here too the conventional translation for *daimon* is "fate." This is how Charles Kahn translates it, though he goes on to articulate the inner meaning of the *daimon* in this fragment at some length, taking the literal meaning to be that a person's so-called fate is determined by that person's choices.[10] This meaning, he writes, "is further enriched if we take the *daimon* literally as 'god' or 'divinity.' For the gods of Heraclitus, the immortals who live our deaths and are dead in our lives, can only be the elemental powers and constituents of the cosmos, from which our life comes and to which it returns."[11]

Whatever the exact meaning of this fragment, clearly Heraclitus was moving from the popular belief in the *daimon* as a divinity who imposes his will on us to something more subjective. What is implicit in Heraclitus becomes explicit in Plato. Plato has Socrates conclude the *Republic* with the myth of Er, a man who is killed on the battlefield, passes into the afterlife, witnesses how souls are processed after death, and is sent back into a new existence.[12] Er is given the privilege of returning to his earthly existence in order to report what he has seen in the afterlife. After the sophisticated arguments of the *Republic*, this myth strikes many as a sorry end to one of the most majestic philosophical studies ever written. Julia Annas finds it vulgar and childish.[13] But despite the features of this myth that scholars might censure as woefully unphilosophical, embedded in it is surely the most astounding passage on human choice to be found anywhere in ancient literature. Souls after death, so Er's story goes, pass either below the earth if they have led evil lives or into the heavens if they have lived lives of justice. After long aeons, when the evil are punished and the righteous enjoy their state of heavenly bliss, the souls are assembled to enter into new lives. A prophet (called in some translations an "interpreter") then takes the lots from the knees of the goddess Lachesis, the Fate whose name identifies her function as "Apportionment," and addresses the souls as follows: "O souls of the day, now begins a new cycle of mortal generation that leads to death. *No daimon will be allotted to you*. Each of you will make his or her own choice. And virtue owns no master. Each of you will have virtue to the degree that you practice it or do it dishonor. The responsibility lies with the chooser. The god is not responsible."[14] After the souls have chosen their individual lives, they are led to the goddess Lachesis, who assigns to each the *daimon* that each has chosen. This *daimon* is the divine ratification of that individual's own choice. The Bollingen translation gives us "divinity" or "deity" for *daimon* in this passage, rather than "fate," but even "divinity" seems too abstract for this personalized *daimon*, who becomes the indwelling presence of the divine in each human soul. But regardless of our choice of words, we see that the old popular meaning has been completely reversed. The individual's *daimon* is allotted to human souls neither in a random way nor by some alien force. Everything depends on the human choice, and it is a choice made in complete consciousness. This choice is then validated by the goddess Lachesis, who, in this myth, far from being "Allotment," has become "Choice." *The god is not responsible.*

This is the message of the chorus in this kommos. "Your fate has not been allotted to you," the chorus admonishes Philoctetes. "The allotment has been your own choice." Philoctetes is his own *daimon*. To translate *daimon* in this passage as "fate" is to erase any idea of relationship from our reading. Who chooses their fate? Fate, almost by definition, is that which cannot be chosen. Relationship is implicit in the Heraclitus fragment, but it is made more explicit in the story Socrates tells at his trial regarding what he calls his *daimonion* (his "little *daimon*"), that personal and private *daimon* who never gave Socrates instructions on any course of behavior but intervened only to caution him against any action that might have a deleterious effect on the welfare of his soul.[15]

The *daimon* who in this kommos enters the dialectic of the play is arguably Sophocles' greatest contribution to the Philoctetes myth. Paradoxically, the hero of ancient tragedy, who often must seem to others as the most isolated of all human beings, the most estranged from the gods, is for all his alienation, potentially the person in the closest bond with his or her own *daimon*. To quote from Emily Dickinson's poem "This Consciousness that is aware":

Adventure most unto itself
The Soul condemned to be
Attended by a single Hound,
Its own identity.[16]

When Philoctetes rails at his *pathos* as a suffering imposed on him by some external force, he keeps it safely objectified, but the tragic hero's fate is never only objective; it must be objective and subjective at the same time. Even if a deterministic interpretation of fate were defensible in reference to the serpent's wound or Philoctetes' expulsion from the Greek army, those dramas are over. Now the chorus speaks from the center of a different drama, which is subjective. The chorus will not allow Philoctetes the escape of an etiology that puts all the blame elsewhere.

The chorus articulates the idea of personal responsibility in three different ways in the same sentence (vv. 1095–96). First, "you have considered yourself worthy of this fate." Lloyd-Jones gives us simply "you have chosen this," but a value judgment is also included here, which Webster addresses in his gloss: "'You deemed this worthy,' i.e., you are responsible for it."[17] The chorus then amplifies on the theme: "This Fate [*Tychē*] does not come from elsewhere or from some greater power." And, finally, it concludes, "You have used your own intelligence in choosing your worse *daimon* over your better."

Philoctetes' problem is no longer his enemies. He is the problem or more exactly, his relationship with his own self. His disease may have begun as a physical injury, but its field has now been enlarged to include rage, hate, and a psychotic solipsism. This is the despair that in Kierkegaard's analysis takes three forms: "being unconscious in despair of having a self (inauthentic despair), not wanting in despair to be oneself, and wanting in despair to be oneself."[18] Until the kommos introduces Philoctetes' *daimon* into the discourse, it has been the assumption of the play that his sickness is physical and is caused by an external agent. But from this point forward, the disease is defined differently and given a different etiology. Whatever that original disease, Philoctetes' present disease is spiritual.[19] Alas, few indeed are the patients suffering from this pathology who can accept the diagnosis and correct the problem. If the pathology is in the self's relations with itself, how is that same self to become its own physician?

The First Antistrophe (Verses 1102–1121)

The chorus speaks the truth, but its attitude is more that of the bishop speaking ex cathedra, and we should not be surprised if Philoctetes cannot hear counsel spoken by a comforter like this. In this first antistrophe Philoctetes continues his funeral dirge as if singing to himself. This disjunct between the protagonist and the chorus is a striking feature of this ode, made more conspicuous because the intention was that Philoctetes and the chorus would bond in a close and intimate relationship to compensate for Neoptolemus's embarrassing failure. But like Job's comforters, this friend brings not comfort but accusation, which leads the invalid to reinforce his own solipsism. After Philoctetes has sung his part, the chorus concludes this antistrophe as it had concluded the strophe, acting still as the sick man's comforter, but cold indeed is its comfort:

πότμος σε δαιμόνων τάδ', οὐδὲ σέ γε δόλος
ἔσχ' ὑπὸ χειρὸς ἐμᾶς· στυγερὰν ἔχε
δύσμοτμον ἀρὰν ἐπ' ἄλλοις.
καὶ γὰρ ἐμοὶ τοῦτο μέλει, μὴ φιλότητ' ἀπώσῃ.
(vv. 1116–20)

[This is your destiny from the gods. No trick of my hand
holds you in this condition.
Direct your deadly curses
at others, not at us.
For *this* is our concern, that you do not thrust from yourself the friendship being offered to you.]

We need Ariadne to thread our way through this maze of contradictions. It is not that the chorus has turned jesuitical. Rather, Sophocles uses the chorus to do his thinking on several levels simultaneously. Philoctetes had bemoaned the sufferings inflicted on him through the "unsuspected and secret words of a cunning mind" (vv. 1111–15), but now the chorus disavows any trickery on its part and insists that Philoctetes' fate is from the gods. This is disingenuous. At the present moment, when Philoctetes is focused on the theft of his bow, for the chorus to deny its part in that conspiracy we take to be an outright lie. How glibly it now absolves itself of its own deceitful ways when deceit is at the very center of the play. This is certainly an instance that exemplifies the argument of Tycho von Wilamowitz-Moellendorff that we should not expect ancient drama to satisfy the criteria of modern naturalism.[20] The problem for interpreters is that the chorus has divested itself of its conspiratorial role and has become Philoctetes' spiritual counselor, thus returning to the role that Hegel understood as the essential function of the chorus in tragedy, to represent "a substantive and more enlightened intelligence."[21] The chorus, distancing itself now both from the trick perpetrated by Neoptolemus and from those who perpetrated the original crime in depositing Philoctetes on Lemnos, presents itself as standing outside the events, viewing them as a priest might see them. Two separate conditions seem to be implied here and differentiated, the external and the internal. While Philoctetes is most deeply hurt by the external events, culminating in the theft of his bow, the chorus works to shift his attention to the context of his destiny. But what satisfaction can a man have in being told that it was his destiny to be robbed by another man pretending to be his friend? The chorus and Philoctetes inhabit two different worlds.

The word that the chorus uses for "the gods" is *daimones* (plural of *daimon*). The word contains ambiguities not hinted at in our English "gods." When the chorus attributes Philoctetes' condition to *daimones*, its earlier gloss on his personal *daimon* still reverberates in our ears. The *daimones* in its present argument could be simply the larger gods, but included in the word *daimones* are also his more personal gods, who are the expressions of his own choices. The contradiction between the arguments of the chorus in the first strophe and the arguments now being put forward is, in part at least, because two conditions are being discussed, with no clear demarcation between them. In the strophe, when the chorus advises Philoctetes that he has chosen his own *daimon*, its reference is to the present moment. If his curses are prompted by the snakebite and then by the treatment he received from the sons of Atreus, those prior events are now irrelevant; hence the choral admonition to Philoctetes to refrain from cursing others for a fate that lies within his own power. Certainly, the *daimones*, the higher powers, are always implicated in the destiny of any hero of Greek tragedy, but the more important issue now, which the chorus articulates as best it can in its opaque fashion, is Philoctetes' relations not with the greater *daimones* of the outside world but with his own *daimones*, who are two aspects of himself. Hegel writes of this complex relation in ancient tragedy between destiny and character: "All that we attribute to the gods must at the same time establish itself as that which is essentially cognate with the spiritual life of particular men. . . . All that is posited in an external relation to man is none the less clearly that which is immanent in his own spirit and character."[22] The artist's function, Hegel continues, is "to introduce a mediating link between the difference involved in these two aspects, to bind them, in short, by a finely conceived thread of relation which, while clearly emphasizing their springs in the spiritual life of man, shall make no less visible the universal and essential element which is therein implied and present as such to the imagination in individual form."[23] This is the function of the chorus in this kommos, to mediate between the inner and the outer and to bind them with a "finely conceived thread of relation." Throughout the play Philoctetes sees himself as impotent. On the contrary, his impotence is self-willed. His will is the problem, not that it is too weak but that it is too strong. Nothing could be stronger than the will of this angry man, but it is completely invested in his now false identity. The chorus ends its response in this antistrophe with the wish that Philoctetes not reject friendship when it is offered. We begin to grasp the strange dynamics of this kommos. This patient's disease has become his badge of honor, his very life; his sick *daimon* has become the only self whom the patient will admit into dialogue with himself.

The Second Strophe (Verses 1123–1145)

The second set of strophe and antistrophe follows the pattern of the first strophic pair, with the burden of the song falling to Philoctetes. He begins both the strophe and the antistrophe with his lamentation, and the chorus concludes both strophes with its briefer response. Philoctetes, imprisoned in his own solipsism, continues to chant his lament as if he has heard not a word the chorus had said, revealing unmistakably that his *pathos* is his wounded pride. He keeps lovingly before his eyes the image of Odysseus standing like an arrogant colossus on the plains of Troy, brandishing his bow and laughing, as if it were proof of one warrior's conquest of another. If Philoctetes were an Odysseus, he would have adapted to necessity, but his *psychē* is made from a different mold. He cannot adapt to what he sees as rank injustice. A passion for justice is a noble virtue, but Philoctetes' pain at the injustice of the world, on the surface one of his most admirable virtues, also reflects a serious disorder. It is an expression of that extremism of which Hegel writes, the one-sidedness of the hero that leads to his fatal collision with all other points of view.[24] Philoctetes' obsession is one-sided not only in his relations with his larger society but also in his relations with himself. Some might be reluctant to apply modern theories of narcissistic disorder to this ancient tragedy, but Philoctetes' disorder certainly exemplifies the kind of problem with self-identity that modern psychology has uncovered. Heinz Kohut writes that aggressions "in the pursuit of maturely experienced causes are not limitless."[25] But the enemy who provokes "the archaic rage of the narcissistically vulnerable is seen by him not as an autonomous source of impulsions, but as a *flaw in a narcissistically perceived reality*. . . . [It is this archaic mode of experience which explains the] fact that those who are in the grip of narcissistic rage show total lack of empathy toward the offender. It explains the unmodifiable wish to blot out the offense which was perpetrated again the grandiose self."[26]

Several elements in the case before us point toward this kind of narcissistic disorder. The first is Philoctetes' rage; the second is the grandiose self. This self is what gives Philoctetes his heroic stature, but it is at the same time a serious flaw. Throughout the play, until Heracles intervenes at the end, Philoctetes never allows for any defect in his own character, though his defects are exactly what the chorus now addresses. The righteousness he lays claim to belongs not to the human sphere but to the gods. Philoctetes validates this grandiose self by invalidating Odysseus at every opportunity and in every possible way. His loathing for Odysseus is pathological. For Philoctetes, Odysseus is a flaw in Nature herself. This is the grandiose self at its most extreme, painting itself as the sum of all perfections, while painting its enemy as the sum of all depravity. The third point of comparison with the narcissism of modern psychoanalysis is that Philoctetes, being impotent to inflict any damage on his enemies, can harm only himself, which further aggravates his fury at his enemies.

Philoctetes calls upon his bow to witness that it has been wrenched from his hands by an act of violence:

ὦ τόξον φίλον, ὦ φίλων
χειρῶν ἐκβεβιασμένον,
ἦ που ἐλεινὸν ὁρᾷς, φρένας εἴ τινας
ἔχεις, τὸν Ἡράκλειον
ἄθλιον ὧδέ σοι
οὐκέτι χρησόμενον τὸ μεθύστερον,
ἀλλ' ἐν μεταλλαγᾷ ‹χεροῖν›
πολυμηχάνου ἀνδρὸς ἐρέσσῃ,
ὁρῶν μὲν αἰσχρὰς ἀπάτας,
στυγνόν τε φῶτ' ἐχθοδοπόν,
μυρί' ἀπ' αἰσχρῶν ἀνατέλ—
λονθ' ὅς ἐφ' ἡμῖν κάκ' ἐμήσατ' ἔργων.
(vv. 1128–39)

[O my beloved bow,
O torn from my loving hands
by force,
surely you witness this with pity,
if you have any intelligence at all,
the friend of Heracles
no longer using you as before
but you must now be plied in the hands
of a cunning man,

witnessing ugly deceit
and a loathsome enemy—
and the countless evils that he plotted against me.]

The uncertainties in the Greek manuscript make translation of this passage difficult. Webster, in explicating the last verses, writes: "Sophocles began as if he were going to say '(1) seeing tricks (2) seeing an enemy (3) seeing the results of the tricks planned by the enemy,' but he actually wrote 'seeing tricks, and an enemy, and the results.'"[27] The confusion is a good reflection of Philoctetes' own tortured line of thought, but we cannot say that Sophocles intended a confusion in syntax to reflect his character's inner confusion. Rather, in such a passage the poet himself speaks on several levels simultaneously and then subjects his thoughts to the intense compression required in ancient lyric poetry.

The first and most significant theme in this passage is love. Philoctetes' love for his bow is the reverse side of his hatred of Odysseus. In his apostrophe to his bow Philoctetes mentions love twice in a single sentence, using the adjective *philos* (dear, beloved) once of the bow and once of his own hands that had held the bow. Lloyd-Jones gives us both: "O beloved bow, bow that was forced out of my loving hands" (vv. 1128–29). When Philoctetes speaks of the bow in his own "dear" hands, we are reminded of the Homeric usage where *philos* pertains to a person's heart, spirit, life, or limbs, which the lexicon advises us to translate as "one's own." Webster reads the Sophoclean usage as conforming to the old Homeric pattern; Philoctetes means merely "my bow, my hands."[28] But this sacrifices some of the intimacy. We do not want to do anything to lessen the force of love in Philoctetes' apostrophe to his bow. The adjective, even if used twice in quick succession, may seem a small detail, hardly more than a manner of speaking. But quite the opposite is true. Philoctetes has lived all these years on Lemnos in a loveless world. His only relationship, to call it that, has been with the nymph Echo, which is a cruel charade of a relationship. Neoptolemus, arriving on the scene, had established a true relationship of the heart, so Philoctetes has assumed, but that relationship has been shown to be as empty as his communications with Echo, or even worse, since Neoptolemus had fostered that relationship with only one intent, to rob Philoctetes of his bow.

Significant here is the psychic projection invested in the bow. The bow, while still in Philoctetes' hands, was his friend. Now, taken from him, it is exalted almost to godhood, magnified by Philoctetes' own narcissism. Between him and his bow, as he now reflects on its loss, is what Martin Buber has called the I-Thou relationship.[29] Once his beloved but now taken from him, it must now look down with pity and horror at the fate of its friend while at the same time surely it will pity itself, forced to witness its own humiliations. This vision, of Philoctetes and his bow gazing on each other and witnessing each other's humiliations, is complex because it includes both being seen and not being seen. Philoctetes first sees in his imagination Odysseus standing somewhere on the shore (at Troy, of course), *laughing*, and brandishing in his hand what once had served as Philoctetes' livelihood, the bow that no one else has ever used. Contrasted here are the uses of the bow, a contrast that is intensified as Philoctetes develops his line of thought. Odysseus is not imagined as using the bow; rather, he stands on the shore, brandishing it as a trophy. For Philoctetes the bow has been a piece of equipment essential for his very survival. He calls on the bow to witness this travesty. "Surely you see," he begins, "*if you have any intelligence at all.*" The bow, once an instrument, has become a conscious being. This is surprising yet intelligible, given that the bow is repeatedly marked as divine, given also the man's projection of his own emotions onto this one and only companion of the past ten years. This now-mindful bow is to witness first that it has been wrenched from the hands of its owner in an act of violence, and then that it is being *manipulated* by a man of violence and deceit.

The bow is to see itself as once *used* by Philoctetes but now *plied* in the hands of Odysseus. Sophocles gives us two verbs for "use" here: *eressō*, of the bow as used in the hands of Odysseus, and *khraomai* when the bow was in Philoctetes' hands. He could have used either of these verbs twice over; either can mean "used" or "plied." The difference in emphasis in the two verbs is slight, or would be slight, if this were, in Hegel's distinction, "the language accompanying ordinary action in actual life."[30] When Philoctetes speaks of the bow in his own hands, his verb for "use" is *khraomai*, a very common verb in Greek and applicable in any context, in connection with any kind of implement or tool. But its primary associations involve not tools but the oracles. The verb in the active voice is spoken of the gods "proclaiming" their oracles. Used in the middle, reflexive mode, it is "to consult the oracle." Only at the end of a long line of development from the religious to the mundane does the verb come to be spoken of in its ordinary sense as "to use." *Khrēstēria*, neuter plural, in time came to mean "the things that are useful," but it is also the common word for "oracles." The bow, to which

Philoctetes sings his sad ballad, is a simple implement, but the implication here is that it is more than a tool; it is an oracle. And this oracle must now witness its own tragedy.

The verb that Sophocles has Philoctetes use of Odysseus "plying" the bow is not the common verb for "to use." It has various associations, but its prime meaning, to be found in Homer, is "to row." The noun built on this verb is the "oar." The image of rowing can then be transferred to anything that might be seen as plying or being plied; the feet, for example, or the bow and arrow. Webster considers the verb to be "colorless" here.[31] True enough; the verb might seem completely neutral, but its associations lean strongly toward ships and oars. The Homeric Odysseus was both master of the oar and master of the bow. Thus the verb, though apparently neutral, helps reinforce the contrast between Philoctetes and Odysseus, each verb making its own slight but significant contribution toward defining the character of the man who uses it.

When Philoctetes speaks of Odysseus as the new owner of the bow, he calls him *polymēchanos* (v. 1135, "of many devices"). This epithet is taken directly from the *Odyssey*, where it is used in a formula a dozen times or more, spoken by characters addressing Odysseus. In the *Odyssey* the epithet is packed with admiration. Not so here. In Philoctetes' mouth, all admiration has been stripped from the epithet. It is spoken with sarcasm and loathing. In the five verses that Philoctetes dedicates to Odysseus in this strophe, he finds for his hated enemy five stinging terms of abuse (vv. 1134–39). First, *polymēchanos*, which Homeric characters might use to express their awe, though here it has come to mean cognitive skills at their basest level. Then *aiskhron* (ugly, disgraceful), *apatē* (deceit), *stugnos* (horrendous), *ekhodopon* (hated enemy). He then rounds off this litany of insult with *kaka* ("evils," generalized). The bow is to witness both its own degradation and at the same time the evil perpetrated against the person of Philoctetes—"all these evils that this man plotted against us" (v. 1145). This diatribe about Odysseus is grandiose narcissism. The bow is made grandiose as the love object, and Odysseus is then aggrandized to serve the villain function, so that our pity for the victim will also be properly magnified.

When Philoctetes brings the name of Heracles into this strophe, the textual confusion leaves us in doubt whether the text would have Philoctetes calling himself "the friend of Heracles" or calling the bow "the prize of Heracles" (vv. 1131–32).[32] Either way the significance lies in the name itself, which forms the apex of the triangle that includes Philoctetes and the bow. The bow represents the only I-Thou relationship that Philoctetes can cling to in his desperate condition, but it in turns enjoys its I-Thou relationship with Heracles. Thus the I-Thou relationship between Philoctetes and his bow has been the outward manifestation of his deepest I-Thou relationship, which was with his friend Heracles. The chorus first grants a certain legitimacy to Philoctetes' complaints but warns him that he might incur *phthonos*, the retributive jealousy, whether from humans or the gods:

ἀνδρός τοι τὸ μὲν ὂν δίκαιον εἰπεῖν
εἰπόντος δὲ μὴ φθονερὰν
ἐξῶσαι γλώσσας ὀδύναν.
(vv. 1140–42)

[A man may justly present his own case
but when he has spoken it is not right for him to spew forth with his tongue
bitter pains that arouse jealousy (*phthonos*).]

Compression and textual problems make this a difficult passage. The sense seems to be that a man may justly speak his own case, but adding invective and insults beyond legitimate complaint only provokes retaliation. These bitter stings that provoke jealousy Jebb translates as "rancorous taunts." Lloyd-Jones read the warning here that Philoctetes should not "thrust out a hateful tongue and . . . give pain." Such translations convey the general sense but fail to mark the root meaning of *phthonos* in the adjective that Jebb translates as "rancorous." *Phthonos* is one of the pillars of ancient Greek tragedy; without *phthonos*, we would have no tragedy. There is a stronger morality here than a warning to Philoctetes to mind his tongue. Once Philoctetes passes beyond legitimate complaint into an orgy of insults and abuse, he may delegitimize himself by arousing, instead of the gods' pity, their anger and punishment. This is the besetting sin of the hero of ancient tragedy, to fix on an attitude so rigid that it must inevitably arouse reprisal whether from the gods or from the human society. Philoctetes is here being reminded of his part in an ancient tragedy, which, though it may owe certain elements to the gods, to Nature, to human society, also requires the hero to assume his own responsibility. The protagonist's extremity leads to hubris, and the consequence of hubris is tragedy.

The chorus concludes this strophe by reminding Philoctetes that Odysseus is not some evildoer. Rather, he is but one among many who have followed orders, and he has acted on behalf of those in command

and worked for a common good. But what meaning has the common good now? The commonwealth, to which the chorus now bids Philoctetes turn his attention, was lost to Philoctetes ten years earlier. Nothing now would give him greater satisfaction than to see that commonwealth go down in flames.

The Second Antistrophe (Verses 1146–1169)

Again, Philoctetes has not heard a word. He is too deeply invested in his pain. He continues his own funeral dirge focused wholly on his deprivation, his impotence, his ruined pride, his inevitable death. Having called on his bow to witness his pitiful state, he turns now to the only possible other witnesses, the birds and beasts that were once his prey, and the thought of them compounds his self-pity. Let them approach now fearlessly; let them witness that he is lame. Webster gives us a graphic sentence:

ἕρπετε, νῦν καλὸν
ἀντίφονον κορέσαι στόμα πρὸς χάριν
ἐμᾶς ‹γε› σαρκὸς αἰόλας.
(vv. 1155–57)

[Come, now is the time to glut your lips on my quivering flesh in the pleasure of revenge.]

Odysseus *plying* the bow and *laughing* on the shore of Troy, the birds *glutting* themselves on Philoctetes' flesh—the narcissism is hard at work building the image of helplessness, vulnerability, degradation.

The chorus responds, now with a stronger note of compassion, urging Philoctetes in the name of the gods to *reverence* Neoptolemus since Neoptolemus has approached Philoctetes in all good will:

πρὸς θεῶν, εἴ τι σέβῃ ξένον, πέλασσον,
εὐνοίᾳ πάσᾳ πελάταν·
(vv. 1163–64)

[In the name of the gods, if you have any reverence for your friend approach him, for he approaches you with all good will.]

For "reverence" the chorus uses a verb based on the noun *sebas*, which signifies the highest form of respect, the reverence given to the gods. Odysseus had used the same root in the prologos in telling Neoptolemus that if he committed himself to this small moment of disgrace he would be venerated as "the most revered of all human beings" (vv. 83–85). Twice in the play Neoptolemus is connected with veneration—the poet's reminder to the audience of his day of the hero cult of Neoptolemus that had developed in the centuries after the Trojan War. That is the external reference of this word, but it also has its significance within the plot as Sophocles has constructed it. In this play we are given to see Neoptolemus earning that reverence. He is being made into a genuine hero who pits his personal conscience against the whole world and is willing to stand firm in his friendship with a sick and odious man despite every disadvantage to his own person. Even more than that, he had entered the play as the trickster. But he has repented and now he comes to Philoctetes as the healer.

"Approach him," the chorus counsels in Webster's translation; "for he approaches you with all good will." We have seen Neoptolemus approach Philoctetes first in the political way, as a pawn in the military strategy, but we have also watched his progress as he moves from a soldier obeying orders to become the dearest of friends. But what a confusion! How is this chameleon to persuade Philoctetes, the least malleable of human beings, that he is truly the friend, not the enemy?

The chorus now asserts that his health now lies within his own power:

ἀλλὰ γνῶθ', εὖ γνῶθ'· ἐπὶ σοὶ
κῆρα τάνδ' ἀποφεύγειν.
οἰκτρὰ γὰρ βόσκειν, ἀδαὴς δ'
ὀχεῖν μυρίον ἄχθος ᾧ ξυνοικεῖ.
(vv. 1165–68)

[But know this, and know it well. It is in your power to escape
this demon. For she feeds on you cruelly,
and he with whom she dwells cannot know
how to endure his ten thousand pains.]

For "disease" the chorus uses the word *kēr* (demon). The lexicon translates *Kēr* as "the goddess of death or doom." *She* is often associated with disease. *She* must be the disease itself in this case, but the sense is difficult because the reference is both to the disease and to the doom it brings.[33] Jebb gives us one aspect of the word in "plague"; Lloyd-Jones gives us the other in "deadly fate." He translates verses 1165–68: "For it is in your power to escape this deadly fate. For it feeds on you cruelly, and he who lives with it cannot learn to sustain the countless pains it brings." Webster gives us a translation closer to the awkward syntax of the sentence: the disease is "'pitiful' to feed' with his own flesh, and 'incapable of teaching him with whom it dwells to endure his countless burdens.'"[34]

This is the first clear indication in the play that Neoptolemus has come to bring Philoctetes assistance in the healing of his wound. Even so, Philoctetes cannot be given the full terms of Helenus's prophecy. That must wait for Neoptolemus to return to the scene since only he can spell out the prophecy in full. But at least the focus is now on the disease. The first and obvious reference in these words is to the physical disease, but it would be a superficial reader who understood this demon to be only physical. A physical disease may be a misfortune, but it is not a tragedy. Tragedy requires that this demon be the disease that eats at the soul. Like the chronic physical disease, it too feeds blindly and teaches nothing. Blindness is in the nature of this disease. In its tentative way the chorus gropes toward an understanding of the sickness that is worse than physical trauma.

The remainder of this kommos is the epode (vv. 1169–1217), the traditional concluding "stanza" of a Greek choral ode. Webster quotes Dale on the emotional impact of these meters: the long epode moves to "a climax of passion in the open dactyls, dying away with despair as it returns to iambic and aeolo-choriambic."[35] Our ideal translation should be mindful of these transitions and of the emotions of passion and despair that they represent.

The chorus's appeal to friendship in the second antistrophe is beginning to have its effect. Now no longer singing in complete isolation, Philoctetes begins, however haltingly, to enter into a dialogue: "Again, again, O friends, dearest of all who have ever visited me, you have reminded me of my ancient pain" (vv. 1169–72). Sophocles works to make the emotion audible to his audience, having Philoctetes speak the same syllable *pa-* three times over in a single verse (1170), twice in the adverb "again" (*palin*), and once in the adjective "ancient" (*palaion*):

Palin palin palaion algēma.

We are taken by surprise to hear the change of tone, with Philoctetes addressing these men of the chorus now as his dearest friends. We are to understand that Philoctetes, for all his self-absorption, has glimpses that they mean him well. Yet, despite their kind intentions, they have reminded him of his ancient pain. And what is that? the chorus asks, to which Philoctetes replies: "If you expected that you could take me back to hateful Troy" (vv. 1174–75). No clearer evidence is needed, if any evidence at all were still needed, that the "ancient pain" is not, or is no longer, the serpent's bite but the wound to the man's self-esteem.

"But we think this is the best for you," the chorus responds. The chorus speaks with kind intention, almost gently as this point, but such a response can only exacerbate the injury and solidify the patient's inner wall of resistance. The impasse is obvious. The merest mention of the wound is sufficient to raise the ego's most solid defense. "Leave me at once," Philoctetes cries, at which the chorus responds that nothing would give it greater pleasure than to be on its way and be done with Philoctetes. But now Philoctetes begs the chorus to stay. His desperation is written in his every syllable. "Control yourself," the chorus replies (v. 1182). Its verb is *metriazō* (to apply measure). Lloyd-Jones gives us "be reasonable." But reason and measure are themselves useless in this ego's pathology since reason itself has brought Philoctetes to this condition. Philoctetes pleads again with the chorus to stay. Unwelcome as its counsel may be, it is his only friend, and if it leaves it takes his last remaining hope with it.

By why should the chorus stay? the chorus asks. For what? Instead of making a direct answer, Philoctetes breaks into a tormented cry:

αἰαῖ αἰαῖ,
δαίμων δαίμων· ἀπόλωλ' ὁ τάλας·
ὦ πούς, πούς, τί σ' ἔτι ἐν βίῳ
τεύξω τῷ μετόπιν, τάλας;
(vv. 1186–89)

[Ai! Ai! Ai! Ai!
Daimon! Daimon! Wretched am I. I am destroyed.
Foot! O Foot! What am I to do with you
in this life, such as is left for me, wretch that I am?]

Virginia Woolf, speaking of the poetic force of ancient Greek, writes that to understand Aeschylus, "it is not so necessary to understand Greek as to understand poetry. It is necessary to take that dangerous leap through the air without the support of words which Shakespeare also asks of us. For words, when opposed to such a blast of meaning, must give out, must be blown astray, and only by collecting in companies convey the meaning which each one separately is too weak to express."[36]

Here exactly is that kind of sentence. *Daimon! Daimon!* We might suppose that the whole play was working to bring Philoctetes to utter this word. Without the word *daimon* Greek tragedy would never have been born.[37] This *daimon*, whom Philoctetes would curse if he could, is not an "it." *He* is the protagonist himself, projected as a divine paradigm. We have just heard the chorus elucidate this *daimon* for Philoctetes as the personification of his own choice, and Philoctetes makes no attempt to reject the chorus's explanation. Hence his anguish. After its sermon, Philoctetes must recognize that his *pathos* is a matter between him and his *daimon*, the one self whom he can recognize as himself and that other hidden self, whom he cannot, indeed dare not, recognize as himself. This is the despair that Kierkegaard writes of, which overwhelms the self, not wanting to be itself and at the same time wanting to be itself.

"Foot! My foot!" Philoctetes moves from the metaphysical to the physical. This crippled foot, which hobbles him, is also his *daimon*, or at least the outward and visible manifestation of that inscrutable Being who sits at the center of his being.[38] "What am I to do with you?" Philoctetes cries. But the foot is not really the problem; it is merely the external locus of the problem. His *daimon* is his will, which is committed to do anything rather than be healed.

Philoctetes begs the chorus once more to stay with him. But why? Has Philoctetes changed his mind? To this question Philoctetes gives no direct answer. Instead, he asks the chorus to forgive him for his intemperate words:

οὔτοι νεμεσητὸν
ἀλύοντα χειμερίῳ
λύπᾳ καὶ παρὰ νοῦν θροεῖν.
(vv. 1193–95)

[There should be no *nemesis* for a man who
in the storm of pain wanders
and speaks contrary to intelligence.]

Nemesēton, from *nemesis*, Jebb translates as "just cause for anger" and adds in his note that "the feeling of νέμεσις is justified only when fair allowance has been made for human weakness." Lloyd-Jones gives us "you cannot resent it." While it may suffice to translate *nemesēton* as a just cause for anger or resentment when used in ordinary contexts, tragedy addresses us in a charged language, which, as Hegel puts it, "gathers and keeps more closely together the dispersed and scattered moments of the inner essential world and the world of action."[39] We lose something if we drop the idea of retribution from this word *nemesēton*. Philoctetes is in a manic state.[40] He confesses that his words are wild; they wander; they do not make sense; they border on transgression. In short, they invite nemesis, and nemesis is one of the cornerstones of Greek tragedy. Philoctetes pleads for compassion, some understanding that his unbridled speech issues from a disturbed mind. Implicit in his plea is the acknowledgment that the chorus has made the correct diagnosis. Perhaps if the chorus will give him more time . . . a change of heart hovers on the horizon.

The chorus senses a breach in the patient's self-defense: "Come with us, poor wretch, as we invite you" (v. 1190). But the nerve is hit again, and the gates into the patient's soul, just barely opened, slam shut again. Although the word is unspoken, we know that the source of Philoctetes' reaction is "Troy," which by metonymy means his enemies. The hope that the chorus might have had in its therapeutic counsels is gone forever. The patient is consumed by his own hate, even as he recognizes that defiance now invites the nemesis from Zeus himself:

οὐδέποτ' οὐδέποτ', ἴσθι τόδ' ἔμπεδον,
οὐδ' εἰ πυρφόρος ἀστεροπητὴς
βροντᾶς αὐγαῖς μ' εἶσι φλογίζων.
ἐρρέτω Ἴλιον, οἵ θ' ὑπ' ἐκείνῳ
πάντες ὅσοι τόδ' ἔτλασαν ἐμοῦ ποδὸς
ἄρθρον ἀπῶσαι.

(vv. 1197–1202)

[Never! Never! Never!
Not even if the god of fire, lord of the lightning,
not even if Zeus himself were to come down and with his thunderbolt
consume me in a blazing fire. Let Troy perish and all those
beneath its walls who had the audacity
to expel from their midst my limb, this poor foot of mine.]

Philoctetes has become a Prometheus in his defiance, but Prometheus never championed his own sickness as Philoctetes does. The obvious allusion is to Heracles, whose body was indeed consumed in flames. But Heracles himself arose from the flames to become a god. No such metamorphosis is promised to Philoctetes. He has reached the end. He pleads for a sword, an ax, any weapon at all. Why? To kill himself. But why should he kill himself when Neoptolemus and the chorus, whom he accepts as his friends, have in their respective ways assured him, albeit still only obliquely, that his going to Troy would restore his honor and even bring him liberation from his suffering. But death itself is not sufficient to assuage this pain. Philoctetes wants not just to die; he wants to butcher himself, to hack limb from limb:

κρᾶτα καὶ ἄρθρ' ἀπὸ πάντα τέμω χερί·
φονᾷ φονᾷ νόος ἤδη.

(v. 1207–8)

[Let me with my own hand behead myself and hack off all my limbs.
Slaughter! Slaughter! That is now my mind.]

The chorus tries to remonstrate. Why should Philoctetes want to perform such a savage act on his own body? His response: that he might join his father in the house of Hades. This is the fantasy of despair. How could Philoctetes, hacking his own body into pieces, look to his father for approval? This father is the heroic ethos personified, what psychoanalysts call the "idealized parent imago," but Philoctetes, measured by that patriarchal standard, is a failure.[41] How could Philoctetes present himself as a broken vessel to this ideal ego and expect either comfort or praise?

To this the chorus has nothing more to say: "We would have left you some time ago and we would be already at the ship, if we did not see Odysseus and Achilles' boy approaching us" (vv. 1218–21). So the chorus concludes its part in this kommos. The therapy has failed; the session is finished. Nothing is left now but to sign off on the case or to pass it into the hands of others with greater therapeutic skills. Enter Neoptolemus to take up again the reins of authority, which he had temporarily passed to his sailors.

What went wrong with the chorus's efforts at mediation? The chorus had seemed to be making some headway as the kommos proceeded, but in the end its best counsels could not penetrate the patient's defense. The chorus and Philoctetes might appear to understand each other on the surface, but at the deeper levels of the psyche they were deaf to each other. Why was their communication impossible? A. J. A. Waldock judges this a flawed tragedy because nothing really happens and we are given only appearances to suggest that events are moving forward.[42] But going nowhere, thought it might seem to us a flaw in the dramatic structure, may have been Sophocles' intention. We are asked to concentrate on a case that goes nowhere.

We who live in the age of psychotherapies can recognize this *pathos*, which has become, as the chorus calls it in this ode, "the plague that devoured his mind" (v. 706, Lloyd-Jones's translation). The chorus has now performed its function, which was to bring reason to bear on the problem, but reasoning and even moral argument cannot dissolve the obstacle. What else is needed? The chorus earlier in the play had identified the problem when it spoke of Philoctetes crawling this way and that "like a child without his loving nurse" (vv. 701–6). The problem is obvious. Philoctetes may need his priest, but before the priest he needs a nurse. The nurse could be either male or female, but at this point in the play, so heavily dominated by the male principle, we long for some nurturing female presence. The only female presence who presides over this play is the vindictive goddess in Anatolia who had exacted a cruel tribute when Philoctetes transgressed on her sacred ground ten years earlier.[43] This play is unusual in being totally male. The three actors are male; the chorus is composed of males. To leave the healing exclusively in the hands of the males is a risky practice when the *pathos* itself is so intricately woven into the male heroic ethos.[44] The chorus advises, admonishes, lectures, but whatever comfort it may bring must be couched in the language of the adult male, and mostly it is judgmental.[45] How different the play would be if the members of the chorus could strip off their sailor's uniforms, become Florence Nightingale, and set up a primitive first-aid station for this wounded warrior.

To talk of nurses is of course anachronistic. Nursing, such as it was, was practiced in the home by the women of the house, but Philoctetes is homeless. The nurse to whom the chorus alludes in the stasimon is not a medical nurse but the infant's caregiver, but both kinds of nurses are needed here. Call her what we will, the person who is needed is someone who understands that Philoctetes needs mothering. A nurse could coax Philoctetes into accepting his medicine within the hour, and the play would be finished, sweetly, smoothly, but inconclusively. The nurse is the absent but longed-for presence. She who is so desperately needed would speak a language different from the language of blame and admonishment issuing from the chorus. Self-destruction may be the true diagnosis in this case, but that truth belongs somewhere later in the therapy. The first necessity is simple creature comfort. The chorus has limited empathy because it keeps itself at a safe distance from the patient, a privilege not given to nurses. Speaking "in the name of the father," the chorus cannot do other than address this invalid as if he were a soldier gone AWOL rather than the man who was suffered violence in the name of that same father who now commands the patient to return to his duty at Troy.[46]

Why does this injured boy not turn to his mother? Because she is nonexistent. In this play of men acting and suffering in a man's world, the mother image has been deleted. The chorus, for all its attempted sympathy, speaks as the emissary of that very father imago that had years ago expelled Philoctetes from the field of honor and now, just as peremptorily, orders him to abandon his seclusion—as if it had been his own choice!—and rejoin his comrades, shifty as they have proved to be.

11

The Exodos

(Verses 1218–1471)

> Great minds against themselves conspire
> And shun the cure they most desire.
>
> Henry Purcell, *Dido and Aeneas*

The exodos (English "exodus") is the final section of a Greek tragedy, the exit.[1] Aristotle defines it as that part of the drama after the last choral ode. "Exit" seems an inappropriate description for a passage extending over some 250 verses. This exodos looks more like a fourth episode; it brings all three actors on stage for extended dialogues, and the chorus is given only the last three verses to give the play its benediction (vv. 1469–71).

In the kommos just concluded, the chorus had introduced self-consciousness into the dialectic of the play, but it merely broached the idea. Enter now Neoptolemus to reclaim the responsibilities that he had passed to the chorus when he exited the theater at the end of the third episode. Odysseus follows him in anxious pursuit. "Will you not explain?" he calls after Neoptolemus as they arrive in the theater again. "Why have you turned around and are speeding on this path with such furious energy?" Odysseus applies the adjective *palintropos* ("turning back," v. 1222) to describe Neoptolemus in this question. Classical scholars can hardly see the word without sensing an intimation of *polutropos* (much-turning), used of Odysseus in the first verse of the *Odyssey*. In this play, however, Odysseus, famous as the master of versatility, has become the man fixed in one attitude while his young cadet has become, it seems, *polutropos*. We also hear in *palintropos* the resonance of the word *palintonos* (stretched back on itself), which Heraclitus had used to describe the harmony of opposites—"when the thing that differs from itself also agrees with itself, like the *back-stretched fitting together* [*palintropos harmonia*] of the bow and lyre."[2]

Neoptolemus explains his "turning back": "I go to undo the *hamartia* that I committed in the past" (v. 1224). Odysseus is appalled: "What you say is horrifying [*deinon ge phōneis*]. What *hamartia* was that?" (v. 1225). We are bemused to hear Odysseus, the rhetorician, now accusing his protégé of being "formidable in speaking." In the prologos Odysseus had coached Neoptolemus in the art of words, but now the youth has found his own voice and the first word he utters in his own voice is the verb *hamartanō*, "I have sinned." That is the fearsome word now hanging in the air. Odysseus in his stunned reply employs the noun itself, *hamartia. Hamartia*? What *hamartia*? The reversal of the play turns on this word.

Aristotle introduced the word *hamartia* into our vocabulary, and it has been a staple of critical theory ever since.[3] But the word was not common in ancient Greek, and it occurs only rarely in the extant tragedies; after all, the tragic heroes are not usually able to discern their hamartia until it is too late to undo the consequences.[4] In this play, however, the character himself identifies his own hamartia and is given time to undo his mistake. It is yet another signifier that identifies Neoptolemus as a tragic hero. Philoctetes' hamartia is necessary to the play, but the hamartia of Neoptolemus is equally important and equally necessary. It is not merely incidental to the play; rather, it is the motive that drives the whole plot. When Odysseus asks Neoptolemus, "What *hamartia*?" Neoptolemus replies: "The one when I obeyed you and the whole army" (v. 1226). The *sophisma* laid out in the prologos is the hamartia of this play. Both Neoptolemus and Philoctetes face their own crisis of conscience, and each character's crisis mirrors the other's. The hamartia of each must be recognized, identified, and corrected so that the two, chastised and purified, can be united to become those two lions whom Heracles describes at the end of the play, going out on the hunt together.

Under further interrogation Neoptolemus explains to Odysseus that he intends to give the bow back to Philoctetes since he obtained it by ugly and unjust means. Odysseus is astounded, seeing the very success of the mission slip through his hands. To his incredulous questions Neoptolemus replies like a teacher instructing one of his less intelligent students: "Must I repeat the same words two and three times?" (v. 1238). Odysseus, flailing for his lost authority, resorts to an outright threat: "There is one who will prevent you from doing this." Who could that be? "The whole host of the Achaean army and I among them" (vv. 1241–43). To which Neoptolemus replies:

σοφὸς πεφυκὼς οὐδὲν ἐξαυδᾷς σοφόν.

(v. 1244)

[You were wise by birth, but nothing you say is wise.]

We are back at *sophos* again. Jebb stresses wisdom: "Wise though you be, thy words are void of wisdom." Lloyd-Jones opts for cleverness: "Clever as you are, what you are saying is not clever!" Here certainly is a passage where we need both meanings and both to be understood simultaneously, if we are to get at the full implications of the thought that brings together ethos, intelligence, cleverness, and wisdom, all in a single and simple line of Greek.[5]

Odysseus replies to the charge that he is not *sophos* by making an accusation of his own:

σὺ δ' οὔτε φωνεῖς οὔτε δρασείεις σοφά.

(v. 1245)

[But neither the things you say nor what you intend to do are wise *sopha* (neut. pl.).]

Lloyd-Jones opts for "cleverness" here, but we need more than "cleverness" at this important place in the argument. Odysseus charges Neoptolemus with a stupid and dangerous lack of judgment. "But if my actions are just, they are stronger than what is *sopha* [neut. pl.]," Neoptolemus replies, speaking ironically and with sarcasm. A new element has been introduced into the debate on justice. An action cannot be *sophōn*, whether wise or clever, if justice is not a component. How could it be just, Odysseus asks, for Neoptolemus to give to Philoctetes what Neoptolemus had procured through the plan of Odysseus? Neoptolemus shifts the ground once more to bring the dialogue back to his *hamartia*, which was also his injustice:

τὴν ἁμαρτίαν
αἰσχρὰν ἁμαρτὼν ἀναλαβεῖν πειράσομαι.

(vv. 1248–49)

[Having committed that ugly act of *hamartia*,
I shall now attempt to take it back again.]

How facile Odysseus seems now with his assurances that Neoptolemus could be a thief and still be revered as both virtuous and wise. Neoptolemus has taken charge of the debate, routing *sophisma* and bringing the discussion full circle to *sophia*.

Odysseus, having lost the argument, now blusters absurdly, threatening Neoptolemus with the sword, as if he could so easily kill the son of Achilles, who is now wielding the bow of Heracles. He has indeed become our comic *graeculus* whom Nietzsche so despised.[6] Neoptolemus threatens to draw his own sword in return, and Odysseus's bluster is over, except for one last threat, that he will report Neoptolemus's insubordination to the Greek army, and the army will punish him (vv. 1257–58). Neoptolemus takes this threat for what it is, a mere piece of theater, proof of Odysseus's failure: "Very wise of you! If in the future you show as much sense, perhaps you will keep your foot out of trouble" (vv. 1259–60, Lloyd-Jones). At this point Neoptolemus turns his back on Odysseus and addresses Philoctetes, calling him from the cave (where Philoctetes has gone to die).

Odysseus is given one more brief scene a few moments later. When Neoptolemus passes the bow back to Philoctetes, Odysseus cries out: "But I forbid it, as the gods are my witnesses, in the name of the sons of Atreus and the whole Greek army!" (vv. 1293–94, Lloyd-Jones). With these words Philoctetes recognizes the voice of Odysseus: "Boy, is this truly the voice of Odysseus I hear?" To which Odysseus himself replies:

σάφ' ἴσθι· καὶ πέλας γ' ὁρᾷς
ὅς σ' ἐς τὰ Τροίας πεδί' ἀποστελῶ βίᾳ,
ἐάν τ' Ἀχιλλέως παῖς ἐάν τε μὴ θέλῃ.
(vv. 1297–99)

[Be sure of it! You see right here the very person
who will convey you to Troy by force
whether Achilles' son wishes it or not.]

But Philoctetes now holds in his hands the sacred weapon against which all threats and arguments are powerless. Philoctetes threatens to take aim and shoot Odysseus. Surely never was a target more desired and better positioned to take a direct hit. But Neoptolemus restrains him (oh bitter frustration!), and Odysseus escapes offstage, his tail between his legs, truly the *graeculus*, bright as a penny when clever arguments are needed but useless when justice, wisdom, and compassion are the issue.

With Odysseus rendered both incompetent and irrelevant, the rest of the play is dedicated to the two characters of true significance. The ethics, serpentine in their windings, have been clarified. Trickery has been ruled out and theft even more so. No person in this drama is going to be taken by a trick, and nothing is to be stolen. Philoctetes is not to be carried off the island against his will. In short, consciousness must emerge victorious.

Philoctetes hears a ruckus outside his cave, a scene reminding us of similar scenes in comedy where the porter of the house is roused by a banging on the door. He emerges and recognizes Neoptolemus, who tries to reassure him of his good intentions, but how can Philoctetes trust him now, having just been tricked and robbed by this seemingly honorable youth? To his resistance Neoptolemus replies with another of those sentences in this play that should be highlighted in red:

οὔκουν ἔνεστι καὶ μεταγνῶναι πάλιν;
(v. 1270)

[*Is there no room, then, for repentance?* (Jebb's translation, italics added)]

Here we watch Sophocles working his way tentatively out of the paradigm of ancient tragedy. Neoptolemus has sinned, to give *hamartia* its most solemn and sacred meaning, and now he has repented. He has become the paradigm of the new hero. Philoctetes is not persuaded of this young man's conversion, given the history of his relations with Neoptolemus. Once again he reverts to the theft:

τοιοῦτος ἦσθα τοῖς λόγοισι χὤτε μου
τὰ τόξ' ἔκλεπτες, πιστός, ἀτηρὸς λάθρᾳ.
(vv. 1271–72)

[That is how you were in your words when you stole my bow,
trustworthy, but in secret deadly. (Lloyd-Jones's translation)]

The verb *kleptō*, used here at the end of the play, takes us back to the opening of the play to remind us that theft is the major crime in this play. It is also linked again with *logos* as if to remind us that the *logos* Odysseus had in mind had theft as its object. Even more fixated in his hatred than before, Philoctetes shouts forth one final diatribe:

πάντα γὰρ φράσεις μάτην·
οὐ γάρ ποτ' εὔνουν τὴν ἐμὴν κτήσῃ φρένα,
ὅστις γ' ἐμοῦ δόλοισι τὸν βίον λαβὼν
ἀπεστέρηκας· κᾆτα νουθετεῖς ἐμὲ
ἐλθών, ἀρίστου πατρὸς ἔχθιστος γεγώς.
ὄλοισθ', Ἀτρεῖδαι μὲν μάλιστ', ἔπειτα δὲ
ὁ Λαρτίου παῖς, καὶ σύ.

(vv. 1280–86)

[Everything you say will be said in vain.
For you will never win my mind to be kindly disposed,
you who by your tricks have taken my life
and robbed me of it. And then you have come to lecture me,
you the most hateful of men, born to the best of fathers.
Die! All of you, especially the sons of Atreus,
then the son of Laertes, then you.]

"No more curses," Neoptolemus replies: "Here, take this weapon from my hand" (vv. 1286–87). This is the second stage in the *peripeteia* of Neoptolemus. The first stage occurred when Neoptolemus came to his senses and decided that he must tell the truth. But his repentance then was only half-complete. Full repentance required that the bow be restored to its owner. Lloyd-Jones conveys the force of this change in his translation of Neoptolemus's words at verses 1291–92: "The act shall make it clear! Come, put out your right hand and be master of your weapon!"

Neoptolemus then tells Philoctetes that with the bow in his own hands again he has no further reason to blame Neoptolemus. Philoctetes agrees and praises Neoptolemus's nature (*physis*)—"you did not have Sisyphus for your father" (v. 1311), the name Sisyphus taking us back to verse 417, when Philoctetes expressed his contempt for Odysseus's base-born nature as the illegitimate child of Sisyphus.

"I took pleasure to hear you speak well of my father, and of me too," Neoptolemus replies. "But hear what I want to gain from you" (vv. 1314–16). Neoptolemus has not severed his relations with Odysseus just to prove his noble nature. He still has his mission to complete, to bring Philoctetes to Troy. But this mission has now doubled in difficulty, since Neoptolemus has determined that Philoctetes must consent of his own free will. *Persuasion* is still required. Neoptolemus, having made his own confession and repented of his *hamartia*, can speak now as a man who has been healed of his own disease. He has become *sophos*, no longer clever but truly wise.

Neoptolemus delivers a long speech, one of the longest in the play (vv. 1316–47). The first lesson that he has for Philoctetes is the same that the chorus had given in the kommos, that Philoctetes must accept his own responsibility:

ἄκουσον. ἀνθρώποισι τὰς μὲν ἐκ θεῶν
τύχας δοθείσας ἔστ' ἀναγκαῖον φέρειν·
ὅσοι δ' ἑκουσίοισιν ἔγκειται βλάβαις,
ὥσπερ σύ, τούτοις οὔτε συγγώμην ἔχειν
δίκαιόν ἐστιν οὔτ' ἐποικτίρειν τινά.
(vv. 1316–20)

[Listen. The fortunes given to humans by the gods,
those must be endured by necessity.
But when people persist in pains
of their own choosing, as you are doing,
it is right that these people be neither excused nor pitied.]

The noun here for "excuse" is *syngnōmē*, still used in everyday parlance in Greece, as in "pardon me," but the verb from which it is derived is *syngignōskō*, which means "to have a fellow feeling for" someone. Those who indulge themselves in their own misfortunes should not be indulged by others. Neoptolemus then makes the meaning more explicit:

σὺ δ' ἠγρίωσαι, κοὔτε σύμβουλον δέχῃ,
ἐάν τε νουθετῇ τις εὐνοίᾳ λέγων,
στυγεῖς, πολέμιον δυσμενῆ θ' ἡγούμενος.
(vv. 1321–23)

[You have become savage, and you will not accept a counselor.
If someone gives you advice, speaking with good will,
you hate that person, considering him an enemy and someone ill-disposed to you.]

Here is the crux of the drama: this disease makes the sick man savage even toward those who bring sympathy and healing. Neoptolemus reviews the arc of Philoctetes' misfortunes since he was bitten by the serpent in the goddess's shrine and calls upon Zeus the guardian of oaths, to be the guarantor of his words:

καὶ ταῦτ' ἐπίστω, καὶ γράφου φρενῶν ἔσω.
σὺ γὰρ νοσεῖς τόδ' ἄλγος ἐκ θείας τύχης,

Χρύσης πελασθεὶς φύλακος, ὃς τὸν ἀκαλυφῆ
σηκὸν φυλάσσει κρύφιος οἰκουρῶν ὄφις·
καὶ παῦλαν ἴσθι τῆσδε μή ποτ' ἂν τυχεῖν
νόσου βαρείας, ἕως ἂν αὑτος ἥλιος
ταύτῃ μὲν αἴρῃ, τῇδε δ' αὖ δύνῃ πάλιν,
πρὶν ἂν τὰ Τροίας πεδί' ἑκὼν αὐτὸς μόλῃς,
καὶ τῶν παρ' ἡμῖν ἐντυχὼν Ἀσκληπιδῶν
νόσου μαλαχθῇς τῆσδε, καὶ τὰ πέργαμα
ξὺν τοῖσδε τόξοις ξύν τ' ἐμοὶ πέρσας φανῇς.
(vv. 1325–35)

[Know this, and write it in your mind.
You are sick with this pain from a god's dispensation,
because you approached Chrysē's sentinel, who keeps watch
over her roofless shrine in secret, her guardian serpent.
And you will never find release from this heavy disease,
not while this same sun rises here in the east, or sets
here in the west, until you come to the fields of Troy,
of your own free will, meet with the sons of Asclepius
who are with us, and from them find relief from this disease,
and with this bow and with me
you are revealed as destroying the city's towers. (italics added)]

First Philoctetes must accept that his wound was caused by his own transgression into the sanctuary of the goddess Chrysē. Three times in two verses this serpent (*ophis*, in Greek) is called a guardian of the sanctuary (vv. 1327–28). This is the first time that we are told explicitly that the serpent's bite was an act of divine retribution, the consequence of Philoctetes' own *hamartia*.

This is certainly a contradiction, that the chorus in the stasimon had sympathized with Philoctetes as a blameless victim, yet now Neoptolemus bluntly undoes that reading and speaks of Philoctetes' suffering as punishment for his transgression into the realm of the divine. No argument can cancel the contradiction. This was the great question with which all the tragic poets wrestled, and the contradiction is to be found in every tragedy. What are the relations between the human will and divine Necessity? Where to draw the line in human affairs between the cosmic forces impinging on the human and the human's own power of choice? Like many Greek tragedies, this play entertains both hypotheses simultaneously, or rather, expresses now one, now its opposite. But to give this contradiction some nuance, Sophocles differentiates between those pains that we must accept, since they are imposed on us by the gods, and those that are self-willed. In the stasimon the chorus had focused on the apparent injustice of Philoctetes' suffering, which seemed radically off the scale, but now Neoptolemus shifts the focus to a separate problem: Philoctetes' own refusal to accept any counsel or therapy. The rhythm of the play calls for Philoctetes to be innocent of any wrongdoing when the play opens so that his anger can seem justified and we will feel pity for this victim so painfully mistreated by his own society. But a hero without a flaw could not become the protagonist of a tragedy. Hamartia must enter into the argument somehow and at some point. Hegel confronts this contradiction: "All that is posited in an external relation to man is none the less clearly that which is immanent in his own spirit and character."[7] The tragic poet's task was to provide that mediating link that Hegel calls the "finely conceived thread of relation" between these two sides of the individual human character. At another point Hegel offers us exactly that finely conceived thread of relation that we need for this play: "Individuals who have aimed at the realization in themselves of a single separate moral power, perish."[8] Philoctetes' assuming into himself what Hegel calls that "single separate moral power"—this is hubris, and in the hubris is his hamartia.

In the stasimon the chorus had *reacted* to the situation with Aristotelian pity and horror. It was an ode of compassion. But sympathy in and of itself is no solution; time now for instruction. Philoctetes must allow for some imperfection in himself; the gods do not punish those who are entirely without blame. There is justice at work. The point is not so much to blame Philoctetes, or even to judge him as in a court of law, but to direct his attention from external conditions back to himself. The problem, as stated first by the chorus in the second kommos, which Neoptolemus now reiterates, is in Philoctetes himself.

The chorus has already informed Philoctetes in the preceding kommos that he can be healed if he so chooses, but it left it to be inferred that such healing would depend on his going with Neoptolemus to Troy. Now at last, and for the first time, Neoptolemus makes the prognosis specific, assuring Philoctetes that this is no idle promise. It bears the validation of the gods, having been delivered to the Greeks by Helenus, the Trojan seer. He even adds a further detail, which we have not expected, that Troy is destined to fall this selfsame summer, and if Helenus's prophecy proves false, the Greeks have his permission to kill him. Needless to say, Neoptolemus learned none of this from Odysseus in the prologos, nor has he learned it from any other source in the interval since the play began. He knows this information now because he needs to know it. He is the prophet.

Neoptolemus goes on to paint a picture of the glory awaiting Philoctetes if he will give his willing consent:

καλὴ γὰρ ἡ 'πίκτησις, Ἑλλήνων ἕνα
κριθέντ' ἄριστον, τοῦτο μὲν παιωνίας
ἐς χεῖρας ἐλθεῖν, εἶτα τὴν πολύστονον
Τροίαν ἑλόντα κλέος ὑπέρτατον λαβεῖν.
(vv. 1344–47)

[Glorious indeed is this possession, to be judged
the one man best of all the Greeks,
then to come into healing hands, then to take Troy, the source of our grief,
and to gain glory sublime.]

Important as the promise of healing and fame is, even more important in this message is the matter of the will. Philoctetes must choose his own healing, a point that Neoptolemus emphasizes in verse 1332 and then again at verse 1343: "Now, since you know this, choose of your own accord to come with us." Choice was of course always implicit. The whole play depends on freedom. Philoctetes' action at Troy would have to have freedom at its base or it would be no act at all. But this idea of freedom, so central to the play, had to wait for Neoptolemus to express it almost at the end of the play after Odysseus's scheme had proved itself a failure.

Philoctetes is moved and unmoved at the same time: "O hateful life, why, why dost thou keep me in the light of day, instead of suffering me to seek the world of the dead?" (vv. 1348–49, Jebb's translation). The word Philoctetes uses for "life" is *aiōn* (Latin *aeon*), which is not life in some abstract sense, the biological phenomenon, but a person's "lifetime." "Why have I been given this life?" Philoctetes asks, addressing his question to life itself, his own life. And the verb that Jebb has translated as "suffering me (to seek the world of the dead)" would be more accurately translated as "dismissed." "Why have you not dismissed me from the light? Why have you not sent me to the land of the dead?" Philoctetes continues to express his pain in a long speech that is more like a soliloquy (vv. 1350–61). He poses questions for himself, which he then answers with counterquestions. How is he to disbelieve this man who has acted with goodwill? His answer is another question: "But am I to give in?" (v. 1352, Lloyd-Jones's translation). *To give in*: this is the crux of his problem. To *trust* Neoptolemus would be *to give in*. Neoptolemus, in returning the bow, has given the strongest proof of his honesty and loyalty, yet even this act cannot cancel the dread of *giving in*.

As he expresses this fear, Philoctetes comes around again to the image of Odysseus, and he beholds himself joined to that villain as to a coworker: "Suppose I yield. How then am I to come into the light, having acted thus? With whom would I talk? Oh these eyes of mine, these orbs that have witnessed all these events that surround me, how could you endure to witness me associating with the sons of Atreus, they who are my destroyers?" (vv. 1353–57). He has poured out his sorrow first to the landscape, then to his bow, to his "life," and now finally to his own eyes, those silent but entirely conscious witnesses of all the wrongs that the sons of Atreus had done him. His eyes are his organs not merely of perception but of self-perception.[9] Philoctetes has legitimate grounds for his anxiety, but behind his fears is a deeper problem, which is the trauma of wounded pride. His concern now is not the past but the future.

In hindsight we can infer that Odysseus's plan was doomed to failure from the outset. How could a man be tricked into joining those he considers his enemies and then to fight on their behalf? Philoctetes dragged off Lemnos in chains and compelled to aim his deadly arrows at the Trojan targets with a Greek dagger held to his throat—that would be a supreme oxymoron. Not simply the bow is needed but of course the archer himself, with both his skill and his intention. The arrow is the very archetype of pure intentionality. Ironically, Odysseus's wit has engineered a situation that activates Philoctetes' worst character traits—worst for himself and worst for the Greeks at Troy—his contempt, his hatred, his rage, his solipsism, his *phthonos*. If he is to die of starvation on Lemnos, let him at least enjoy the sardonic pleasure that his absence from Troy may bring down the whole Greek empire. Odysseus had informed Neoptolemus that persuasion would be useless, and so it is.[10]

Philoctetes' self-absorption leads him back to Neoptolemus. "And *you*," he cries with emotion-burdened intensity: "I am amazed at you" (vv. 1362–72). Neoptolemus should not be going to Troy, and he should be doing everything in his power to keep Philoctetes from succumbing to the Greek blandishments. "These men have insulted you," he continues. His Greek becomes more forceful: "They have acted with hubris against you." This puts Neoptolemus in a difficult spot since the story that he had used to win Philoctetes' trust was entirely a lie invented for purposes now all too obvious. Philoctetes then pleads with Neoptolemus to keep the promise he had once made, that he would take Philoctetes back to his own home in Greece. For this, he says, Neoptolemus would win "a double thanks" from Philoctetes and "a double thanks" from Philoctetes' father. Lloyd-Jones translates the word here as "gratitude," but "gratitude," can hardly convey the rich spiritual meaning of the Greek word *kharis*. *Kharis* is "grace" as an act of kindness; it is also "gratitude" when it is a grace given in return for grace. "Be gracious," Philoctetes pleads, "and you will receive a twofold grace from me and a twofold grace from my father." The deeper truth, which a man in Philoctetes' condition could never see, is that were Neoptolemus to take Philoctetes to Greece instead of to Troy, they would both lose grace.

Philoctetes has boxed Neoptolemus into one final aporia. Neoptolemus cannot now confess that his story was a lie. Would such a confession bring the necessary persuasion into the argument? Has Neoptolemus really changed his character? And can he claim repentance if he continues to serve under Odysseus? Neoptolemus has cleared his conscience first by confessing to his part in the plot and then by the return of the bow, but one misdemeanor remains, perhaps the greatest of them all, which is to continue his association with corrupt men. If Neoptolemus severs his connections with the Greeks at Troy, so Philoctetes concludes his argument, Neoptolemus "will not seem to have been born with a nature like theirs." This is a powerful argument. Character has been made so fundamental to the play that it is difficult to brush it aside now. Neoptolemus had used character as an argument himself, speaking of Philoctetes as having a savage nature, but Philoctetes has seized the higher ground, making character his most important argument. How could Neoptolemus accuse Philoctetes of any flaw in his character while Neoptolemus's own remains so conspicuous?

Neoptolemus makes one last appeal to Philoctetes to trust him, to come to Troy, where he can find healing for his disease, but Philoctetes remains fixated on his wounded pride and on the shame that Neoptolemus ought to feel at associating with Odysseus and the Greeks. Neoptolemus reaches his limit: "It is time for me to give up words, and time for you to continue as you are living now, without salvation" (vv. 1395–96). Philoctetes in his turn makes his final appeal: "Yes, enough words. Leave me to suffer the sufferings that I must endure. But what you promised me, placing your right hand in mine, to escort me home—do this, my boy, and no more delay, no more talk of Troy" (vv. 1397–401),

To this Neoptolemus responds with an act that must stand as one of the astounding moments in Athenian tragedy: "If that is how it seems to you, let us be on our way" (v. 1402). Character has won the day, or so it seems. This is the third and final stage of the *peripeteia* in the *pathos* of Neoptolemus. If Philoctetes will not change his course, then integrity, as Neoptolemus now perceives it, calls for him to make the change and ally himself completely with Philoctetes against all the other Greeks. In the *pathos* of Neoptolemus, Odysseus and Philoctetes are the two contestants for his soul, and Philoctetes has now emerged as the winner. It might seem a victory for honesty and courage, for true friendship over the false facade of friendship. Yet this is a specious victory, a victory for sickness over health. The prophecy, as delivered through Neoptolemus, is emphatic. Philoctetes can be healed of his disease only if he returns with Neoptolemus to Troy. If Neoptolemus takes Philoctetes to Greece, Philoctetes may continue to exist but will be forever sick in both body and mind. And Neoptolemus, far from bringing Philoctetes to his salvation, will have become himself a victim, first a victim to his own false story and then a victim of Philoctetes' own sickness, joining Philoctetes in his sickness to prove the strength of his friendship. If Philoctetes chooses Greece over Troy, he forfeits not only his health but his destiny. And Neoptolemus will suffer a similar fate. He will have rejected his own destiny. With whom would he converse in Greece if he were seen everywhere as the son of Achilles who had refused to take his father's place on the plains of Troy? He would have no friend but Philoctetes, and sickness would be their bond.

The stratagem laid on Neoptolemus's shoulders in the prologos has become completely unraveled. We return to the problem of the two plots. The bond that was forged between Philoctetes and Neoptolemus was to be a mere facade in the political plot. But when Neoptolemus grasped the hand of Philoctetes and gave his word that he would never leave Philoctetes nor ever allow Philoctetes' bow to fall into other hands, he inadvertently gave up his false persona and became the character in another drama as staged by Philoctetes, in which ethos takes precedent over politics. Neoptolemus has promised that he and Philoctetes are joined as one, and Philoctetes has made him his *symparastatēs*. Here, then, is the final test. Will he be true to his word by repudiating the self he agreed to be before he made his promise to Philoctetes?

Philoctetes is jubilant. He has won a great victory, but at great cost, that he must live in pain for the rest of his life and meet with disgust wherever he goes, both for his loathsome physical condition and because he has turned his back on his own good *daimon*. But this cannot be the end of the story. How then to find the ending that will be true to the necessities of the myth and at the same time invest the myth with its spiritual value?

Philoctetes must fulfill his destiny at Troy, as must Neoptolemus; those were essential elements in the Trojan myth. From the moment of Neoptolemus's realization in the stasimon that the victor's crown must go to Philoctetes, we glean that persuasion is essential. Hence the conundrum. Every form of persuasion is tried, but this is not a disease that capitulates to argument. Philoctetes' problem, which Neoptolemus put forth in the boldest way, is that he needs repentance. Just as Neoptolemus needed to come to repentance and correct his own *hamartia*, so also must Philoctetes come to his repentance. Sophocles is moving in this play to the realization, which Socrates more clearly articulated, that an injury done to another is in reality only done to oneself. To spite Odysseus, Philoctetes can only spite himself. For Neoptolemus too it is the same dilemma though worked out in a different way. Neoptolemus comes to the point where he acts as if his own integrity depends on his validating Philoctetes. But to validate Philoctetes, he must invalidate himself. How can a man who has invalidated himself ever validate another person? The virtues prized in the heroic code are those that aggrandize the self at the expense of the other, but that paradigm has brought Philoctetes to his despair. Neither the chorus nor Neoptolemus can lead Philoctetes through the dialectic that bridges the abyss between the self and the other. Philoctetes in rejecting his good *daimon* had alienated himself not only from all other human beings but most of all from himself. If the play were to end here, it would indeed be a tragedy.

12

Heracles

Deus ex Machina

> Renunciation is the cornerstone of wisdom, the condition of all genuine achievement. The gods, in asking for a sacrifice, may invite us to give up not a part of our food or our liberty but the foolish and inordinate part of our wills. The sacrifice may be dictated to us not by a jealous enemy but by a far-seeing friend, wishing we may not be deceived. If what we are commanded to surrender is only what is doing us harm, the god demanding the sacrifice is our own ideal. He has no interests in the case other than our own; he is no part of the environment; he is the goal that determines how far we should proceed in order to realize as far as possible our inmost aspirations. When religion reaches this phase it has become thoroughly moral. It has ceased to represent or misrepresent material conditions, and has learned to embody spiritual goods.
>
> George Santayana, *The Life of Reason*

> There is a human loneliness;
> A part of space and solitude,
> In which knowledge cannot be denied,
> In which nothing of knowledge fails,
> The luminous companion, the hand,
> The fortifying arm, the profound
> Response, the completely answering voice,
> That which is more than anything else
> The right within us and about us,
> Joined, the triumphant vigor, felt,
> The inner direction on which we depend,
> That which keeps us the little that we are,
> The aid of greatness to be and the force.
>
> Wallace Stevens, "The Sail of Ulysses"

The most problematic issue in Sophocles' *Philoctetes* is the epiphany of Heracles with which the play concludes. One of the stage devices used in the ancient Athenian theater was a platform that could be rolled out above the heads of the human actors when a god made an appearance in the play. Whence the Greek phrase, which has come into English via Latin as *deus ex machina*, "the god (speaking) from the machine." Plato introduced this idiom into our vocabulary, both naming the device and explaining its dramatic function. In the *Cratylus*, in the discussion on the origin of human language, he has Socrates say that in human affairs we must always search for a human etiology. To invoke the gods as the ultimate causes would be no explanation at all but a confession of failure. We must not, Socrates says, do as the tragic poets do: "When they are in a state of *aporia*, they flee to their machines, bringing out the gods on high."[1] Heracles' appearance in this play is this machine in its most flagrant use. While this epiphany would certainly earn Plato's condemnation since the god's interference aborts the process of human reason, it also seems plainly a violation of simple dramatic plausibility.

When Plato has Socrates speak of the tragic poets' machine, he uses it as a metaphor to refer to a principle that was indeed fundamental in the thinking of the tragic poets, one to which he was vigorously opposed, that gods would interfere in human action to cause human failures or suffering. But without the gods supervising, scheming, or interfering, there would be no Athenian tragedy. Whether the tragic poet employs the machine or not, every tragedy depends ultimately on the ideological machinery of the gods. Whether visible or invisible, malign or benevolent, the gods are the operators in the human drama, turning the cogs and wheels and tripping the levers of human action. In many of the tragedies that we possess today, some god is the agent who precipitates the catastrophe. In the *Philoctetes*, however, Heracles is brought in on the machine not to precipitate the tragedy but to prevent it. This is doubly problematic. A god who instigates a human tragedy may be unacceptable in Plato's cosmology, but the concept has a certain human plausibility. Human actions, however well intentioned, can be undermined by what humans in times of stress are likely to call the will of the gods.

Heracles' action in this play is implausible in that the action has been proceeding inexorably in one direction, and only when each human character has reached his final and irrevocable position does Heracles appear, and with one short pronouncement he effectively erases the whole development of the plot. The issues of this play could certainly have been resolved in human terms, but the point of the play is that in the complexity of human affairs, reason and logic reach a dead end.[2] For Sophocles, Heracles must be not only the logical but also the necessary solution.

Cedric Whitman has made a vigorous defense of Heracles' intervention in the play. He acknowledges the problem but only to dismiss it as unreal and as of no consequence: "Heracles is no ordinary *deus ex machina*; he does not solve a difficulty otherwise insoluble."[3] But this play is built as a series of ascending aporias, the final and most significant of them all requiring the epiphany of Heracles, which brings the play to its close. Why is Heracles needed? And why is this no ordinary deus ex machina? Heracles speaking from the machine proclaims that both Philoctetes and Neoptolemus must return to the myth, which their human actions had threatened to undo. Philoctetes, heroic as he is in his endurance and in the force of his will, has misunderstood the nature of the true heroic ethos. "The play has two 'endings,'" R. P. Winnington-Ingram notes, "and it would contradict its whole trend and the whole artistry of Sophocles, if the 'second ending' deprived the 'first ending' of all its values."[4]

The real conflict of the play, first staged as if it were a contest between Philoctetes and his enemy Odysseus, centers in fact on the problems of the misalignment of the self. For Philoctetes to leave Lemnos for Greece would be no victory but, in fact, a failure, for Philoctetes would thereby separate himself from his true self. Whitman reads Heracles' intervention as aesthetically and dramatically consistent with the rest of the plot because he sees Philoctetes as morally blameless: "Philoctetes was right, and needed no correction."[5] But correction is exactly the reason for Heracles' precipitous arrival on the scene. Before we can approve of Heracles' intervention, we must first acknowledge that Philoctetes is in error. His error has been pointed out both by the chorus in the second kommos and by Neoptolemus in the exodos. Philoctetes is a sick man who can be healed only if he willingly joins the Greeks at Troy, but the physical disease is not the problem at the end of the play. The sickness has become what Kierkegaard calls "the sickness unto death," for which, according to Kierkegaard's diagnosis, there is no healer but God.

When Philoctetes persuades Neoptolemus to join him in deserting the Greek cause at Troy, he suffers from the illusion that he has the stamina to endure his physical disease as he has already endured it for ten years on Lemnos but fails to see that he would drag out his days with the same disorder that has now deranged his mind and caused him suffering as acute as his bodily affliction. Neoptolemus, in turn, also fails to see that in siding with Philoctetes he has consented to take on himself the same moral sickness. Consciously to forsake the hero's vocation might seem an honorable virtue when the grounds for the desertion are as virtuous as they seem in this play, but this is renunciation in its weakest form. It would lead Neoptolemus to no higher plane. He would be at best half a man, a man who had forfeited his own destiny, indeed his own health, to bond himself with a sick man. The ferocity of his conflict with Odysseus blinds Philoctetes to the tragedy of his own choosing, that as a sick man he has surrendered himself to his sickness, preferring sickness to health, and he wins Neoptolemus to the same point of view.

Whitman calls Heracles "the archetype of Philoctetes' greater self, the pattern of his glory."[6] He calls our attention to the importance of *aretē* in Heracles' speech but reminds us that *aretē* "is a specifically mortal attribute." This is true. We never hear of a god deficient in *aretē* or called on to prove his or her own *aretē*. It is unusual to hear of a god celebrating his own *aretē* as Heracles does here. We recognize a certain blurring of the distinctions that are normally maintained in tragedy between the hero of tragedy and the hero of religious cult, and the figure of Heracles allows for that blurring. He proved his *aretē* by his human achievements, but he was also rewarded with immortality itself.[7] In the cult on Mount Oeta, where Heracles was honored, and no doubt Philoctetes too would have shared in that cult, Philoctetes would have been honored as both a human and a god.[8] But normally tragedy focuses on the events that lead to the hero's death, leaving the hero's cult out of the picture, with a few exceptions, as in this play and in Sophocles' final play, *Oedipus at Colonus*. Heracles, as an exceptional case, both fully heroic and fully divine, leaves a certain implication hanging in the air that Philoctetes will come to enjoy a similar glory when he joins Heracles in their religious cult on Mount Oeta in years to come.

The relations between Heracles and Philoctetes were closer, we are to understand, than between any other two heroes, but until Heracles' appearance they remain only implicit, signified by the bow passed from Heracles to Philoctetes. Now, with Heracles himself arriving on the scene, the implicit is made explicit. Philoctetes has through his own *aretē* won back his stolen bow, and that *aretē* is now acknowledged and rewarded by the epiphany of Heracles. This is indeed an extraordinary affirmation, but the *Philoctetes* is an extraordinary play. A snakebite as the origin for a tragedy; a timeline that begins in tragedy and ends in triumph; a prophecy that is used and misused; a strategy that both depends on and is undone by a trick; a protagonist who is sicker than any other protagonist in tragedy yet holds in his hands a sacred weapon that gives him, a single man, power over two great civilizations; a tragic fate that is undone through love and compassion—to these anomalies we can add Heracles as the final anomaly. Perhaps his entry into the play is to mark it as a new kind of tragedy.

If human *aretē* is immortal, Whitman continues, it is because "it is a god in man, the yardstick by which he measures himself against fate and circumstance, and even the gods themselves."[9] This is true, but a truth hardly ever so boldly articulated in ancient Greek poetry as in this play. To speak of *aretē* as "a god in man" would strike Athenians' ears as a strange truth indeed, though it was to become a commonplace some centuries later. What justifies Whitman's speaking of Heracles as Philoctetes' inner god is the emphasis in the play on the personal *daimon*, which in this play is not some external necessity but that living presence that abides within the will of Philoctetes himself. Whitman calls Heracles Philoctetes' "greater self," which is borne out throughout the play. Over the entire play hovers the figure of Heracles as Philoctetes' Eidos, his Platonic Idea of himself.[10] It is hard to think of another tragedy in the Athenian repertoire where the bond between the protagonist and his personal god is so essential not only in the construction of the protagonist's own character but also in his rescue from the disaster of his own choices.

When Philoctetes hears the voice of Heracles, he exclaims: "O Thou who has made Thyself visible in the length of time, Thou who hast uttered this longed-for sound, I will not be disobedient to Thy words" (vv. 1445–47). We scarcely hear this tone, this degree of intimacy between god and man, in the whole history of Greek tragedy before this play. We are to understand at this point that the bond between Heracles and Philoctetes is of a different nature than the customary bonds between heroes and their gods. Heracles, transcending both his suffering and his human condition, has become the signifier of transcendence. Now he calls upon Philoctetes to transcend his condition, not the failure of his will but rather its misdirection, and the hatred that eats at his soul. Only in transcendence can Philoctetes attain his immortal *aretē*. The other Sophoclean tragedy that centers on transcendence is *Oedipus at Colonus*, produced posthumously shortly after this play was produced. These plays taken together suggest that Sophocles himself, in the long years of his meditation on human fate, was moving toward his own transcendence.[11] If Heracles is needed to speak from the machine as Philoctetes' "greater self," this is because a greater self is needed to release Philoctetes from his fixation on his injured self, where he has concentrated the entirety of his intelligence and his will. Philoctetes' worse *daimon* feeds on hatred and revenge, but since that hatred is impotent, it turns on the hater himself and like a virus multiplies with every passing day until it becomes his total identity. It is dramatically convincing that a self so crippled by its own narcissism would yet have the power to lure an unsuspecting youth into the web of its disorder, as Philoctetes lures Neoptolemus to join him in failure.

Kierkegaard defines the sickness of the spirit as a perpetual and irreconcilable conflict when the self both wants to be itself and is unwilling to be itself. Certainly Philoctetes does not want to be the self he is on Lemnos, crippled and destitute. But he would be pathologically deluded if he thought that his condition could be cured by his retreat into the emptiness of his home. Nonetheless, Philoctetes' greatest fear, which he expresses in language bordering on blasphemy, is that if he were to return to Troy, he must give up the self with which he has become identified on Lemnos. Whitman reads Heracles' epiphany as a complete validation of Philoctetes: "Philoctetes was right and needed no correction; he was victorious, and therefore needed no consolation."[12] But where is the victory in self-ostracism?

Relevant here are what psychoanalysts call "pathogenic beliefs."[13] Such beliefs may be false, but they are adaptations, attempts "to understand the dangers of the world and by understanding to avoid them."[14] These beliefs "weaken a person's control of certain kinds of behavior."[15] Philoctetes is of course a fictional character, but Sophocles has attributed to this character certain pathological traits that were no doubt as deeply embedded in Sophocles' own culture as they are in ours.

The two endings of the play that Winnington-Ingram has observed are the outcomes of the two different plots. The first play centers largely around the external events, and the presiding spirit over these events, as the chorus makes clear, is Philoctetes' evil *daimon*. But in the middle of this plot begins the second play. In biological evolution, Henri Bergson has noted, life overcomes the obstacles presented by inert matter "by dint of humility, by making itself very small and very insinuating, bending to physical and chemical forces, consenting even to go a part of the way with them, like the switch that adopts for a while the direction of the rail it is endeavoring to leave."[16] So in this play the two plots at first travel, as it were, on the same tracks, but they diverge more conspicuously as the play unfolds until it must be revealed that the one track leads to sickness and the other to health. The focus of the second plot is the inner war that Philoctetes wages within himself, and the presiding spirit of this plot is Philoctetes' good *daimon*. To have a tragic plot reversed in the end by a man's good *daimon* is to take tragedy in an entirely new direction.

Kierkegaard writes that the torment of the soul at odds with itself can be so acute that it drives the self into a demonic rage.[17] Even if God and the angels were to offer this self a cure for its torment, Kierkegaard writes, such a person would refuse the help; once this person

> would gladly have given everything to be rid of this agony, but he was kept waiting, and now all that's past; he prefers to rage against everything and to be the one whom the whole world, all existence, has wronged, the one for whom it is especially important to ensure that [he] has his agony at hand, that no one will take it from him—for then he would not be able to convince others and himself that he is right. . . . Ah! demonic madness; he rages most of all at the thought that eternity could get it into its head to take his misery away from him.[18]

We may not observe this ultimate despair in the world around us, Kierkegaard adds, but the poets ascribe it to their characters—"the real poets, who always lend their creations this 'demonic' ideality, to use the word in the purely Greek sense."[19]

Sophocles certainly endows his characters with this kind of rage, but in no other character is this rage so clearly shown to be the effect of the war of the man's inner *daimon* with himself. Throughout the play Philoctetes is driven by a rage that is almost superhuman in its scope. When the play opens, Philoctetes has been excommunicated from human society, and for ten years he has survived this condition imposed on him by external agents, first by the snakebite and then by the religious scruples of his peers. But as the play unfolds, we come to understand that the stark landscape of Lemnos, which was at first the external environment, has become internal. Its harshness has become his harshness. So ruthless is his demonic rage that he will go so far as even to rob Neoptolemus of his soul, so that they can become partners, allied in his hate and rage. Neoptolemus too must become demonic.

Hannah Arendt has described our human condition as an evolutionary process.[20] At the first stage the human is the *animal laborans*, imprisoned in the cycle of the life process, "forever subject to the necessity of labor and consumption." This human, merely an animal, can be redeemed "only through the mobilization of another human capacity, the capacity for making, fabricating, and producing of *homo faber*." From *animal* to *homo faber*, but yet one further transcendence is required. *Homo faber* can "be redeemed from his predicament of meaninglessness, the 'devaluation of all values,' and impossibility of finding valid standards in a world determined by the category of means and ends, only through the interrelated faculties of action and speech, which produce meaningful stories as naturally as fabrication produces use objects."[21]

We can trace this evolution in the character of Philoctetes as Sophocles has drawn him. Cast out from human society, Philoctetes is reduced to bare animal survival. In time he adapts sufficiently to his hostile environment to become *homo faber*; a primitive life to be sure, yet he has fabricated around himself a world—a rudimentary wooden cup, an herb for his pain, a bow to supply him with food, leaves for a bed, a cave to be his makeshift home, flint stones to make his fire. Now the time has come for him to reenter human society, where speech and action go together to produce "meaningful stories." But here exactly is where the process is arrested. The only meaningful story for Philoctetes now is "meaninglessness." The only way Philoctetes can see to fabricate a meaningful story for himself would be to sever all his connections with human society, except Neoptolemus, whom he has persuaded to join him in renouncing meaningful human society and human action.

What is the root of Philoctetes' problem? Why can neither Neoptolemus nor the chorus acing as his surrogate persuade Philoctetes to choose health over disease? He must change his story, but how can he do that? Neoptolemus has done his best to enable Philoctetes to change his story. He has returned the stolen bow and has proved himself a man of his word. The promise given will be the promise honored. A promise, as Arendt puts it so eloquently, creates an island of security "in the ocean of uncertainty."[22] Neoptolemus has given Philoctetes that security both at the level of the *animal laborans*, through the return of the instrument on which his physical survival depends, and at the level of what Arendt calls "the interrelated faculties of action and speech." If Neoptolemus can repent of his false persona, why is repentance impossible for Philoctetes?

A self so incapacitated cannot be its own physician.[23] What would convince a man who has enshrined his worse *daimon* as his god to then declare this *daimon* to be no more than an idol? What would be required for Philoctetes to give up this *daimon*, which, in bitterest irony, is the source both of his comfort and of his pain? The cure, in a word, is forgiveness. But forgiveness was not in Philoctetes' vocabulary. His refusal to forgive his enemies is the passion that drives this drama through almost fifteen hundred verses. When Neoptolemus returns from the ship in the exodos to make one last attempt at persuasion, he instructs Philoctetes to engrave in his heart the word that Neoptolemus now brings him regarding the oracle that commands Philoctetes to return to Troy. But Philoctetes cannot engrave this story in his heart, because already engraved there is a more compelling story, which is of his own composition. That story, which consumes him as ferociously as the demon that eats at his foot, though it will never give him release in death, is constructed along two axes: the injuries done to him by his enemies and his need for revenge. As he dwells on his injuries, so grows his need for revenge.

"Without being forgiven," Arendt writes, "released from the consequences of what we have done, our capacity to act would, as it were, be confined to one single deed from which we could never recover; we would remain the victims of its consequences forever."[24] Revenge, she continues, is "the natural, automatic reaction to transgression."[25] Philoctetes' rage has turned him into an automaton. His actions are by now not actions but reactions.[26] If the entire Greek army were to be destroyed at Troy, it would be inadequate compensation for the wrong done to him.

Forgiveness was not in Sophocles' vocabulary. We can search through pagan Greek literature without finding forgiveness articulated as a necessary principle of social behavior. Not even in Plato's ethical system does forgiveness find a place. Socrates did not need to forgive his accusers because no person could do evil to a just man whether in life or in death.[27] Today we can hardly imagine an ethical system that did not hold forgiveness to be one of the greatest virtues. Arendt, noting that the "discoverer of the role of forgiveness in the realm of human affairs was Jesus of Nazareth," goes on to argue that though Jesus articulated this principle in religious language, that is "no reason to take it any less seriously in a strictly secular sense."[28]

If Heracles is to be our lodestar, he cannot be the paradigm of forgiveness, for he is as unforgiving in his death as in his life. Sophocles drew his plot and his characters from the epic tradition, and in that source the heroic code reigned supreme.[29] In his Philoctetes, Sophocles has given us the most extreme portrait of the negative side of that ethos, which knows only one remedy for pain received, which is to inflict a heavier pain on one's enemy. His Heracles, god though he might be, must still speak from within that heroic vocabulary.

Absent forgiveness, Sophocles had to address Philoctetes' pathology from a different angle. The emphasis must fall therefore on *aretē*, the primary heroic virtue. Even so, the *aretē* for which Heracles stands as the paradigm in this play is something different from the virtues most prized in the heroic ethos. Heracles introduces the word at verse 1420. Webster translates the verse as "I won immortal excellence, as you can see," and adds: "This is a difficult phrase." Indeed it is, since Sophocles has coded three different messages into a single word, a forceful example of the density of Sophoclean language:

καὶ πρῶτα μέν σοι τὰς ἐμὰς λέξω τύχας,
ὅσους πονήσας καὶ διεξελθὼν πόνους
ἀθάνατον ἀρετὴν ἔσχον, ὡς πάρεσθ' ὁρᾶν.
καὶ σοί, σάφ' ἴσθι, τοῦτ' ὀφείλεται παθεῖν,
ἐκ τῶν πόνων τῶνδ' εὐκλεᾶ θέσθαι βίον.
(vv. 1418–22)

Webster refers us to Jebb for a fuller exposition of the problem. Jebb translates the passage as follows: "First, I would tell thee of mine own fortunes,—how, after enduring many labors, I have won deathless glory, as thou beholdest. And for thee, be sure, the destiny is ordained that through these thy sufferings thou shouldst glorify thy life."

When we first read the word *aretē*, our instinct is to take it in its primary sense as "valor," the heroic virtue par excellence. But here, as Jebb notes, Heracles uses it to mean "esteem," or as Jebb puts it in his commentary, "reputation won by merit."[30] It is something Heracles "acquired" through his trials and labors. Jebb cites a passage in the *Symposium* (208d) where Plato uses this same phrase, *athanatos aretē*, to mean "the reputation which survives on earth," something close to the Homeric formula *aphthiton kleos*, "imperishable fame." But *athanatos aretē* here has a second meaning when applied to Heracles: he won not only the immortal fame that heroes enjoy on earth but immortality itself. His *aretē* was through his suffering to achieve the sublime. The phrase *athanatos aretē* as Heracles uses it signifies, therefore, both his fame and his apotheosis. To get at these two contradictory meanings, Jebb parses *athanatos aretē* in verse 1420 to mean both "deathless glory" and "glorious immortality," taking each of the two words in the phrase in two separate senses, *aretē* being both fame and immortality and *athanatos* being "imperishable" in the one case and "immortal" in the other.

In verses 1421–22 Heracles seems to promise the same fate for Philoctetes: τοῦτ' ὀφείλεται παθεῖν, "the same fate is owed to you." But of course their fates were not at all the same. As Heracles continues his sentence, he parses τοῦτο παθεῖν to mean in Philoctetes' case not immortality but the glory he will win on earth for killing Paris. Used of himself, Heracles means his divinity, but applied to Philoctetes it is to signify the glory to be enjoyed by a hero such as Philoctetes who is endowed, if we may be so bold, with a spark of that divinity. The link between the two meanings of the phrase is transcendence. "I transcended my sufferings," Heracles says, "and achieved my glory, as you can see. So the same will come to pass for you. You must transcend these present sufferings to attain your glory."

In using the word *aretē*, Heracles passes over its primary meaning, but that meaning cannot be forgotten. It is embedded in the word itself. No one hearing the word in ancient times could fail to include within its semantic field its original sense of heroic valor. Heracles both proved his *aretē* by his labors and won "deathless *aretē*" as his prize. He himself had used the word in its primary sense in the first episode when he told Neoptolemus that the latter alone had through his *aretē* earned the privilege to touch the sacred bow (v. 669).

What would this *aretē* signify in the late fifth century and, in particular, in this play? The evolving definition of *aretē* in ancient Greek thought is one of the persistent themes in Werner Jaeger's *Paideia*, and this is a good example of that persistence.[31] To illustrate Jaeger's point, the TLG gives us over six hundred instances of the word *aretē* in Plato's *Dialogues*. The *Meno*, one of the shorter dialogues, yet with over one hundred instances of the term, focuses on one target: what is *aretē*? Is the *aretē* the same whether for free person or slave, adult or child, man or woman? With the *Meno* at hand, we can see that both Sophocles and Plato (or Sophocles and Socrates) were pursuing the same question. What would "valor" or "virtue" mean in the case of a cripple, expelled by his society and consumed by hatred, both of his enemies and of himself? *Aretē* is the word that binds the three heroes—Heracles, Philoctetes, and Neoptolemus—into a common destiny. It is that point where the human and the divine intersect.[32]

Surely we are to infer that the *aretē* of which Heracles speaks, while it still retains its most archaic meaning, is at the same time something new since it seems to call, if only obliquely, for the hero's renunciation of his self-destructive passions. What makes possible the elision of the old Heracles and the new in this play is that trajectory not granted to any other Greek hero, which took Heracles from his human life to the sublime state of divinity itself.[33]

Heracles himself was never required to seek forgiveness in the old myth though on several occasions he was punished or sent in search of purification. Yet for all his transgressions, against both humans and gods, he was welcomed into the company of the gods and made a god himself. Irreversibility is the distinguishing mark of the tragic protagonist's destiny. The irreversibility of human action is what we call fate.[34] But if reversibility is to be our theme, and if we must scan the ancient mythic tradition for our paradigm, that paradigm too we find in Heracles. Heracles may have gone to his death as the most unforgiving of heroes, but in death he himself was forgiven.

"The decisive moment," Kierkegaard writes, "only comes when man is brought to the utmost extremity, when in human terms there is no possibility. Then the question is whether he will believe that for God everything is possible, that is, whether he will have faith."[35] When a person finds this faith, Kierkegaard continues, the despairing self is eradicated; "in relating to itself and wanting to be itself, the self is grounded transparently in the power that established it."[36] Heracles in his own person represents these two selves that Kierkegaard has described as bound together in mutual antagonism. No other character in Greek tragedy is more demonic in the rage caused by this split personality than the Euripidean Heracles, who in his insanity kills his own wife and children, mistaking them for his enemy. Yet this same demonic self came in the end to be grounded in the power that established it, in his case Zeus, the supreme god who was also his biological father. When Heracles appears on the machine in this play, he is the spokesperson for the new Sophoclean doctrine, according to which the demonic rage of the split personality can be cured when the person's selves are grounded in that higher power that established them.

Whitman is tempted to see in Heracles' intervention "a Christian act of grace," but he is quick to reject such a reading: it "would be unfortunate, to say the least, because grace is for the unworthy."[37] But grace (*kharis* or *charis*) was deeply interwoven into Greek thought long before the Christian era. How would Pindar have celebrated the beauty of the dance and the style of the young male athletes if grace were not in his vocabulary? If we search for grace in the ancient heroes, Heracles once again becomes our paradigm. What human, what hero was ever more graced than Heracles? And what greater grace than to pass his divine bow on to Philoctetes?

Heracles, in fact, uses the word "grace" (*kharis*) in his speech from the machine, though it is never translated as such:

I have left my seat in heaven and come here
as a *grace* to you,
to tell you the counsels of Zeus
and direct you on the path you must follow.
(vv. 1413–16)

Here again the lexicon points us to a shortcut when it informs us that *kharis* when used in the accusative (*kharin*) can have an adverbial sense, "for the sake of." We need impute no deeper meaning in Heracles' announcement than that he has come "for Heracles' sake." But if this visitation from a heavenly being, which reverses a plot headed into catastrophe—if this is not grace, what more do we need that would allow us to introduce the word "grace" into this context?

The grace given to Philoctetes at the end of this play is not the only proto-Christian element in the play. The most prominent is the figure of Heracles himself. In our modern age we are likely to focus more on Heracles' brutishness and his hubris, but in antiquity he was celebrated as much for his virtue as for his vices. For all his excesses, Heracles was taken as a paradigm of the moral hero. In the *Trachiniae*, in which Sophocles gives Heracles voice to speak, in effect, his own eulogy, Heracles raves at the labors that have been imposed on him, which he contrasts with his own heroic virtue, but not a word does he utter to suggest that he owns any responsibility for the poisoning that he is now suffering at the hands of his wife Deianeira.[38] To modern eyes, his death is well deserved. Yet, far from being some sordid act of revenge by his wife, it is snatched from her hands, as it were, and made into his crowning glory by his own choice of immolation as an end more sublime than to be poisoned by his long-suffering wife. In that play Sophocles gives Heracles a final speech so heroic that it ensures that his end, however deserved it may be by our standards, will be elevated to a martyr's death.[39] Helen Foley writes of the "moral chaos" that this Heracles introduces into his house when he loses control of his erotic desires and brings his captive Iole into his marriage bed.[40] But we find not a hint of this agent of moral chaos to contaminate the atmosphere of the *Philoctetes*. Instead, this Heracles is much the same Heracles who moves into Rome and from Rome enters into the consciousness of the Western world, to become, as in Annibale Carracci's painting *The Choice of Heracles*, the very model of the Christian hero, made to choose between Pleasure and Virtue.[41] This is the Heracles whom we must see if we are to comprehend his significance in Sophocles' *Philoctetes*—the flawed human being rescued from himself, purified and transfigured.[42] Speaking ex machina above Philoctetes' head, this Heracles, so imperfect in his human frame but perfected through suffering, brings into the play ideas of transformation that would be more fully articulated in the centuries to follow. In the customary tragic pattern, what makes a life story a tragedy is a great hero's fall from the pinnacle of success into catastrophe. Here the pattern is reversed. The hero begins in tragedy, which he must surmount if he is to come into his glory.

Faith is the necessary element in Kierkegaard's paradigm of the self reconciled to itself and made whole, the anchor that holds the self secure in that higher power to which the self owes its being. Certainly Philoctetes must have this kind of faith, a trust in the goodness of the gods and in the virtue and value of his own destiny. When Philoctetes chooses Troy over the illusory comfort of a retreat to his home in Thessaly, he must move out in trust—trust in his friends, trust in Heracles, and trust most of all in himself. The promise given to him via the oracle and proclaimed by Heracles may be, as Arendt puts it, his island of security in the sea of uncertainties. But a promise is an empty thing in itself, mere words. The words, if they are to become fully a promise, must first be authenticated by the moral integrity of the person who speaks the words, but then they must be taken on faith.

When Philoctetes consents to accept this promise, he turns to the island of Lemnos to say his farewells. He prays to the island to send him on his way with fair sailing and "without blame" (*amemptōs*, v. 1465). What is this talk of blame? Who is to be blamed, and for what? It is an enigmatic adverb in this context. Jebb takes the meaning to be "so that I shall have no cause to complain," but acknowledges that others "understand, 'without complaint on *thy* part,'—because I leave thee, or have changed my resolve."[43] But "that I have no cause to complain" is surely the weaker reading, and "complaint" seems a weak translation for a Greek word that contains the idea of blame. Throughout the play, blame is the ever-present theme. Blame drives the action throughout. Almost every word Philoctetes utters from beginning to end is heavy with blame. Blame radiates from him in all directions. Wherever he turns his eyes, he sees blame written large across his landscape. The chorus in the preceding kommos fends off from itself this all-encompassing blame—"we are not to blame," it says (vv. 1118–20). While the chorus accepts the inscrutable gods as responsible for the origin of his suffering, it insists that for his present condition Philoctetes has no one to blame but himself. Now at last, as he leaves the island, he prays to be sent on his way *free of blame*. His acceptance of the promise requires him to take back his blame. He no longer has the privilege of blaming Odysseus. May the promise be secure!

The person to be cleared of blame is Philoctetes himself, not only for deserting his island but, more important, for deserting the self he had chosen to become on Lemnos. During his years on Lemnos, Philoctetes had constructed his being in hatred and rage, which, as he saw them, were grounded in piety and justice.[44] But now a higher power has intervened to reorient his understanding. Philoctetes must now forgive himself for what must seem a great betrayal of that self in which he has invested his honor and his righteousness. Lemnos, in its unforgiving inhospitality, had become his Ground of Being, but his new Being is to be grounded now in the powers that he names in his plea for forgiveness (vv. 1466–68): "great Moira, and the intelligent counsel of my friends, and the all-powerful Daimon, who has brought these things to fulfillment" (vv. 1466–68).

When the topography of Lemnos is first presented to our eyes, its distinguishing feature is sterility. But now, when Philoctetes asks for his island's blessing on his departure for Troy, it blossoms. Many have commented on the lyricism in these last words of the play. Knox has written that Philoctetes "is bound for Troy now, for the world of men and great deeds, the world too of his enemies—of Odysseus, of lies, craft, and stratagem. . . . And though he is content to go, the farewell to his island shows his love for it, for the scene of his lonely endurance and suffering—that island, which, like so many islands in the *Odyssey*, was a form of death, of oblivion, but also a tempting haven."[45] Pietro Pucci, noting that in this final speech Philoctetes invokes the nymphs, Hermes, Apollo, Moira, and Zeus, writes that he leaves "the horizon of nature" and enters into the world.[46] We might clarify that the horizon of nature as shown in the earlier part of the play is sterile and toxic. The nymphs of the watery meadows, whom Philoctetes now discovers, are nature transmuted and made humane. To these divine names, we should also add those whom Philoctetes calls his "friends" (his *philoi*, those who love him). Indeed, this farewell is filled with love, as if Philoctetes were seeing with new eyes the self he had been on Lemnos, seeing himself as he had been seen by the great gods themselves and by those whom he now understands to be his friends. Philoctetes sees that he is loved.

What has not been adequately recognized is that the island has been transformed. Where we saw sterility, we now see fertility. The cave, once so primitive, has become "the chamber that shared [his] watch." Now, instead of the stagnant pools, we are told of "the liquid nymphs of the meadows" (v. 1454). Instead of Echo babbling back his words in a cruel parody of human conversation, Philoctetes speaks now of a different kind of echo in "Hermes' mountain," which in Knox's translation is rendered

sent me back
the voice of my lamentation,
the echo of the storm in my heart.[47]

Echo, no longer a noise, has become a sympathetic vibration. Finally, we hear Philoctetes speak of fountains and of "the Lycian drink" (v. 1461).[48] This must allude to a fountain or spring named after Apollo Lykios.[49] From late antiquity came a legend that Apollo, to alleviate this hero's suffering, had caused two fountains to arise on the island—one of water, the other of wine.[50] We heard nothing of such bounty in the earlier descriptions of the island, nor would we have the same play if we had come upon Philoctetes sitting at his leisure outside his cave, enjoying the refreshments of sweet water and honeyed wine.

The island has been transformed by human vision. Once unsympathetic, it has become sympathetic; once austerely masculine, it has become feminine. Once a prison, it has become the hospital. Seamus Heaney in his translation endows Philoctetes in his final speech with a certain light-headedness that diverges conspicuously from the more stately ethos that Sophocles ascribes to Philoctetes at this point, but its jubilation fits well with this context: "But I can't believe I'm going. My head's light at the thought of a different ground and a different sky"—as if the old cripple had suddenly become Zorba the Greek.[51] We might add in parentheses that Philoctetes does not need to wait for Troy to find this new ground and this new sky. Already newness is everywhere he looks.

Earlier in the play the chorus had spoken of Philoctetes crawling on the ground like a child without his nurse (vv. 701–6). Now the island, we discover, once so stony, so unforgiving, has been his nurse; it has become fertile, feminine, nurturing. Philoctetes needs no forgiveness from this gracious soil. The elements that once seemed the cruelest punishments have become his nurses; the brackish waters have turned into well-watered meadows, playful nymphs, and streaming fountains. The joyful presence that Philoctetes now discovers suffused throughout the island is, of course, his own joy reflected back to him. The nurses, standing now on the steps of the hospital, wave Godspeed to their favorite patient as he passes through the gates and hobbles down to the ship that will take him to Asclepius himself and back into his own life. Their work is done. *Va con Dios*, as they say in the Latin countries; *go with God*.

When Philoctetes defends himself in his prayer for the island's acceptance of his departure, he names as the third of the three powers to whom he owes his conversion "the all-conquering Daimon, who has brought these things to their fulfillment" (vv. 1467–68). The conventional reading here is that this all-conquering Daimon is Zeus; as Jebb puts it, this Daimon "is clearly Zeus, whose ordinances Heracles came to announce."[52] But if Zeus is so clearly intended, why should the poet vex us with ambiguity? Is there no virtue in ambiguity?

To read this Daimon as Zeus is not an error, but it is a simplification of a complex issue.[53] True, Greek tragedies conventionally come to their conclusion by leading us out of the human agon and directing us back to Zeus. "Zeus on Olympus is the dispenser of many things," so the chorus concludes Euripides' *Medea*. "The gods bring to fulfillment the things that were unexpected; what was expected they do not bring to completion, but the god finds a way for that which was unexpected."[54] At the end of the dialectic, as at the beginning, must stand the gods, who engineer and dispense everything, the good and the bad. Always at the end of a Greek tragedy, the gods appear, if not literally on the machine, then in the final benediction. Zeus is always at the end of every pathos, the final and absolute deus ex machina.

The all-conquering Daimon to whom Philoctetes credits his change of heart may be a formulaic truism for Zeus. But the poet's discretion in leaving this Daimon unnamed allows for, indeed encourages, an amplitude of significances. Philoctetes' "Daimon! Daimon!" is the most anguished utterance in the whole play. Now, as the characters and the chorus walk out of the theater, Philoctetes invokes the Daimon one last time, this Daimon being that greater divinity who has brought Philoctetes' will back into alignment with his own good *daimon*.

The great Daimon whom Philoctetes now recognizes as the power enabling him to transcend his precious solipsism can be none other than what in Kierkegaard's analysis is his very Ground of Being. Who can this Daimon be but the transcendent Self who guides every living self to his or her own self-consciousness?

Appendix

The Problem of Helenus's Prophecy and Its Relationship to Neoptolemus

It is an accepted fact that the Athenian dramatists violate our canons of naturalistic realism, but the reasons for this practice have received less attention.[1] Greek drama, as a composite of elements both primitive and modern, had functions that are not indigenous to our modern drama. The single element that most differentiates ancient tragedy from our own is religion. Shakespeare may tease our imagination with a ghost, with witches, a magician, or a soothsayer, but these ventures into the supernatural seem more like artistic tropes than manifestations of a genuine personal religion. We accept them as stage devices rather than as theology.

The religion of this play puts modern readers in a peculiar quandary. While most of the world's population has or has had a religious orientation toward the world, the modern exegetes of Greek tragedy are likely to belong to that minority that is indifferent, or even actively antagonistic, to religion. P. E. Easterling, pondering the significance of Helenus's prophecy for this play, writes that it "*could* be offering some sort of illumination of the gods' purposes or some meditation on the relation between man and man," but she would be surprised if it were.[2] She expresses a view common among present-day scholars that the religion of this play, such as it is, is of little consequence. But to detach the religion is to take the heart out of Greek tragedy. The story told of Sophocles, that he was made a hero after his death and given a cult title, "Dexios," for having received Asclepius into his home as a snake—would this be told of a man with only a casual attachment to his religion? The story may be completely apocryphal, and we certainly do not need such a fable to argue our case when the evidence for Sophocles' piety is plain to see, in the *Philoctetes* no less than in any other play. Sophocles' ode to the grove of the Eumenides at Colonus, generally acknowledged to be one of the finest odes in ancient Greek poetry, was not the composition of a man for whom religion was merely ornamental. Destiny itself would drop out of our consideration of Greek tragedy were it not the mark and proof of a divine dispensation. We can study *Hamlet* without referring once to destiny but certainly not the *Philoctetes*.[3]

Our difficulties are exacerbated because, on one hand, as post-Enlightenment humanists, we are often advised to brush aside the religious language in our study of Sophocles, while, on the other hand, we are cautioned not to import into our reading any insights to be gleaned from modern psychological theory. Thus we are placed under the double restraint in our reading of a Greek tragedy that we are not to read a play as it might have been received by an ancient Athenian, for whom the gods were still a living presence, nor are we to impose any of our modern insights into the nature of the soul.

An additional challenge is that modern concepts of religion have been founded on monotheism, which thinks in Platonic absolutes—either providence or free will, reason or opinion, *logos* or *mythos*, with no middle ground in between.[4] In pagan Greece, however, religion was a fecund field where a thousand flowers bloomed. Gods could come and go in a profusion of colors, shapes, and tones. The world was populated by a dense throng of gods, thousands of them, some as solid as Gibraltar, others as ephemeral as the mists that cluster and disperse in endless variations around the mountain peaks.[5] In the fifth century philosophy had certainly brought fierce rational judgments to bear on the vibrant poetry of the old religion, yet that religion was still largely intact, if only because polytheism was ubiquitous and as sinuous as a serpent.[6]

The Athenians saw monuments of their religion everywhere.[7] On every street were temples or shrines, modest or magnificent. Every poem was a celebration of divinity. No doubt the vendors' stalls around the stoa teemed, as they do today, with votive figurines of one sort or another for those wanting to make some public declaration of their piety. The fragrance of the burnt offering rising from countless altars was a constant remembrance of what Plato called *koinonia,* that communion between the seen and the unseen. Cities had not yet been paved over by human technology. Nature was everywhere, in birth and in death, in the wind, the moving stream, the lightning flash, the rolling thunder. Religion infiltrated every aspect of human experience, every thought, every image, every hope, every fear. Athenians attended the festival of Dionysus to engage themselves in the sacraments of their religion. And Sophocles understood his role to be not entertainer but prophet and teacher, with the responsibility to uphold the religion while also to deepen his fellow citizens' understanding of its meaning and function.

Our modern understanding of religious belief begins in dogma, but dogma had little place in ancient Greek religion, except when it might be conveniently used as a judgment to convict Socrates for being a heretic. Even to think in such terms as "gods" is to oversimplify the manifold that is ancient Greek religion. Heroes were as much part of that religion as the gods, and not just as a subcategory. Among the heroes, some were the Panhellenic heroes of epic and others were local, some of them hardly known beyond their own neighborhood but each, great or small, with his or her own sphere of influence, his or her own catalog of blessings and miracles.[8] All the characters in this play, the three humans no less than Heracles, were heroes in the Panhellenic religion; each of them, in short, was *worshipped*. Greek tragedy had as one of its missions to trace the relationships between the gods and the heroes, since on these relationships depended the fructifying benevolence of the gods on human life and labor.

One of the religious aspects of the *Philoctetes*, generally ignored, is its presentation of the process by which Philoctetes and Neoptolemus become heroes, how, in short, as humans they rise up to become more than human, to become *daimones*, the conduits of the divine for their own communities. In the extant tragedies, more often the protagonist has already achieved heroic stature, but the *Philoctetes* begins with two men who are heroes *in potentia* and takes them step-by-step through the transformative process. They are not yet heroes when the play opens. They have not yet won, or proven, the *aretē* that is the sine qua non of the true hero. Philoctetes has not been to Troy; he is a cripple who has been sequestered from the field of battle for ten years. Neoptolemus has arrived at Troy, but his career still lies ahead of him. Each has his own marks of his latent heroic stature: Philoctetes owns the bow of Heracles, and Neoptolemus claims descent from Achilles. By the end of the play they have become heroes. Heracles brings them, as it were, their certificate that they have passed the tests; they have been initiated and are now ready to shoulder the responsibilities of their destiny.

The prophecy given to the Greeks by Helenus is the vehicle for this transformation. Without that prophecy this play would never have seen the light of day: Philoctetes would never have been brought from Lemnos back to Troy, nor would the Greeks have conquered Troy. The prophecy states the essential program that ties the beginning and the end of the drama together. The play begins with the theology of the serpent; it ends with the theology of the Daimon. Between the two lie perhaps a thousand years of intellectual history. A prophecy is needed to bridge this great divide and a character within the play with shamanic skills to guide our thinking from serpent to Daimon. The prophecy given to the Greeks by Helenus had brought two names together, Philoctetes and Neoptolemus, as the agents necessary for the fall of Troy. It was the genius of Sophocles to see in this link the ground of his whole drama.[9] As the action unfolds, we trace how the prophecy guides these two men through their missteps, misjudgments, and deliberate misrepresentations of the truth, to their inexorable destiny. When the chorus in its final benediction calls on the nymphs of the sea to be these men's saviors on their homeward journey, we have already seen how Neoptolemus and Philoctetes have been saved from themselves, each from his own weaker self, to become in their turn the two lions rampant, the saviors of Hellas.

The whole play must derive from that prophecy, and here is where our structural problems begin. Philoctetes cannot be merely a person; he must be a man through whom the divine can manifest itself. And if the play must be driven by the prophecy, the prophecy itself cannot be stated at the beginning of the play explicitly and in its entirety. It must unfold in stages if it is to be made the basis for a tragic plot. This dramatic use of the prophecy requires that it be disassembled and reassembled in such a way as to be the skeleton of the plot.

In discussions of Helenus's prophecy there seems to be an implicit assumption that there was once a text of the prophecy, archived somewhere like a decree voted by the Athenian assembly, and debates arise regarding Sophocles' fidelity to the original text and whether the spectators watching the performance in 409 BCE would be comparing his use of the prophecy against the well-known text. There is even talk of Sophocles using the prophecy in such a way as to create surprise among the spectators. We should be clear at the outset: there never was a written text of this prophecy. Like every other element in the myth, the prophecy comes to us from oral tradition. It is a necessary ingredient in the story of the fall of Troy; without it, there would be no story. Equally obvious, if there were such a text and it were read to Philoctetes in the first episode of this play, that would be another way to cancel the story.

This prophecy would not have been complicated. It would have stated simply that the Greek victory at Troy would require the two men, Neoptolemus and Philoctetes, to be brought to Troy, and would no doubt include the additional point that Philoctetes in going to Troy would receive honor on the battlefield and healing from Asclepius (or his sons). Questions have arisen as to whether the prophecy stipulated that Philoctetes himself must come with the bow or whether Heracles' bow in itself would be sufficient to bring down Troy.[10] We cannot imagine that a prophecy introduced into the myth at some distant point long preceding written texts would fuss with such a quibble. Of course Philoctetes was to be brought to Troy with his bow and *because* of the bow. This was the bow of Heracles. It belonged to Philoctetes and was not to be handed about like some ordinary weapon. In the absence of any text to which Sophocles or either of his two predecessors could refer, it rested with Sophocles to treat the prophecy as an artistic construction that could be made to serve his own dramatic purposes.[11]

The complications inherent in the use of the prophecy are further aggravated by introducing Neoptolemus into the process, first to bring that prophecy to fulfillment and then to reveal its deeper spiritual meaning. These two factors, the prophecy that brings both Neoptolemus and Philoctetes to Troy and the addition of Neoptolemus to this plot, account for those instances where the drama violates our criteria for naturalism. Neoptolemus himself has his own complications. A figure taken from the epic tradition (remembered more for his hubris than for his piety), he must be made into a plausible human character. This requires him to be multifaceted. He must be, depending on the situation of the moment, ignorant, partially ignorant, yet sometimes completely knowledgeable. These shifts derive from his three separate roles: to be at times the antagonist in Philoctetes' tragedy; at other times to become the protagonist in his own tragedy; and finally, to serve yet another function as the leader of the chorus. Sophocles' invention of Neoptolemus as a character was an inspiration, but it introduced certain structural illogicalities. He is a study in contradictions; some we can attribute to the necessities of the character, which is made intentionally contradictory, and some to the requirements of the form, which must mold the character to a much older tradition. As a persona, he must be at first a novice in the art of deception who, as the play progresses, acquires knowledge and understanding.[12] But even more important as a character is his responsibility to be the chief spokesperson for the prophecy (until Heracles intervenes at the end of the play). Neoptolemus must be both ignorant and knowledgeable, ingenuous and wise, a hero and a villain, yet ultimately his most important role is to serve as spokesperson for the gods.

The problems inherent in the dramatic use of the prophecy first appear in the prologos. Neoptolemus is called upon to be the trickster of the play, yet if he is to be the trickster, he must first be tricked himself. He cannot be apprised of the full content of the prophecy. In the first episode, the "merchant" informs us that Odysseus had captured the seer Helenus as if he were an animal bagged in the hunt—"a beautiful trophy." So too with Philoctetes. He too is to be a beautiful trophy for Odysseus. Neoptolemus must be given only as much information as is necessary for him to enter into the conspiracy but not so much as to overshadow Odysseus as the arch-strategist. Neoptolemus is to invent a story that he has been greatly abused by the sons of Atreus and by Odysseus himself, but Odysseus is explicit about the objective of the mission: "If this man's weapons be not taken, it is not possible for you to ravage the fields of Troy" (vv. 68–69). Later in the prologos Odysseus states the objective even more plainly: "You must exercise cleverness to see how you may become the thief of those invincible arms" (vv. 77–78). The arms must be captured, and theft is the only viable method. The theft is Sophocles' contribution to the story. The plot requires Neoptolemus to know only enough to convince him that theft is the necessary, indeed, the only possible strategy. The bow must be stolen. This is the first great manipulation of the prophecy.

Odysseus emphasizes that the theft will be a gain for Neoptolemus. How so? Neoptolemus asks, to which Odysseus replies: "These arms alone will take Troy" (v. 113). Neoptolemus is surprised: "But surely I, so you said, am to be the one who sacks the city" (v. 114). To this Odysseus replies: "You cannot do it without these arms, nor can they be effective without you" (v. 115). We are to infer that Odysseus has given Neoptolemus one half of the prophecy, that Neoptolemus is the man destined to take Troy, and now he has added a new detail, that Neoptolemus will also need Philoctetes' bow. We might suppose that if the man's bow is stolen, the man himself will surely follow, but the question is left open because the emphasis in the prologos must be on Neoptolemus himself, who must suppose that the fall of Troy depends on him alone, and that his success in turn depends on his acquiring Philoctetes' bow.

In the parodos the problem is given a different orientation. In the first strophe and antistrophe the chorus plays the role assigned to it, to be Neoptolemus' assistant and accomplice. But in the second strophe its thoughts turn from obedience to Neoptolemus to pity for Philoctetes. This transition is natural enough because pity is the necessary emotion, and in expressing sympathy for Philoctetes, the chorus serves one of its most important functions, to provide the emotional resonance for the drama. But it also has another function, which transcends its part in any individual play, which is to make Philoctetes into a *tragic hero*, not simply a hero in our modern sense of the term, but a hero as defined in that most ancient of forms, tragedy itself. Its second strophe, in shifting our attention to Philoctetes, elevates the play to the religious domain, where tragedy has its true meaning and function. This chorus assigned to be Neoptolemus' servant may seem to be speaking as a character, but in fact it has for the moment shed that persona and stepped into the most primitive role of the chorus in Greek tragedy, to be the protagonist's community and witness (and celebrant) of his passion.

The chorus, in its transition from deference to compassion, opens the field for Neoptolemus too to step out of his role as a character in a specific play and to become the archetypal leader of a tragic chorus. A few minutes before the chorus entered the *orchēstra*, Neoptolemus had known almost nothing about the story of Philoctetes. Now he has become the voice of wisdom, speaking with the authority of a prophet defending the ways of the gods and explaining that even Philoctetes' terrible fate is enclosed within the divine plan. If we have missed the cue in the strophe and antistrophe that the chorus has assumed the original function of the tragic chorus, Neoptolemus's response leaves no doubt as to the dynamic here. He has become the individual separated out from the chorus to become its *hypokritēs*, who, as George Thomson argues, was originally the "interpreter," that person in the chorus gifted with the power to interpret dreams and oracles.[13] Neoptolemus now interprets the meaning of the prophecy as if he were giving the chorus a lecture on the nature of tragedy itself.[14]

Neoptolemus's surprising shift from character to interpreter alerts us to the play's bifurcation into two plays running on two different and divergent tracks. The play initiated by Odysseus concentrates on the theft of the bow and secondarily on the capture of Philoctetes himself. The other play summons us to ponder the nature of tragedy itself and suffering as an essential component of human existence. As Edmund Wilson puts it so eloquently, this play is as much about the wound as the bow.[15]

Next, the first episode glances at the prophecy from yet another angle. Neoptolemus cannot say anything of the prophecy first because he knows only that part that affects him and because the dynamics require that Philoctetes be fooled by a trick rather than be convinced by any message from heaven. Thus the dialogue between Neoptolemus and Philoctetes must proceed on the track established by Odysseus in the prologos. Their negotiations proceed as planned. Philoctetes is completely won over by Neoptolemus's false story and is anxious to board Neoptolemus's ship; needless to say the bow will go with him. And then the merchant arrives on the scene. His appearance seems hardly necessary. Nothing now prevents the successful conclusion of the mission. Why this new masquerade, with a man arriving in breathless haste to talk of plots at Troy against both Philoctetes and Neoptolemus? Here we concede a point to Waldock. This unneeded third person seems to support his argument that Sophocles kept contriving ways to extend the plot by adding to it what passes for various complications.

This merchant, a spinner of tales like Odysseus, tells three separate stories, each attached to the other. In his first fiction, he tells Neoptolemus that the Greek commanders have discovered his defection from the army and have sent Phoenix and the sons of Theseus to intercept him and bring him back to Troy by force. Neoptolemus plays his role of the ephebe in wide-eyed astonishment. He wonders why Odysseus was not chosen for this assignment. Whereupon the merchant tells his second fiction, of a second mission sent out from Troy, headed by Odysseus and Diomedes. And what would be the purpose of this mission, and where was it headed? The merchant, affecting the anxiety of messengers bringing unwelcome news, blurts out that Odysseus and Diomedes are en route to this very island, having sworn before all the Greeks to bring Philoctetes back to Troy, either persuading him with a word (*logos*) or taking him by force.

Now it is Philoctetes' turn to express his alarm. What would lead the Greeks to send Odysseus to capture him? This question invites the merchant's third tale, and here we are now told the story of the capture of Helenus and his prophecy (vv. 604–20). This, it seems, is the principal purpose of the merchant's arrival, to inform both Neoptolemus and Philoctetes of this hitherto unknown element in the prophecy, that Philoctetes is needed at Troy in person. The prophecy has revealed that the Greeks would not capture Troy unless they "could bring this man from the island where he now lives, *persuading him with a word [logos]*" (vv. 611–13). No mention can be made of Neoptolemus being needed at

Troy, since he at this very moment is acting as if he were sailing away from Troy at top speed. The merchant rounds off his tale: Odysseus, hearing this prophecy, has promised that he will bring Philoctetes back; he thinks he can bring him of his own free will, but if the man is unwilling, he will bring him to Troy by force.

In the prologos Odysseus had emphasized the bow. Now the time has come to shift the emphasis from the bow to the man himself. Even so, one element in the prophecy is still left unsaid, and for obvious reasons: that Philoctetes, once brought back to Troy, would be healed of his disease. Philoctetes, so the merchant reports, must be persuaded in words, but the words that might have the most persuasive effect must still remain unspoken so that the game may go on.

The merchant's appearance serves several functions since it is addressed to three separate audiences. His most obvious purpose is to impress on Neoptolemus the urgency of the moment, but his news is also intended to intensify Philoctetes' anxiety to be off the island once he has been told that his archenemy is chasing him down and will take him to Troy by force if necessary. Philoctetes is inflamed with anger:

οἴμοι τάλας. ἦ κεῖνος, ἡ πᾶσα βλάβη,
ἔμ' εἰς Ἀχαιοὺς ὤμοσεν πείσας στελεῖν;
πεισθήσομαι γὰρ ὧδε κἀξ Ἅιδου θανὼν
πρὸς φῶς ἀνελθεῖν ὥσπερ οὑκείνου πατήρ.
(vv. 622–25)

[Oh, wretch that I am. *He*, that vile pest, he swore
that he would persuade me and bring (me) to the Greeks?
I could as soon be persuaded to rise up into the light from Hades' realm
once I had died, like his father (Sisyphus).]

We are the third audience to whom the merchant's news is directed. While his mix of truth and half-truth will certainly increase Philoctetes' anxiety, we are to deduce that its confusion will hinder rather than further the plan. The merchant's sly fictions achieve the very thing against which Odysseus had cautioned Neoptolemus. He has alarmed Philoctetes. If Neoptolemus can manage to get Philoctetes on board his ship immediately, and certainly that must the intention of the merchant's message, the mission can be saved. But in the brief time required for Philoctetes to gather his equipment, another event intervenes and the game is lost.

Waldock criticizes C. M. Bowra for reading the play as if it had a hidden key, which Bowra argues is to be found in the misinterpretation of the oracle.[16] Helenus has said that Philoctetes must be *persuaded* to come to Troy. But the mission's failure depends on Odysseus himself, who fails to understand the meaning of persuasion. Bowra quotes an excellent passage from the poet Theognis, which bears on this problem:

Straighter than rule or square or line of compass
Cyrnus, must that man be, keeping guard,
To whom the priestess gives the sign at Pytho
And declares god's voice from the rich shrine.
For naught to help you shall you find by adding,
Nor be sinless if you take away.[17]

Absolute fidelity to an oracle's text must be the interpreter's rule, so Bowra argues. But if that is the message of the *Philoctetes*, Waldock argues, it would have been "a muddled technique."[18] He reasons that such an interpretation, depending entirely on the characters' misapplication of the oracle, an oracle that is not given until almost halfway through the play, is to assume too much of the characters themselves and of the audience watching the performance. They, the characters of the drama, are left in the dark, and so are we. Here again, we must remember that there was no written text of the prophecy that either Sophocles or his audience could consult.

Certainly, we are never told explicitly that Odysseus failed because he used the wrong kind of persuasion, but the point is made so lucidly by the action itself that it need not be put into words. The necessity of persuasion is not a key buried somewhere deep in the play that would require some clever scout to decipher. It would be obvious to any Athenian watching this play that if Philoctetes is to be brought to Troy, it must be by persuasion. All three Philoctetes plays depend on persuasion for the success of the mission. Therein lies the drama. Sophocles needed to find a different method of persuasion than those used by Aeschylus or Euripides. The confusion that Bowra sees in the characters' misapplication of the terms of the prophecy can all be referred back to the insertion into the plot of Neoptolemus, who must at one moment be a character in the drama and at another the spokesperson for the community.

When the merchant, reporting on the events at Troy, says that Odysseus has publicly promised that he will bring Philoctetes to Troy by persuasion or by force, the idea of force is introduced to inflame

Philoctetes' fears and make him desperate to board Neoptolemus's ship. Force of itself would be useless; the threat is meant as a rhetorical gambit. The merchant reports that Odysseus thinks he can bring Philoctetes of his own free will (v. 617), and that idea, that Philoctetes can be persuaded by Odysseus, is the only issue to hold Philoctetes' attention: "Is this not a marvel, my boy, that the son of Laertes would expect to win with *soft words* and display me from his ship to the assembled Argives? I would as soon listen to my most hated enemy, the viper who has deprived me of my foot" (vv. 628–32).

In the prologos Odysseus insists that Philoctetes cannot be taken by force. He must be won over by words. This, we later learn, is exactly the merchant's message: Philoctetes must be persuaded by words. Odysseus's *sophisma* depends entirely on the persuasive force of words, but his argument to Neoptolemus is that such persuasion can be achieved only through subterfuge. Philoctetes must be caught as an animal might be baited and trapped. The merchant's function is to speed the process, to get Philoctetes on board the ship as quickly as possible lest some mishap might ruin the plan. We with the broader horizon of spectators know the impediment that looms over the scheme. The political plan is about to be broken by Neoptolemus's spiritual transformation, by his veneration of the godhood in the bow, by his mystical experience in the cave, and by his witnessing the agonies of his personal friend Philoctetes.

The next point where the complication in Neoptolemus's role comes to the fore is in the first kommos, when Philoctetes lies on the ground unconscious, with Neoptolemus holding his bow and the chorus pressing him to seize the moment to escape with the bow. Here Neoptolemus again assumes his oracular role to explain to the chorus that taking the bow alone would be no victory: "His must be the crown." (v. 841). Again, Neoptolemus speaks with a knowledge and an authority beyond what we could expect from his part in the prologos. What is the source of this authority? Can we explain the inconsistency here by referring to Neoptolemus's increasing insight into the nature of the mission?

In the next episode, following the kommos, Neoptolemus admits to being in the state that he calls "my present *pathos*" (v. 899). Philoctetes surmises that Neoptolemus is offended by Philoctetes' disease, but Neoptolemus understands that he himself is the offense. Unable to tolerate himself as a liar, he discloses the plot, and the game collapses once and for all. Neoptolemus begs Philoctetes to withhold his anger until Neoptolemus can explain. Explain what? "[My intention is,] first, to save you from this evil, and then to go with you and ravage the land of Troy" (vv. 919–20). "This evil" implies Philoctetes' disease, and so we would understand it if we knew about the prophecy of Philoctetes' healing at Troy. But this would be an allusion with meaning only for the audience since, in strictly naturalistic terms, neither Neoptolemus nor Philoctetes can yet know anything of that element in the prophecy. "Evil" is generic; it could mean simply Philoctetes' terrible isolation on Lemnos. But this is the closest we get in the third episode to any hint that Philoctetes could be healed at Troy, or that Neoptolemus and Philoctetes have a destiny in common as leaders of the Greek forces at Troy. Again, Sophocles leaves unsaid the argument that might have most influence on Philoctetes. The consequences of the confusion that Odysseus has brought to the argument must be allowed to play themselves out.

Philoctetes is outraged not only at the trick played on him. It is an outright theft, but even more shameful, Neoptolemus has robbed a wounded man of the instrument of his survival. Neoptolemus is de facto both a thief and a murderer. While the two men parlay, ineffectively on each side, Odysseus returns to the scene, to bluster and threaten. Now that persuasion has failed, force is the only option left, though it is to be no more effective than persuasion. Just as the merchant by his appearance in the first episode had put persuasion even further out of reach, so now Odysseus, returning to the stage to reclaim his authority, only alienates Philoctetes even more. His presence ruins all chances of compromise or accommodation, since now the author of the theft is fully revealed. Persuasion is a ruined strategy, exactly as Odysseus had foretold.

The third episode ends with Odysseus and Neoptolemus moving offstage and the chorus left in the theater to save the situation. But what can the chorus do that Neoptolemus has left undone? Neoptolemus still holds the bow; that much seems nonnegotiable. The only point still left unsaid that might have persuasive power is the promise of healing for Philoctetes at Troy. But this promise must still be kept concealed. With Odysseus and Neoptolemus gone, the chorus and Philoctetes enter into the second kommos of the play. Now the chorus rises to its full stature in its traditional role, as the elder of the tribe whose function is to interpret for the protagonist the deeper meaning of his pathos. Even now, however, the information that Philoctetes can find healing at Troy must still remain unspoken. The chorus, unable to speak those words of comfort, can use this kommos to deepen the spiritual values, to talk of healing but still only obliquely.

The chorus here is finished with the role assigned to it in the parodos to guard its master's interests. Now it has shifted into another function, to serve as Philoctetes' community. The emphasis moves in this kommos from Philoctetes as victim to the harder truth that Philoctetes must accept his own responsibility for his part in his pathos. The chorus listens to Philoctetes' lamentation and grants his grievances a certain legitimacy but it warns him that the violence of his words may cross the line to invite *phthonos* (anger and retaliation, whether from humans or from the gods) and calls on Philoctetes to honor the friendship that Neoptolemus is offering him. The chorus introduces two words laden with religious significance to steer the play to its true spiritual meaning. First, in referring to Philoctetes' disease, the chorus calls it a demon (*kēr*) and admonishes him that escape from its voracious attacks is within his own power. This is the first time that anyone has spoken directly of the disease to Philoctetes and certainly the first time that Philoctetes has been told that he can liberate himself from the disease. In the third episode Neoptolemus had spoken of freeing Philoctetes from his "evil," but the chorus now clarifies that the evil is his disease.

The chorus then introduces a second word to assert the central truth of this kommos even more forcefully, counseling Philoctetes that he of his own intelligence has chosen his worse *daimon* over his better. In popular thought both of these words, *kēr* and *daimon*, signified external and supernatural agents, but the chorus is revising the old mythology to make them both internal and subjective. Some sicknesses may come from malignant spirits, but there is also a disease of the will, when the will wills its own disease. We could not have reached this understanding if such a truth had been spoken, whether by Neoptolemus or by this chorus, earlier in the play. This discovery of the self must unfold in stages; it must be pieced together, inferred first from words spoken, then from the evidence of the disease itself, and finally from its effects both on the sick man and on those who witness his sufferings. Even now, however, one piece of information must still remain unsaid.

The second kommos ends when Neoptolemus returns to the stage to correct his error, by which he means his theft of the bow. Returning the bow to Philoctetes gives him the authority to resume his function as the *hypokritēs* and to carry forward the spiritual truths that the chorus had begun to expound. At last in the exodos the critical information can be given, that both honor and healing await Philoctetes at Troy. But that information must be framed within the larger religious question. Just as the chorus in the previous Kommos had finished with its conspiratorial role, so Neoptolemus is finished with his role as a dramatic persona and is now fully invested in his priestly insignia. Neoptolemus warns Philoctetes that humans must endure the fortunes given to them by the gods, but people who persist in pains of their own choosing should be neither pitied nor excused (vv. 1316–20). For the first time, Philoctetes himself is told in the plainest terms of his complicity in his own suffering; furthermore, he deserves neither tolerance nor pity. Neoptolemus now unfolds the whole story for Philoctetes, explaining that the pathos as a whole is a complex weaving of the gods' intentions and the human contribution. Philoctetes' wound at the sacred shrine was in accordance with divine order, but his present attitude is his own responsibility and for that he deserves no sympathy at all. In conclusion, Neoptolemus insists that Philoctetes must come of his own free will to Troy, where he will be healed by the sons of Asclepius and "will sack Troy with [Neoptolemus] and the bow" (vv. 1332–35).

Where did Neoptolemus acquire this knowledge? Certainly not from Odysseus. It enters into the play through two motives. On one hand, Sophocles has unfolded the prophecy in stages because the plot depends on the mishandling of the prophecy. But more important, the drama is focused primarily not on the external events of the plot but on its inner meaning. Now at last, thirteen hundred verses into the play, in the exodos, Philoctetes is given the information that might have been immediately persuasive if it had been told to him at the beginning of the play, that, as Neoptolemus now tells him, he is to be recognized as the best of the Greeks, that he is to be healed, and that, finally, he is to achieve surpassing glory for his part in the fall of Troy (vv. 1344–47). Of course this prophecy could not be delivered to Philoctetes at the beginning of the play, nor even to Neoptolemus, yet now Neoptolemus must speak as if he had known the full extent of the prophecy from the beginning since he has been anointed to be the prophet to reveal the prophecy and to expatiate on its meaning.

Another motive driving the plot is that Neoptolemus is introduced into the plot not simply as a supporting actor but as a full character with his own crisis of conscience. When the play begins, he consents to involve himself in deceit when persuaded that his action is for the common good and that he will personally reap a greater glory for his small malfeasance. But in the exodos he has matured into a sage. A sage is needed if the play is to move beyond sophistic cleverness, and who else could be this sage but Neoptolemus (who is given impeccable credentials as the son of Achilles)? And what strategy is more dramatically effective than to have Neoptolemus, if he is to emerge at the end as the sage, to play the fallen angel who is then rehabilitated?

Sophocles has structured the plot so that even when Neoptolemus has done his part to rehabilitate himself, by admitting his role in the conspiracy and by returning the bow to its rightful owner, the atmosphere has become so clouded with deceit that the proofs of his good faith do not have enough weight to change Philoctetes' mind. Instead, Philoctetes takes advantage of their friendship to win Neoptolemus over to his point of view, and Neoptolemus thereby surrenders his slowly gained moral authority by transferring it to Philoctetes. This adds one new complication to the plot, that the man whom Neoptolemus himself had said should not be excused or pitied for his self-willed suffering, whom the chorus has charged with choosing his own evil *daimon*, should emerge from the conflict as the voice of friendship, health, and conscience.

This is the ultimate irony. Neoptolemus had told the chorus that the victor's crown must go to Philoctetes, and so it does. At the end of the play Philoctetes has won the victory over Odysseus, over Neoptolemus, and even over the whole Greek army. But like Homer's Achilles, he has won his victory only at the price of increasing his own pain. This outcome, of course, cannot be allowed to stand. It is a defiance of destiny, and the plot, so cleverly manipulated as if to circumvent the old myth, must be brought back into the myth's embrace. But the more important issue is that Philoctetes' triumph if left untreated would be a victory for sickness over health, for self-hatred under the appearance of self-affirmation. The deus ex machina, who was not needed, we infer, by either Aeschylus or Euripides, must now be introduced into the plot.

The *Philoctetes* is a complex play. Despite Waldock's criticism that the overriding problem of the play is "stubborn *immobility*," more happens in the play than he is prepared to grant, and on several different levels.[19] Its complexity results from the several different strands woven together. We are given the language of politics, the language of myth and religion, the language of therapy, and the language of the self. The play's emphasis on rhetoric is so strong a theme that politics has garnered much of the attention of modern critics, but disease is as important a theme as rhetoric. The disease takes us first deep into the primal complexes of superstition and taboo, of transgressions against divine prerogatives, of gods jealous of their territories, of scapegoats and ritual purity. But ultimately, the disease is the disease of the will, as the chorus explains in the second kommos and as Neoptolemus reaffirms in the exodos. The nucleus of the play is the self, the self traumatized both by the physical disease and by society's horror, which must make the diseased person into a monster to preserve the purity of the tribe.

This play arose not in the mind of a logician but rather in the intuition, which Bergson describes as a fringe that surrounds the intellect.[20] Bergson defines intuition as sympathy. Readers who read this poet's thoughts with that kind of intuition may sense the poet's meaning that amid all the vicissitudes of life, even in disease, even in utter aloneness, at the center of human experience there abides the self, the individual *daimon* who is uniquely himself or herself and at the same time, in this poet's creed at least, bears the image of the divine.

Notes

Introduction

1. Eco, *Kant and the Platypus*, 34. He adds: "Through this continuous reinvention of language, the Poets are inviting us to take up again the task of questioning and reconstructing the World and of the horizons of the entities in which we calmly and continuously thought we lived."

2. Dio Chrys., *Discourse* 52.

Chapter 1. The Problem of Translation

1. Quoted in Gadamer, *Truth and Method*, 11.
2. Ibid., 12.
3. Ibid., 5.
4. Ibid., 268.
5. Ibid., 270.
6. Ibid.
7. Ibid., 271–73.
8. Ibid., 273.
9. Ibid., 14.
10. Hippoc., *De morbo sacro*. I am grateful to my colleague William Mullen for bringing this text to my attention.
11. All translations are by the author unless otherwise noted.
12. See Santayana, *Interpretations of Poetry and Religion*, 147–65, for his essay "The Absence of Religion in Shakespeare."
13. Ibid., 152, 154.
14. Ibid., 157.
15. Gadamer, *Truth and Method*, 273.
16. Ibid., 111.
17. Ibid., 12.

18. All quotations of the play are from H. Lloyd-Jones and N. G. Wilson's edition of the plays of Sophocles.

19. Gadamer, *Truth and Method*, 79.

20. Frame, *Myth of Return*.

21. For a very perceptive study of Sophocles' use of language, see Budelmann, *Language of Sophocles*, esp. 93–132 on the *Philoctetes*.

22. Eliot, "Tradition and Individual Talent," 49–50.

23. Gadamer, *Truth and Method*, 408.

Chapter 2. The Strong Poet

1. Bloom, *Agon*.

2. Bloom, *Anxiety of Influence*, xxiii.

3. Ibid.

4. Ath., *Deipnosophists* I.20e. Some have claimed, however, that Sophocles did not dance in the nude but in his cloak.

5. Ibid.

6. On this poem, see Austin, "Theocritus XVI."

7. Nagy, *Best of the Achaeans*, 18.

8. Havelock, *Preface to Plato*, chap. 2. Plato's quarrel with Homer has been much discussed since Havelock. For an overview and his own interesting perceptions, see Bloom, *Where Shall Wisdom Be Found*, chap. 2, "The Greeks: Plato's Contest with Homer."

9. Borges, "Pierre Menard," 51.

10. Ibid., 50–51.

11. On the toxic effect of the competition, see Slater, *Glory of Hera*.

12. Nietzsche, "Homeric Contests," 38.

13. Ibid., 37.

14. See Goldhill, "Language of Tragedy," 55, on the *chorēgos*; Easterling, "Form and Performance," 153, on the actors.

15. Cartledge, "Deep Plays," 14. "The competitive element which was implicit in all forms of Greek poetic activity grew in proportion as art became the centre of public life and the expression of the whole political and intellectual outlook of the age. Accordingly, it reached its highest point in drama" (Jaeger, *Paideia*, 1:268).

16. Pl., *Symp.* 175e, 194b.

17. Goldhill, "Audience of Athenian Tragedy," 55.

18. Jaeger writes of this continuous process of competition of the dramatic poets that it "made taste extraordinarily sensitive to any falling off in the great tradition and to any diminution in the power and depth of the influence which tragedy exercised" (*Paideia*, 1:268–69). Herington notes that the competitive pressures of the "song culture" of archaic Greece "may be partly responsible for the extraordinary combination of vitality and technical excellence which

amazes us in the archaic poems that reached the Alexandrian library" (*Poetry into Drama*, 62–63).

19. Arist. *Poet.* 1451b.

20. Ibid.

21. Herodotus, *Historiae*, 5.67.

22. Sheppard, "Attic Drama in the Fifth Century," in *Cambridge Ancient History*, 5:129. Easterling argues that the Athenian theater involved displacement, in time and place, because the issues explored were explosive enough to provoke violent reactions "if the audiences were not kept aware of the essentially metaphorical status of everything enacted before them" ("Form and Performance," 172).

23. See *Oxford Classical Dictionary* (1949), 282, "Dio Cocceianus."

24. Dio Chrys., *Or.* 52.

25. Ath., *Deipnosophists* 8.39.

26. On this ideology, see Hall, *Inventing the Barbarian*.

27. See Stanford, *Ulysses Theme*, on the different approaches to the character of Odysseus over the centuries.

28. Odysseus is "in many respects a degenerate descendant of the Homeric hero" (Knox, *Heroic Temper*, 124). See also Kirkwood, "Persuasion," 430; Craik, "*Philoctetes*," 26.

29. Rose, "Sophocles' *Philoctetes*"; also Rose, *Sons of the Gods*, 56–57.

30. Cf. Segal, *Tragedy and Civilization*, 296: Philoctetes' life is bounded by "the hostile sea on one hand and the wild rocky terrain where he hunts on the other, both spaces beyond the pale of civilization."

31. Herington makes good observations on what he calls "the forests of myths," in which the ancient Greeks lived and moved: "For the Greek poet at any time in the song-culture period, Homer and all the line of great singers who followed him were in constant re-performance before the community, as alive, as available and as potent in rivalry as any contemporary poet" (*Poetry in Drama*, 62).

32. On the *Philoctetes'* relations to the events of its own time, see Jameson, "Politics and the 'Philoctetes.'" See also Goldhill, *Reading Greek Tragedy*; Goldhill, "Audience of Athenian Tragedy"; Vernant and Vidal-Naquet, *Myth and Tragedy*, 26; Hall, *Inventing the Barbarian*.

33. See Lloyd-Jones, *Justice of Zeus*, who argues against those who would see in Greek tragedy a liberalism regarding the gods.

34. Levi, "Greek Drama," 157.

35. See Goldhill on Homer's "privileged place in Athenian cultural life." The Homeric poems, he notes, "provided a resource of normative images of the world and ways to relate to the world that informed all aspects of Athenian culture" ("Audience of Athenian Tragedy," 127). "The ubiquitous presence of the myths and their high-born people in the tragic theater of democratic Athens does not seem to have presented contemporaries with anything like the problem

that it poses for modern scholars" (Griffin, "Sophocles and the Democratic City," 76). Easterling notes that the aristocratic bias of the Homeric poems could "easily be reinterpreted to suit a democratic society. The notion of the 'best people' (as Louis Gernet pointed out) could be transferred from one kind of elite, an aristocracy, to another, the citizen body" ("Form and Performance," 172). But cf. also Hall: "Tragedy offers no simple 'reflection' of the social processes of Athens: it transformed them while assimilating them into its own medium" ("Sociology of Athenian Tragedy," 93). Also "Greek Tragedy does its thinking in a form which is vastly more politically advanced than the society which produced Greek tragedy" (ibid., 125). The *Philoctetes* is a casebook of these competing pressures. The characters of this play are only very distant cousins of their Homeric namesakes. If it were not for the constant echo of the epic in the names, in the language, and in wholesale episodes, we could see more clearly that this play is hardly Homeric at all. The studied Homeric references scattered throughout the play reveal Sophocles' own anxiety to make his ideas persuasive. To achieve that end, they must seem entirely *Homeric*.

36. Burian, "Myth into *Muthos*," 190.

37. Bloom, *Map of Misreading*, 19.

38. "It remains not arbitrary nor even accidental to say that everyone who now reads and writes in the West, of whatever racial background, sex or ideological camp, is still a son or daughter of Homer" (ibid., 33).

39. Thomson, "Introduction," in *Aeschylus*, ed. Robert W. Corrigan, 24.

Chapter 3. The Prologos

1. This is the accepted modern interpretation of the origins of tragedy, derived largely from a few remarks in Aristotle and other fragmentary pieces of testimony from ancient sources. For the evidence, see Pickard-Cambridge, *Dithyramb, Tragedy and Comedy*. For a contrarian view, see Else, *Origin and Form*.

2. See Thomson, *Aeschylus and Athens*, 181

3. On the competition between these two Homeric heroes to be judged, in the formula used in the *Iliad*, "best of the Achaeans," see Nagy, *Best of the Achaeans*, 15–58.

4. On the horrors provoked in the Greek leaders by this disease, with its stench and noise, see Stephens, "Wound of Philoctetes"; Padel, *Whom Gods Destroy*; Kott, *Eating of the Gods*.

5. Segal notes that this play makes no mention of any altars on Lemnos (*Tragedy and Civilization*, 292). This absence points to the religious vacancy on the island, since it is uninhabited except by Philoctetes, who has been certified by his peers at Troy to be a nonperson and therefore beyond the pale.

6. Burkert, *Greek Religion*, 55–59; also Burkert, *Homo Necans*, 3–8.

7. Attali, *Noise*, 26–27; see also Dworkin, *Reading the Illegible*, esp. 46–49.

8. Burkert, *Greek Religion*, 73.

9. Attali, *Noise*, 27–31, on music as a simulacrum of sacrifice.

10. Webster translates the word as "thwarted" and notes, "The word is so common that Jebb is wrong in seeing an allusion to 'tripping' a wrestler" (Sophocles, *Philoctetes*, note at v. 432). But why should we prefer that Sophocles would assume this to be a dead metaphor, meaning no more than Odysseus being thwarted?

11. On this evolution in thought, see Nestle, *Mythos*; Snell, *Discovery of the Mind*, 191–226.

12. Kirk and Raven, *Pre-Socratic Philosophers*, frag. 235; Kahn, *Art and Thought of Heraclitus*, frag. 35.

13. For translations of this *Encomium*, see Dillon and Gergel, *Greek Sophists*, 76–84; Freeman, *Ancilla*, 131–33. No date can be given with any confidence for the publication of Gorgias's *Encomium*, but we might hazard the 420s, when he was at the height of his popularity. Dodds argues for 387–385 BCE as the probable date for the publication of Plato's dialogue, the *Gorgias* (*Gorgias*, 24).

14. In Sophocles, *Plays and Fragments*, Jebb, at v. 50, writes: "The sentence begins as if the form were to be, δεῖ. . . γενναῖον εἶναι, μὴ μόνον τῷ σώματι, ἀλλὰ καὶ γνώμῃ: he must show his true-bred spirit, not merely *physically*, but *morally*—i.e., by bringing himself . . . to aid plans which may be repugnant to him." But morality is not of primary importance here; rather, cleverness is the faculty most required in the circumstances.

15. Vidal-Naquet suggests that in this play Neoptolemus "passes through the ephebic initiation" (*Myth and Tragedy*, 169) and that Heracles' words at the end of the play, when he commands Philoctetes and Neoptolemus to stand by each other on the battle line, recall the ephebic oath. Jebb writes: "Odysseus calls on Neoptolemus to prove himself a true son of his sire . . . by complete loyalty to his mission" (Sophocles, *Plays and Fragments*, note at v. 51). Knox objects that this interpretation "neglects the awkward fact that the last thing in the world Achilles thought of was 'loyalty to his mission'" (*Heroic Temper*, 187n18). But the Achilles who functions as the paradigm for Neoptolemus is no more the Homeric Achilles in this play than its Odysseus is Homer's Odysseus. The Homeric characters are reconstructed as needed for the ethos of this play.

16. Pl., *Ap*. 24b, 26b.

17. On the theme of inherited excellence, see Rose: "The will to humanize, to universalize the sufferings specific to the ruling elite, is the founding ideological gesture of the new tragic form" (*Sons of the Gods*, 189). Easterling notes: "It is interesting that the essentially aristocratic bias of the Homeric poems and of much choral lyric could so easily be reinterpreted to suit a democratic society. The notion of 'the best people' (as Louis Gernet has pointed out) could be transferred from one kind of elite, the aristocracy, to another, the citizen body" ("Form and Performance," 172).

18. See Lattimore's translation of Hom., *Il.* 18.380, where he renders the "knowing mind," said of Hephaestus, as "with his craftsmanship and his cunning."

19. Hom., *Od.* 11.609–14. I have used Murray's translation, which Stanford quotes in his edition, as an excellent expression of the uncanny nature of *technē*.

20. Gorg., *Hel.*, 10, trans. by Dodds in his edition of Plato, *Gorgias*, 8.

21. Sophocles, *Plays and Fragments*, Jebb at vv. 54–55.

22. See Austin, "Great Soul Robbery," for a fuller discussion of the history of the word and its place in this play.

23. Hom., *Il.* 22.161.

24. This point is well made by Claus, *Toward the Soul*, but its implications have not been fully understood.

25. Pl., *Gorg.* 464a.

26. Gorg., *Hel.*

27. Ibid.

28. Hom., *Il.* 23.103–7.

29. See Kahn, *Art and Thought of Heraclitus*, 126–30, for his commentary on this fragment. On the significance of this fragment, he quotes Wilamowitz-Moellendorff ("Heraclitus is the first to have given serious thought to, and had something to say about, the soul in man"). Also for Reinhardt, Heraclitus gives us "for the first time a psychology worthy of the name" (Reinhardt, *Parmenides*, 201, quoted in Kahn, *Art and Thought of Heraclitus*, 127). Worth noting in this context is Heraclitus frag. 113A (Kahn), where Heraclitus says that the *psychē* is the least bodily thing (*asōmatōtaton*).

30. See Kirk and Raven, *Presocratic Philosophers*, 205.

31. Snell, *Discovery of the Mind*, 27.

32. Pl., *Phdr.* 261a.

33. Pl., *Phdr.* 271c10.

34. Claus, *Toward the Soul*, 69.

35. Eur., *Hec.* 87–88.

36. Pl., *Phd.* 64c.

37. Soph., *OT* 63–65; 93–94.

38. See Rohde, *Psyche*. "The sense of beauty that produced the men and women of Sophocles arose from a vast new interest in the *souls* of tragic characters. It was a manifestation of the new ideal of areté, which for the first time emphasized the central importance of the psyché, the 'soul,' in all culture" (Jaeger, *Paideia*, 1:279).

39. Burnet, "Socratic Doctrine of the Soul."

40. Pl., *Ap.* 29 d–e.

41. Burnet, "Socratic Doctrine of the Soul," 140.

42. Ibid., 156.

43. Pl., *Minos* 321a4. Paul Shorey argues that the first half could not have been written by Plato but adds that it is hard to imagine who else could have written the second half (in which this quote appears). He considers its ideas to express orthodox Platonic thought (*What Plato Said*, 425).

44. "The *agathos* traditionally is he who is held to be most effective in assuring the security, stability and well-being of the social unit, in war and peace" (Adkins, *Moral Values*, 60).

45. "In war, the *agathos* is still the effective fighter; and it remains *kalon* to succeed, *aischron* [disgraceful] to fail" (ibid.).

46. ὁ ἀγαθὸς καὶ σοφὸς γεωμέρτης (Pl., *Hp. Mi.* 367e.2). In Plato's *Phaedo* 63b6, Socrates uses the same expression of the gods whom he expects to meet after death: θεοὺς ἄλλους σοφοὺς τε καὶ ἀγαθούς.

47. "The play of Sophocles that is most remarkably involved in the workings of shame, the expectation of it and its attempted avoidance, is the *Philoctetes*" (Williams, *Shame and Necessity*, 87).

48. Neoptolemus cannot mean, as some readers have taken it, that he is willing to put up with the shame: "This he will not do; if it becomes present to him, he cannot put up with it, and this becomes clear to him later, when he changes his mind. Neoptolemus, although he himself is an heroic warrior, is one for whom the standard by which he measures his own worth quite clearly involves values beyond so-called competitive success, though he is open to the attractions of that too, which is why he can be temporarily seduced" (ibid., 88). In my view, Neoptolemus represents two personas; on one hand, he fits the paradigm of the old heroic virtue, but, on the other, he is also the new Athenian ephebe who is talked out of his shame by the new kind of rhetorician, who promises sophistication in place of the old virtues.

Chapter 4. The Parodos

1. Wilamowitz-Moellendorff, *Die dramatische Technik des Sophokles*.

2. "As of old in tragedy formerly the chorus by itself performed the whole drama" (Diog. *Laert.* 3.56, quoted in Pickard-Cambridge, *Dithyramb, Tragedy and Comedy*, 70).

3. For the ancient testimony on the origins of tragedy, see Arist., *Poet.* 48b–49b; and Pickard-Cambridge, *Dithyramb, Tragedy and Comedy*. See also Herington, *Poetry into Drama*, for good observations on the contributions of myth and the lyric genres to the formation of tragedy.

4. Thomson, *Aeschylus and Athens*.

5. Pickard-Cambridge, *Dithyramb, Tragedy and Comedy*, 86.

6. Else, *Origin and Form*.

7. Information given by Poll. 4.123, cited in Pickard-Cambridge, *Dithyramb, Tragedy and Comedy*, 71, 86; see also Pickard-Cambridge, *Theater of Dionysus*,

131. Pickard-Cambridge, giving other instances where eleon is a carving table or a chopping block, has difficulty imagining that a table used for carving the sacrificial animal could become the platform on which the chorus danced its celebration of the sacrifice.

8. Pickard-Cambridge, *Dithyramb, Tragedy and Comedy*, 71, 86.

9. Pickard-Cambridge, *Theater of Dionysus*, 131.

10. Freud, *Totem and Taboo*, 192–94. My understanding of tragedy has been deeply influenced by Frazer and Freud, especially by Freud's *Totem and Taboo*. This is definitely disputed territory; many classical scholars reject almost every item in these modern scholars as they pertain to the evolution and function of tragedy.

11. Ibid., 193.

12. See Sophocles, *Plays and Fragments*, Jebb's note on v. 837.

13. The theological element is mostly treated today as insignificant. See, for example, Stephens, "Wound of Philoctetes." On the problems resulting from the addition of Neoptolemus to the plot, see the appendix to the present volume, 211–12.

14. "The Hero of tragedy must suffer; to this day that remains the essence of tragedy" (Freud, *Totem and Taboo*, 193).

Chapter 5. The First Episode

1. Hall, *Inventing the Barbarian*, reminds us that one aspect of the ideology of Greek tragedy was to affirm the Hellenic identify as against the "barbarian." Sophocles, in placing the emphasis on the Greek language in this passage, would send the signal throughout the whole theater that everything in this play was Greek through and through.

2. "Philoctetes says that being without a polis is equivalent to being dead (1018)" (Hall, *Inventing the Barbarian*, 97).

3. Blundell writes that Odysseus is less the sophist than the politician. Such politicians "show evidence of sophistic influence. Like them, however, he is not so much a sophist as an embodiment of the kind of political opportunism for which some sophistic theories offered a conventional intellectual justification" ("Moral Character of Odysseus," 328).

4. Sophocles, *Philoctetes*, Webster's note at v. 391.

5. Ibid. Reinhardt disagrees with those scholars who argue that Sophocles "blindly surrenders to the pathos of each moment without expecting his audience to consider the past or the future." He goes on to argue that Sophocles "is playing a game with the situation: this is clearly reflected in the way in which the harmony of the solemn formula is disturbed—for there is no longer anything sacred or pious in the intention that would correspond with the sacred nature of the invocation" (*Sophocles*, 171).

6. Blundell considers Odysseus in this play simply a politician who is

influenced by the ideas of the sophists ("Moral Character of Odysseus," 328). But the vituperation heaped on Odysseus by Philoctetes, including accusations of his illegitimate birth and his slavish character, goes far beyond what might be said of a politician.

7. Thersites is introduced in a "way that strikingly confuses him with Odysseus" (ibid., 322).

8. Belfiore, *Tragic Pleasures*, writes of Greek education as teaching the young to love the fine and be disgusted at the shameful. The simple moral issue is made more complicated here because Philoctetes, with his disease and his wildness, is disgusting, yet Neoptolemus is called on to love him.

9. See Ringer, *Electra and the Empty Urn*, 101–25, on the metatheater of Sophocles' *Philoctetes*, with Odysseus the playwright (*didaskalos*) within the play, and Neoptolemus "a surprising combination of internal actor, a character playing a 'role' within his role and onstage audience to Philoctetes' suffering" (104). See also Easterling, "Form and Performance," 169–71, on this play within the play. Also Burian, who notes that "the scene refers to its own deceptiveness" (Myth into *Muthos*, 170).

10. Hamilton, "Neoptolemos' Story in the *Philoktetes*," approaches this aspect of the play as a presentation of two stories; the first story, as told by Neoptolemus, is based on a lie, hence must be corrected by the story told later by Heracles, which is the truer model for Philoctetes' action.

11. On the bow, see Harsh, "Role of the Bow." The bow is the "most integrally incorporated of all material objects in Greek tragedy" (Taplin, *Greek Tragedy in Action*, 89). "No visual symbol in Sophocles has a more powerful and far-reaching ethical and psychological meaning than the bow of the *Philoctetes*" (Segal, *Interpreting Greek Tragedy*, 122).

12. Kosak, "Therapeutic Touch and Sophocles' *Philoktetes*," has interesting observations on the therapeutic touch in this play and on the anxieties shown in Greek tragedy, here and elsewhere, about the relations implied when one man touches another. Less attention has been given to this element in the play, Neoptolemus's desire to *touch* the bow, and Philoctetes' response that he may *touch* it, though later, not at this present moment. This touch is as much fraught with anxiety as the physical touch of man and man (Philoctetes and Neoptolemus).

13. See Lada-Richards on Neoptolemus and the showing of the bow, which "would have suggested a whole string of ritual associations falling into the realm of Eleusinian mystic initiation" ("Neoptolemos and the Bow," 180). The *proskynesis* in the cave is part of that initiation into the mysteries.

14. Webster calls this "the young soldier's reverence for a great weapon" (note at v. 656).

15. Webster notes that "if Neoptolemus can get the bow, the plan as formulated by Odysseus is complete (68, 77, 116), but Neoptolemus is not thinking of this here; his emotion is genuine" (at vv. 660–61).

Chapter 6. The Stasimon

1. Sophocles, *Plays and Fragments*, Jebb's note at vv. 676–729.

2. "Whereas Neoptolemus is ensnared by reason and argument, he is rehabilitated principally through emotion. It is through compassion (οἶκτος, ἔλεος) that he is brought to an empathetic understanding of Philoctetes' suffering" (Hawkins, "Ethical Tragedy and Sophocles' 'Philoctetes,'" 345).

3. Nagy, *Best of the Achaeans*, gives a good exposition of this process whereby the heroes, worshipped in their local cults, rose to achieve Panhellenic status by their place in the Panhellenic epic. Particularly important for the study of tragedy is his discussion of the relations between the *kleos* of the hero (his eventual fame) and his grief and pain. See his chapter 6, "Lamentation and the Hero," 94–117; also Frye, *Anatomy of Criticism*, 206–19, on tragedy as "The Mythos of Autumn."

4. No discussion of Greek tragedy is complete without reference to *pathos*, which entails ideas of suffering, punishment, and guilt. Thomas Gould defines pathos in tragedy as the "catastrophic suffering, undergone by some great figure, man or god, far in excess of the sufferer's desserts" (*Ancient Quarrel*, ix). See also Kott for a bleak view of this way of thinking in Greek tragedy; he quotes Frye: "In tragedies of a sick society the central figure is often a victim, and the victim's nature is too big for his fortune" (*Eating of the Gods*, 9). See also Frye, *Anatomy of Criticism*, 206–23, for a good essay on these paradoxes inherent in tragedy.

5. See Thomas Gould on Aristotle's dilemma, to find in tragedy "the right balance between injustice (required for pity for a *pathos*) and justice" (*Ancient Quarrel*, 53). Aristotle found a compromise: "There would be injustice, insofar as we see a good man come to grief, but also justice, insofar as some significant blame could be traced to the (imperfectly) good man's own actions" (54).

6. The isolation of Philoctetes from all human company, one of the most marked features of this play, has been noted by many. See Knox: "The Sophoclean hero acts in a terrifying vacuum, a present which has no future comfort and no past to guide, an isolation in time and space which imposes on the hero the full responsibility for his action and its consequences. . . . Sophocles presents us for the first time with what we recognize as a 'tragic hero'" (*Heroic Temper*, 5). Segal mentions the absence of altars on Lemnos; Philoctetes, removed from society, is cut off from religion (*Tragedy and Civilization*, 242). Segal notes "the inhuman savagery of the island" (308). Rose treats the isolation on Lemnos as representing the first stage in the sophistic theory of social evolution. The setting, in this reading, is not just to enhance the artistic or dramatic effect of the play, but presents a strong anthropological framework for the play, the "primitive, presocial stage" of sophistic theory ("Sophocles' *Philoctetes*," 58). See also Frye: "The center of a hero's tragedy is in the hero's isolation" (*Anatomy of Criticism*, 208).

7. Claus, *Toward the Soul*, 69. On *psychē* in this play, see my earlier essay "The Great Soul Robbery."

8. Sophocles, *Philoctetes,* Webster's note at vv. 712–13. See also Jaeger (*Paideia,* 1:279, quoted in chap. 3, n.38, of this volume) on the "vast new interest in the *souls* of tragic characters."

9. Herodotus, v. 67. For a fuller discussion of this passage, see Pickard-Cambridge, *Dithyramb, Tragedy and Comedy,* 101–5.

10. Heracles is a compound of the most extreme polarities, which add their aura to the figure of Philoctetes, first in this ode and in the play as a whole. Silk writes: "Heracles represents *both* those deep immortal longings which all men feel or repress, and which the Greeks felt to be too dangerous to admit, *and* the huge but human sufferings and dislocations that are felt to go with them" ("Heracles and Greek Tragedy," 127). For a discussion of the Heracles myth in the context of Indo-European myth, see Puhvel: "Heracles' career is punctuated by three great crimes. . . . These misdeeds resemble most closely the 'three sins' of Indra" (*Comparative Mythology,* 242). On the tensions in the hero figure, he observes: "The warlord himself could be an equally self-willed individualist and from inspired and inspiring leader shade over into a lone-wolf kind of figure. The warrior thus had an ambivalent role as a single champion or part of a self-centered corps or coterie, both a society's defender or its potential internal menace" (242). On the double nature of Heracles, see also Kott: "The myth of Hercules remained broken up until the end of the classical period and was never put together in a complete whole. . . . A thousand years later the Hercules on Roman reliefs, conquering a wild boar or a hydra, became the model for St. Michael or St. George slaying the dragon. Hercules the savior . . . bears a striking resemblance to the archangels storming the gates of hell." Heracles "became a Christ figure. Christ is even called 'the Christian Hercules'" (*Eating of the Gods,* 113).

11. Hamilton, "Neoptolemos' Story in the *Philoktetes,*" analyzes the two opposing stories enacted in this play. This ode completely ignores Neoptolemus's story, and the part of the chorus in bringing that story to completion; instead, it sings throughout of that other story, of which Heracles is the paradigm.

12. See Finkelberg on the cult of Heracles on Mount Oeta. She suggests that Heracles' apotheosis may have originated in Athens in the sixth century. The familiarity of this cult to Athenians who might be watching Sophocles' *Trachiniae,* which depicts the full horror of Heracles' death, would make that play "a far more profound tragedy" ("Second Stasimon," 140). The same cult, but now including also the cult of Philoctetes, would enhance the meaning of this ode and also Heracles' appearance at the end of the play. "Anyone accustomed to think archetypically of literature will recognize in tragedy a mimesis of sacrifice" (Frye, *Anatomy of Criticism,* 214).

Chapter 7. The Second Episode

1. On this scream, which surpasses any language, see Knox, *Heroic Temper,* 130–31; also Kott on the horror of the wound and Philoctetes' suffering: "Sophocles, the most cruel of Greek tragedians, never shrinks from the physical image

of agony" (*Eating of the Gods*, 166). See also Stephens, "Wound of Philoctetes," 166–67. Stephens argues that many scholars, taking the wound "as a literally insignificant, but symbolically fertile, stage prop" turn the play "into a trite, even dramatic, conflict between good and bad" (168).

2. Neoptolemus in this play has generated considerable debate. This is understandable. The figure of Neoptolemus is one of the most remarkable inventions in all of Greek tragedy. It also represents one of the most complex ideas in Greek tragedy. All the deeper issues of the play—language, character, plot, truth versus deceit, means versus ends—come to a focus in Neoptolemus. He provokes, therefore, a wide spectrum of interpretations. At one extreme is Calder, "Sophoclean Apologia," who does not believe that Neoptolemus changes between the beginning of the play and the end. Carol Gould gives a good survey of the recent scholarship on this issue. She argues that only Philoctetes is shown as having a moral character. Neoptolemus, she argues, "is striking not so much for his pity for the wounded hero, but for the instability of his emotions" ("Moral Dilemma," 212). She goes on to say that he "prefigures a personality Plato describes in his *Republic*—the democratic soul, the person whose values are all on a par, with none prior to another, the person whose choices are arbitrary, as if selected by lot (*Rep*. 8.561a–562a)" (ibid.). It is difficult for me to accept that Sophocles would invent one of the most interesting and innovative characters in Greek tragedy only to have us believe that this character, the son of Achilles, has none of the virtues of Achilles but from beginning to end is as corrupt as the Odysseus of this play, and utterly callous. To Gould's thoughtful suggestion that Neoptolemus represents Plato's "democratic soul," we might counter that Plato is much more concerned with the perfected soul than with the soul in its growth toward perfection. Even the morally upright soul must become such by trial and error. At the opposite end is Kitto: "The part of Neoptolemus has a much wider range than any other extant in Greek tragedy. . . . If any Greek play can be said to show development of character, it is this one" (*Greek Tragedy*, 299). The various readings of Neoptolemus can be situated like points along this line. Kott sides with Calder: "But this Neoptolemus, who grows morally and whose character changes exists only in Kitto's reading of the play. The heroes of Greek tragedy, and especially Sophoclean tragedy, do not change, nor do those in the subplot rise to heroic heights. From the beginning of the drama to the end, Sophocles' Neoptolemus is a young man who is devoured by ambition and whose unchanging trait is instability" (*Eating of the Gods*, 178). This reading presents several challenges. First, Neoptolemus is unlike other characters in Greek tragedy. Second, Neoptolemus is far from being a subordinate character. His part in the plot is not a subplot; it is the play itself. When Heracles appears at the end of the play, he treats Philoctetes and Neoptolemus as equals; they will range at the front like two lions. The two were associated in the ancient myth, but the myth brought them into convergence only at Troy. Sophocles' invention is to bring them into conflict and convergence on

Lemnos. Thus he has woven the fortuitous coincidence of the myth into the dramatic structure of this play, making Neoptolemus go through his own tragic crisis. For views more sympathetic to Neoptolemus as a character, see Goldhill, "Great Dionysia," 118–23; Kirkwood, *Study of Sophoclean Drama*, 158–60; Nussbaum, "Consequences and Character," 25–53; Heath, *Poetics of Greek Tragedy*; Blundell, "*Phusis* of Neoptolemus," 104–15; Stokes, "Two Questions on Sophocles' *Philoctetes*"; Belfiore, "*Xenia in Sophocles' Philoctetes*." In the appendix to the present volume, 211–12, I address the complications in plot and character brought into the play by having Neoptolemus introduced as a character.

3. Kott considers this play as bleak as any play in the ancient tragic repertoire (*Eating of the Gods*, 162–85), and certainly it could be argued that Phthonos as used here is an essential element in that bleak landscape. When Sophocles introduces words like "Phthonos" (Jealousy), he reminds us of the root and origin of tragedy.

4. On the volcano on Lemnos, see Jebb's commentary at v. 800 and his appendix, pp. 242–45. He gives us a note of mythological significance for this play, that "Lemnos was celebrated in antiquity, and down to very recent times, for producing a kind of earth which was believed to have a medicinal value in various maladies, and more especially to be an antidote for poisons" (243). He quotes Galen's description of the hill from which this earth is taken as "looking exactly as if it had been burned—both in color, and by the absence of all vegetation" (244). This is a provocative suggestion, that Lemnos was barren yet at the same time had healing properties in its earth.

5. Belfiore, "*Xenia* in Sophocles' *Philoctetes*," adds that a strong element in the bond created between Philoctetes and Neoptolemus is *xenia*, that formalization of a friendship between two persons originally strangers, who become as close as family. *Xenia* was an institution supported by many unwritten and divine laws.

6. The question of character in Greek tragedy is complex and controversial. The older view is that we are misled if we search for "character" in Greek tragedy. Lloyd-Jones notes with approval the view of Tycho von Wilamowitz-Moellendorff that Sophocles "cared nothing for consistency of character; the behavior of his people was always determined by the situation of the moment" (*Greek Epic, Lyric, and Tragedy*, 404). Heath considers that in this play Neoptolemus's hostility to deception is an extreme position, that Sophocles was oversimplifying a more complex problem. He questions whether Neoptolemus can be said to mature as a moral agent ("Sophocles' Philoctetes," 142–45). Easterling argues that Neoptolemus's question (at vv. 755, 895, 908, 974, 1393) "'What am I to do?' gives a clear signal to the spectators that his moral perplexity is a significant dramatic issue" ("Form and Performance," 162). See also her earlier essay "Constructing Character in Greek Tragedy"; Pelling, *Characterization and Individuality*; Gill, "Bow, Oracle, and Epiphany," 98–99, at Neoptolemus's growing moral repulsion at his theft of the bow; also Blundell, "*Phusis* of Neoptolemus,"

104–15. We can agree that Sophocles perhaps oversimplifies the political issue—the use of theft and deception to achieve a necessary political objective—the nature of Greek tragedy as a performance for a large and diverse public makes for simplifications. Yet Sophocles has created in Neoptolemus a character of greater complexity than any character in his other plays, and it would be peculiar for the poet to invest so much of his art in this character only for the character to have no effect on the plot or the moral issues. Kirkwood writes that Sophocles has placed clues so that we see that Neoptolemus's change of mind happens over a period of time. He speaks of "careful psychological accuracy in Sophoclean characterization. Of course the psychological accuracy is not for its own sake. Psychology here subserves plot development, but that does not make it any less real" (*Sophoclean Drama*, 160). I am grateful for the insights in a paper written by Jason Herman for the Philoctetes course that I taught in 2002.

7. C. Gould, "Moral Dilemma."

8. The question of Neoptolemus's character is bound up with the larger issue of decision making in Greek tragedy. On this point, see Snell, *Discovery of the Mind*, 101–8; Rosenmeyer, "Decision-Making," 187–218; Buxton, *Persuasion in Greek Tragedy*. Rosenmeyer writes: "Decision-making on stage, the dramatized contemplation of alternatives, and the consequent selection of one of them for enactment, is a subordinate feature in Greek drama" ("Decision-Making, 194). He adds: "In tragedy, it is obvious that technical choices, the selection of the better means toward a goal, were of less interest than the great moral dilemmas" (ibid., 213). This is true, but the *Philoctetes* differs from most other tragedies in this as in many other respects. The moral issues are certainly of paramount importance, and they can be rendered down to one: are humans to be used by other humans as a means, or are they ends in themselves? This play, in my view, revolves around the idea of *personhood*. The shifting dialectic as this question is formulated gives decision making an extraordinary role in the plot. We see both Philoctetes and Neoptolemus wrestling with the concept of their own personhood. This play represents this struggle as a complex enigma, which includes destiny, social obligations, character, relations to the gods, and the quest for personal *eudaimonia*.

9. Arist., *Rh.* 1371a21. "Cherished" is J. H. Freese's translation, his attempt to differentiate in English the two words that Aristotle uses for "love." See the Perseus texts.

Chapter 8. The First Kommos

1. Sophocles, *Plays and Fragments*, Jebb's note at vv. 827–64.

2. "Thus, the climax of the tragedy, corresponding to the crucial moment, the agon, in the passion of Dionysus, was commonly cast in a distinctive form which embodied the remains of the primitive dithyramb—a musical dialogue between the leader and his *thiasos*" (Thomson, *Aeschylus and Athens*, 187).

Thomson also writes that the normal place for the kommos "is immediately before or after the tragic crisis. It is properly a 'beating of the breast'—that is to say, a *thrēnos* or lament" (ibid.) The kommos form is used twice in this play; once here, and then again almost at the end of the play, vv. 1081–1217, and both occur at moments of crisis. Here, where Neoptolemus joins with the chorus, it is his crisis; later, when Philoctetes is the singer, the crisis is his. Kirkwood notes that the kommoi in this play "achieve what might be called the basic function of the kommos—to signal and emphasize moments of great emotional stress" (*Study of Sophoclean Drama*, 190).

3. The word has prompted a number of readings. Jebb calls it "'dream-light,'—such as illuminates the visions that come in sleep" (Sophocles, *Plays and Fragments*, Jebb's note at vv. 830–31). He adds that Pausanias (2.10.2) records seeing a statue of Hypnos (Sleep) at Sicyon. The chorus, in singing this ode, calls on Hypnos as *Paion*, that is, the "Healer." This statue of Hypnos in Sicyon stood near the Asclepeion, and "Aigle" (Gleam or Radiance) was also the name of the daughter of Asclepius. Jebb notes also that these verses remind us of a statue of Hypnos now in Vienna: "The Sleep-god is advancing softly; his head is bent; a kindly smile is on his face; his eyes are half-closed; and in his outstretched right hand he holds the horn from which the poppy-juice (μηκώνιον [*mekonion*]) is to be shed on weary mortals. The right hand (as replicas show) once held a poppy-stalk—answering to the ῥάβδος [*rhabdos*] with which Hermes seals the eyes of men" (Jebb's note at v. 827). Pucci suggests that this is the light that emanates from the presence of the god (Sophocles, *Filottete*, Pucci's note at vv. 830–31).

4. Sophocles, *Plays and Fragments*, Jebb's note at v. 837.

5. Ibid., Jebb's note at vv. 839–40.

6. For further discussion of this problem, see the appendix to the present volume, 211–12.

7. "In a new meter, the hexameter, the medium of heroic poetry and divine prophecy, he states clearly what his objective has so far been as he renounces it forever" (Knox, *Heroic Temper*, 131). Segal writes of the paradoxes of this situation: "The sleeping invalid who lies collapsed before the strong, erect Neoptolemus looks like anything but the bearer of the crown of valor at Troy. Yet Neoptolemus begins to have a glimpse of the true strength and valor beneath the devastated exterior of the older man" (*Interpreting Greek Tragedy*, 123).

8. Pl., *Resp*. 10.613b–c.

9. "Neoptolemus' men are doggedly loyal to the stratagem even after the youth himself has grown sick of it" (Kirkwood, *Study of Sophoclean Drama*, 187).

Chapter 9. The Third Episode

1. In the fifth-century debates, the two terms *physis* and *nomos* (nature versus custom or convention) were in constant use. Much has been written on this

debate in ancient Greece. See Annas, *Introduction to Plato's Republic*, 7; Adkins, *Moral Values*; Carlevale, "Education, *Phusis*, and Freedom," 46. In the older culture, under assault in the fifth century, ethos was rooted in nature (*physis*). The innate ethos of the boy would be nurtured by a basic education in music and literacy, and in the manly skills to be acquired in athletics and physical exercises. But the most significant component of the old education was the young man's association (*synousia*) with the older men of his class. Carlevale discusses this education in its relevance for this play.

2. On the respective value of the cooperative versus the competitive values in Homer and more generally in ancient Greek thought, see Adkins, *From the Many to the One*; Cairns, *AIDOS*.

3. "Neoptolemus is not truly himself but a persona—a walking, talking deception" (Carlevale, "Education, *Phusis*, and Freedom," 39).

4. Webster suggests that Sophocles has given this sound *papai* to Neoptolemus at this point to indicate that "Neoptolemus' mental agony is parallel to Philoctetes' physical agony" (Sophocles, Philoctetes, note at v. 895).

5. On this crisis, see Easterling, "Form and Performance," 162; see also, on language in the play as a whole, Goldhill, "Language of Tragedy," 141–45. "The function of words used on stage is not so much to establish communication between the various characters as to indicate the blockage and barriers between them . . . to locate the points of conflict" (Vernant and Vidal-Naquet, *Myth and Tragedy*, 42, quoted in Goldhill, "Language of Tragedy," 136).

6. Herodotus (5.67) writes that the people of Sicyon celebrated *ta pathea* (the sufferings) of the hero Adrastus with "tragic choruses." This is our oldest extant reference to tragic choruses and to the content of such choruses. For a good study of *pathos* in ancient Greek, in its usage in religion and in Aristotle, and for its bearing on Greek tragedy, see T. Gould, *Ancient Quarrel*.

7. *Pathos* was honored by the Greeks "as the most vital moment in religion and art, feared by others as an enticement to sacrilege and irrationality" (T. Gould, *Ancient Quarrel*, ix).

8. Aultman-Moore notes the double entendre in the word *ethos* as used in this passage. Philoctetes assures Neoptolemus (v. 894) that he needs no assistance; his own customary habit will get him to his feet. Neoptolemus internalizes this and translates it into moral terms. His *pathos* "stems from some deep *interior* disturbance" ("Moral Pain," 310). Neoptolemus translates Philoctetes words into a question that he directs at himself: "Will my customary character, my true moral identity, set me upright" (310).

9. On shame culture, see Dodds, *Greeks and the Irrational*; Adkins, *Moral Values*. Williams does not believe that when Neoptolemus decides to put aside shame in the prologos (v. 120), he does not mean "'I'll put up with the shame." Williams argues that Neoptolemus, while cast in the mold of the heroic warrior, "is one for whom the standard by which he measures his own worth quite clearly involves values beyond so-called competitive success" (*Shame and*

Necessity, 88). Whatever meaning Sophocles intended Neoptolemus to associate with the idea of shame in the prologos, in the crisis of this episode he has moved Neoptolemus to a much deeper sense of shame.

10. Decision making is a profound element in ancient Greek tragedy. See Snell, *Discovery of the Mind*, 99–108; Rosenmeyer, "Decision-Making." Note Snell on choice in the plays of Aeschylus: "In Aeschylus, the hero's choice becomes a problem whose solution is contingent on nothing but his own insight, but which is nevertheless regarded as a matter of compelling necessity" (103). Since Neoptolemus seems to be a lesser character in this play than Philoctetes, the obvious protagonist, it is insufficiently recognized that Neoptolemus is required to make three momentous decisions in the play (disclosing the *sophisma*, returning the bow, and joining forces with Philoctetes), all strictly based on his own insight, and each sufficient to place him in the company of the tragic protagonists of the Athenian theater. See Kitto on the character of Neoptolemus: "If any Greek play can be said to show development of character, it is this one. If the spiritual journey which befalls Neoptolemus is not very close indeed to the real theme of the play, Sophocles has miscalculated badly, for we cannot imagine that any responsive audience would have been disposed to give its serious attention to something else" (*Greek Tragedy*, 299). On the question of character, see also Easterling, "Character in Sophocles," 138–45. She writes: "There are times, if we are honest, when we are made uneasy by the extremely public nature of his characters, as indeed by that of all characters in Greek tragedy. This is no doubt because the Greeks were interested in individuals as part of a community much more than in the individual's unique private experience, a difference of attitude which is sometimes hard for us to share or appreciate" (145).

11. "By the later fifth century the Greeks had their own distinctions between a shame that merely followed public opinion and a shame that expressed inner personal conviction" (Williams, *Shame and Necessity*, 95). Williams also notes: "The play of Sophocles that is most remarkably involved in the workings of shame, the expectation of it and its attempted avoidance, is the *Philoctetes*" (87). On shame in this play, see also Konstan, *Emotions of the Ancient Greeks*.

12. Cf. Kott: "The delegates of authority always begin with the Great Necessity. . . . If a prisoner believes in the Great Necessity he is lost forever" (*Eating of the Gods*, 172).

13. For Pandora as artifice, see Hes., *Theog.*, 569–89; *Op.*, 59–82.

14. The two instances in Sophocles where the usage of the word *psychē* implies it as "the seat of knowledge" both occur in this play (v. 55, in the prologos, and here in this passage, vv. 1013–14): "These instances belong to the very close of the century and anticipate the usage of the next" (Burnet, "Socratic Doctrine of the Soul," 156).

15. Knox notes that Odysseus treats Philoctetes like a slave, but even more important for the play's theme are the scathing references to Odysseus's slavish condition (*Heroic Temper*, 134).

16. Knox, *Heroic Temper*. See especially his first two chapters.

17. Hom., *Od.* 8.216–25, translation by Albert Cook.

18. See Sophocles, *Philoctetes*, Webster's note at v. 1055 on the motivation here, and his reference to A. E. Hinds (in Webster, *Tragedies of Euripides*, 177). Webster at v. 1055 takes up the possibility that "Odysseus is playing his last card: 'we don't need you.'" But he considers this maneuver to be too complicated for the audience watching the play. On the contrary, it is not at all complicated. The issues are boldly underlined: the terms are victory or defeat. Odysseus has already insisted that neither force nor persuasion can achieve the objective in this present instance. Guile is all. It would not be difficult for clever Athenians of the fifth century to assume that Odysseus, in airily dismissing all debate and threatening to wield the bow himself, would be still working his *sophisma*. Now that Neoptolemus has failed, Odysseus must take over the plot himself.

19. See Shay, *Achilles in Vietnam*, for his discussion of the importance of trust in the military environment of the *Iliad*.

20. On the "name of the father," see Lacan, *Four Fundamental Concepts of Psycho-analysis*, 281–82.

Chapter 10. The Second Kommos

1. Aristotle understands that tragedy developed from earlier improvisations, "from those leading out the chorus of the dithyramb" (*Poet.* 1449a). On this point, see Pickard-Cambridge: "It cannot be doubted that Aristotle thought of the [first] actor as the *exarchon* of the dithyramb. . . . The *exarchon* must have been transformed into an actor, when he delivered a speech (not a song), in which the chorus did not join in" (*Dithyramb, Tragedy and Comedy*, 90). In an ode like this kommos, while Philoctetes remains at all times the "actor," he has taken on the attributes of the *exarchon* of the ode, leading the song, with the chorus making the response.

2. Sophocles, *Philoctetes*, Webster's note at v. 1081.

3. The normal place for the kommos "is immediately before or after the tragic crisis. It is properly 'a beating of the breast'—that is to say, a *threnos* or lament" (Thomson, *Aeschylus and Athens*, 187).

4. Hegel, *Hegel on Tragedy*, 65.

5. Ibid.

6. Ibid., 325.

7. "The root *dai-* is ambiguous," because the verb *daiō* "means to divide, not to apportion" (Burkert, *Greek Religion*, 420n3). But surely division, at least when undertaken by a divinity, is apportionment.

8. The hero's misfortune can be summed up as his *daimon*: "In Greek there is a word for this type of divine power, which is not usually individualized and which takes action at the very heart of men's lives, usually to ill-fated effect and

in a variety of forms: It is *daimon*" (Vernant and Vidal-Naquet, *Myth and Tragedy*, 36). The strength of this play lies in its thesis that one's *daimon* is one's own choice.

9. Diels, *Die Fragmente der Vorsokratiker*.

10. Kahn, *Art and Thought of Heraclitus*, 260–61.

11. Ibid., 261.

12. Pl., *Resp.*, 617.

13. Annas, *Introduction to Plato's Republic*, 349.

14. Pl., *Resp.*, 10.617

15. Pl., *Ap.*, 31D. Socrates calls this presence *theion* and *daimonion*, "something both divine and daemonic." He adds that Meletus had in jest made this part of the indictment against Socrates; presumably he is referring to the charge made by Meletus that Socrates did not accept the gods that the city worshipped but believed in "other new *daimonia*." For a lengthy discussion in antiquity regarding Socrates' *daimonion*, see Plutarch, "On the Sign of Socrates" (*De gen.*), *Mor.* 575A–598. In that dialogue, Galaxidorus argues that it was no more than Socrates' keen perception of chance omens such as a sneeze or a passing remark. Another interlocutor, Simmias, offers a more profound analysis, bringing out its semantic significance as a kind of *daimon*. For him Socrates' *daimonion* was certainly the expression of an intimate relationship between Socrates and the gods.

16. Dickinson, *Poems of Emily Dickinson*, 358, no. 817.

17. Sophocles, *Philoctetes*, Webster's note at v. 1095.

18. Kierkegaard, *Sickness unto Death*, 43.

19. On the wound: "Inwardly it is correlative of Philoctetes' bitter soul, the poisonous hatred rankling in him all these years" (*Tragedy and Civilization*, 316). Cf. Kott: "The incurable wound is a sacred wound as well. The serpent is an archetype of the invisible becoming visible. Philoctetes became a leper to people because he was chosen to fulfill his given role" (*Eating of the Gods*, 168).

20. Wilamowitz-Moellendorff, *Die dramatische Technik des Sophocles*, argues that much effort has been misspent by modern scholars to give subtle psychological interpretations to the characters of Greek tragedy, whereas dramatists, especially Sophocles, shared little of our modern interest in character consistency. Their characters' behavior was determined more by the poet's understanding of the dramatic requirements of the moment. Character has for moderns become the most essential aspect of tragedy, but Wilamowitz-Moellendorff follows Aristotle in arguing that the characters of ancient tragedy are there for the plot, rather than the plot serving to reveal character. For Easterling's remarks on this topic, see above, 239n10.

21. Hegel, *Hegel on Tragedy*, 65.

22. Ibid., 141.

23. Ibid.

24. "The individuals who have aimed at the realization in themselves of a single separate moral power, perish" (ibid., 325).

25. Kohut, "Thoughts on Narcissism," 149.

26. Ibid., 148–49. Kohut cites Melville's *Moby-Dick* as a great example of "the insatiable search for revenge after a narcissistic injury" (125).

27. Sophocles, *Philoctetes*, Webster's note at v. 1136.

28. Ibid., Webster's note at v. 1128.

29. Buber, *I and Thou*.

30. Hegel, *Hegel on Tragedy*, 292.

31. Sophocles, *Philoctetes*, Webster's note at vv. 1134–35.

32. On the problems in the text and possible constructions, see Sophocles, *Philoctetes*, Webster's note at v. 1132.

33. On the wound, see Padel: "In tragedy, one of the sharper models of *theia nosos, nosos* [*disease*] caused by a divinity, and how it impinges on others, is Philoctetes' festering foot. A 'raw-minded' nymph sent it because he trod on her snake in that cave shrine" (*Whom Gods Destroy*, 158). "Sophocles did not put his heart into this argument" (Mandel, *Philoctetes*, 24–25). It is true that for Sophocles the emphasis is much less on the original "fault" than on the present, when Philoctetes has the power to free himself from his illness. But, as Mandel writes, "this tale of disturbing Chryse may have been deeply rooted, as we shall see, in the pre-Trojan myth. It takes us back to a world of brutal spirits who punish accidental infractions without the slightest consideration of pure or impure motive. No wonder it flits in and out of Sophocles' work without leaving a trace" (ibid., 25). Philoctetes' wound "is god-sent, deserved," deserved because gods punish humans for "'not noticing, "forgetting, and treading on sacred snakes" (Padel, *Whom Gods Destroy*, 201). Stephens also dismisses the grounds for Philoctetes affliction as superficial; of the explanation given at vv. 191–200, he writes that this "is hardly a sophisticated analysis" ("Wound of Philoctetes," 157). The harsh treatment of this "noble and innocent hero," he continues, leaves modern critics annoyed and "understandably, tempts us into supplying some teleological explanation" (ibid.). But the etiology of Philoctetes' physical disease and its place in the divine order could not be more plainly stated. In this kommos and then in the subsequent exodos, where Neoptolemus lays forth the complete story, Philoctetes' responsibility is stated at several points and in several different ways.

34. Sophocles, *Philoctetes*, Webster's note at v. 1167.

35. Ibid., Webster's note at vv. 1081–1217.

36. Woolf, "On Not Knowing Greek," 7.

37. Concerning this *daimon* of tragedy, Vernant writes of the tragic hero in the grip of "a daemonic power in every way beyond him . . . a sinister *numen* that manifests itself in many guises" (Vernant and Vidal-Naquet, *Myth and Tragedy in Ancient Greece*, 35). In this play, however, the protagonist is explicitly told that he holds the power over this *daimon*. This is not that same tragic *daimon* such as we see in Sophocles' *Ajax* or in Euripides' *Heracles*.

38. On this wound, see Kott: "Religious scholars and anthropologists consider a wound in the leg and difficulty in walking signs of relations with

chthonic deities" (*Eating of the Gods*, 167). "The incurable wound is a sacred wound as well" (168).

39. Hegel, *Hegel on Tragedy*, 291–92.

40. Madness of one kind or another is one of the great themes of ancient Greek tragedy. There is no agency in this play that makes Philoctetes insane; it is easy to overlook, therefore, the full extent of his irrational state. But see Padel: "Madness, disease, pollution, divine anger, all reinforce each other's meaning. The images interplay. We may see them as separate fountain jets. But in Greece they make one stream" (*Whom Gods Destroy*, 158).

41. Kohut, *Self Psychology and the Humanities*, 100. The motivation for self-mutilation and suicide in psychotics is "due to the fact that a break-up of the body-self has occurred and that the fragments of the body-self that cannot be retained within the total organization of the body-self become an unbearably painful burden and are therefore removed" (139).

42. Waldock, *Sophocles the Dramatist*, 196–97.

43. "The wound's force is that of a devouring woman, the prostitute or the wandering witch" (Greengard, *Theater in Crisis*, 44). "The inhuman savagery which surrounds Philoctetes on his island is closely bound up with the mysterious goddess, Chryse, 'the golden.'" (*Tragedy and Civilization*, 308). The "Mother" appears in the first choral ode of the play when the chorus, in the parodos, claims that it had called on the Great Mother to witness the injustices done to Neoptolemus by the leaders of the Greek army. Given the absence of the female presence in the play, this choral song is doubly ironic since there never was a call to the Great Mother; it is part of the invention. Concerning this choral entrance, Reinhardt writes that "the traditional form, the pathos of tragic misfortune together with the support given to it by the entry of the chorus, is deprived of the original meaning and brought instead into the interplay of illusion and reality" (*Sophocles*, 180). For a fuller discussion of the broader question of females in Greek tragedy, see Foley, *Female Acts in Greek Tragedy*.

44. Both the *Ajax* and the *Philoctetes* "belong in their different ways to the pathology of heroism" (Winnington-Ingram, *Sophocles*, 305).

45. Even in tragedies with female characters who "struggle with the conflicts generated by the particularities of their subordinate social position, their demands for identity and self-esteem are still designed primarily for exploring the male project of selfhood in the larger world" (Zeitlin, *Playing the Other*, 347).

46. See Lacan on "the-name-of-the-father," as the signifier of the Father who, insofar as he signifies the law, "is certainly the dead father" (*Four Fundamental Concepts of Psycho-analysis*, 281–82).

Chapter 11. The Exodos

1. The names for the parts of a Greek play are given by Aristotle, *Poet*. 12 (1452b).

2. Heraclitus, frag. 51 (Diels); Kahn, *Art and Thought of Heraclitus*, 78.

3. The protagonist of a tragedy ought not to be "outstanding in either virtue or justice, and should not fall into misfortune through evil and depravity, but through some kind of *mistake* [*hamartia*]" (Arist., *Poet.* 13 [1453a]).

4. For a fuller discussion see Bremer, *Hamartia*; for a brief overview, see Kittel, *Theological Dictionary*, 1:293–302. Bremer defines *hamartia* as used by Aristotle in *Poet.* 1453a as "'*tragic error*,' i.e., a wrong action committed in ignorance of its nature, effect, etc., which is the starting point of a causally connected train of events ending in disaster" (*Hamartia*, 63). It is not, he argues, a "tragic flaw," i.e., some kind of moral weakness or defect of character. We are advised to avoid any Hebrew or Christian sense of "sin" in our interpretation of *hamartia* in the pagan authors, but where it appears in Greek tragedy, it certainly connotes the gravest kind of moral offense. In Aeschylus, *Agamemnon*, the word is used twice in its strongest sense; at v. 537 the herald who brings the news of Agamemnon's victory at Troy says: "Twofold is the penalty the sons of Priam have paid for their *hamartia*." At v. 1197, the house of Atreus falls under the same indictment, as Cassandra says: "Can you bear witness and swear an oath that you have not known the ancient *hamartias* [pl.] of this house?" Cf. also Aesch., *PV* 9, where Kratos (Strength) explains that Prometheus must now pay the penalty for his *hamartia* against the gods, when he gave fire to humans. In Soph., *Ant.* 1257–60, the chorus, seeing Creon carrying the corpse of his son Haemon onto the stage, observes, "He bears in his hands the reminder, if it is lawful to say so, that this ruin came not from some external source but because he himself committed this *hamartia*." In such instances, where *hamartia* leads to tragic consequences, while it is certainly error, it seems to point strongly in the direction of moral wrongdoing.

5. Gorgias again adds an interesting perspective on *hamartia* when he links it with *sophos*. In his *Palamedes*, frag. DK 26, he has Palamedes argue that if he were wise (*sophos*), he would not have committed the crime (using the verb *hamartanō*); and if he had committed the crime, he was not *sophos*. Freeman translates thus: "If I am wise, I did not err. If I erred, I am not wise" (*Ancilla*, 136). But Palamedes is here making his defense against the charges brought against him by Odysseus, that he had betrayed the Greeks to the Trojans, for which, if true, he would deserve the death penalty. Surely we need some stronger idea than "error" in this passage.

6. On the comic Odysseus in this play, see Taplin, *Greek Tragedy in Action*, 37; Kirkwood, "Persuasion," 430.

7. Hegel, *Hegel on Tragedy*, 141; see above, 160.

8. Hegel, *Hegel on Tragedy*, 325; see above, 160–61.

9. Cf. Virginia Woolf: "She looked up over her knitting and met the third stroke and it seemed to her like her own eyes meeting her own eyes, searching as she alone could search into her mind and heart, purifying out of existence that lie, any lie" (*To the Lighthouse*, 63).

10. On the *phthonos* of the dead, see Johnston, *Restless Dead*, 190–93. On human *phthonos*, she writes: "The envier desires not so much to obtain what someone else has as to deprive the possessor of it. . . . Satisfaction of many types of envy, therefore, comes only from ensuring that no one else possesses what you cannot possess" (190).

Chapter 12. Heracles

1. Pl., *Cra.*, 425d.
2. See Winnington-Ingram: Sophoclean irony derives from "invoking a transcendental realm from which more permanent realities of the world emerge as inherently intractable to mere human efforts, either at comprehension or control" (*Sophocles*, 267). See also Taplin, "Significant Actions," 35–36.
3. Whitman, *Sophocles*, 187. Heracles' epiphany has been the subject of much discussion. For various views, see Kirkwood, who argues that Philoctetes' acceptance of Heracles' command has little to do with Philoctetes' reintegration into the Greek army but serves to fulfill "the relationship of heroic excellence established between Philoctetes and Neoptolemus" ("Persuasion," 425). On the quality of Heracles' speech, see Kitto: "Nowhere in the whole of Sophocles is there a speech less impressive than this one which he wrote for Heracles" (*Greek Tragedy*, 105). See also Pucci, "Gods' Intervention," 31–36. He recognizes Heracles' epiphany as an element extraneous to the preceding human drama and writes: "It is autonomous in character and encroaches, as an alien discourse, on the end of the play" (31). See also Rabel, "Sophocles' *Philoctetes*," 301; Podlecki, "Power of the Word," 245. Both Whitman and Kirkwood argue that Heracles' appearance is not a real epiphany. Kirkwood writes: "Heracles' appearance is not a matter of 'entrance.' He has been in the play from the beginning" (426). But the bow and the god's actual appearance are two different matters. His live appearance is an example of the deus ex machina both in the technical sense and in Plato's sense of the term, as a god brought into to resolve a problem for which there is no other solution.
4. Winnington-Ingram, *Sophocles*, 267. See also Taplin: "The play reaches at 1217 a real, though morbid, end" ("Significant Actions," 36). But then the play begins again after v. 1217, with its momentum provided by "the personal moral sense of Neoptolemus" (ibid.). See also Robinson, "Topics in Sophocles' *Philoctetes*," 51–56.
5. Whitman, *Sophocles*, 188.
6. Ibid., 187.
7. This distinction, between the hero of local civic cults and the hero of epic, is complex, since it is an intricate weaving of cultural attitudes based on such oppositions as human and divine, present and past, death and immortality. See Nagy, *Best of the Achaeans*, esp. chap. 10, 174–210.
8. On Heracles' cult on Mount Oeta, see Sophocles, *Plays and Fragments*,

Jebb's note at v. 1431; also Burkert, *Greek Religion*, 210. Burkert relates the theme of immolation and apotheosis in the Heracles myth to Near Eastern tradition.

9. Whitman, *Sophocles*, 187.

10. In evaluating Heracles' epiphany, perhaps we should consider that one of the greatest of all anomalies in ancient Greek myth was that Heracles was both a human and a god.

11. Blundell argues that Heracles' intervention "demonstrates the impasse to which the characters have been brought by their various incompatible claims and convictions. The arrival of Heracles pinpoints the insoluble nature of the conflicting demands on Neoptolemus and Philoctetes. In particular, it confirms the danger of Help Friends/Harm Enemies in two different ways. Philoctetes is unable to live up to both principles, and is forced to sacrifice one to the other. Neoptolemus is unable to help all his friends, and must choose between them at severe cost to himself" (*Helping Friends and Harming Enemies*, 224). Heracles, she argues, represents *philia*, friendship based on shared values. Amid the contradictions, trust must be created.

12. Whitman, *Sophocles*, 188

13. Weiss and Sampson, "Unconscious Pathogenic Beliefs."

14. Ibid., 70.

15. Ibid., 68.

16. Bergson, *Creative Evolution*, 109–10.

17. Kierkegaard, *Sickness unto Death*, 103.

18. Ibid., 103.

19. Ibid., 104.

20. Arendt, *Human Condition*, 236.

21. Ibid., 236.

22. Ibid., 237.

23. "No stronger impression arises from the resistance during the work of analysis than of there being a force which is defending itself by every possible means against recovery and which is absolutely resolved to hold on to illness and suffering" (Freud, "Analysis Terminable and Interminable," 242).

24. Arendt, *Human Condition*, 237.

25. Ibid., 241.

26. Winnington-Ingram, *Sophocles*, 311: when a hero suffers a wrong it "totally dominates his mind, it divides his world into friends and enemies."

27. Pl., *Ap.* 41d. Plato opens a space in his eschatology for forgiveness when he has Socrates discussing the fate of certain sinners in the underworld, those who have committed acts of passion, either manslaughter or acts of violence against a parent (*Phd.* 114a–b). Such crimes are grave, Socrates says, but they *can be healed*, if the criminals lived in repentance after their crimes and if after death they are released from Tartarus by those whom they have wronged. Several ideas are brought together here in a nexus of associations—transgression, purgatory, penitence, forgiveness, healing, and rebirth—but their connection is

barely more than an intuition, and the remedy is limited to only one class of wrongdoers.

28. Arendt, *Human Condition*, 238.

29. On the ethics of this code, see Blundell, *Helping Friends and Harming Enemies*, esp. chap. 6, 184–225, on the *Philoctetes*.

30. Sophocles, *Plays and Fragments*, Jebb's note at v. 1420.

31. Jaeger, *Paideia*; see esp. 201–22. See also Herington: "The sagas could show male and female characters who illustrated almost every tint of the moral spectrum" (*Poetry into Drama*, 68).

32. Budelmann quotes a passage from Lesky that perfectly captures the meaning of *aretē* at this point in the *Philoctetes*: "The deep piety which has made Sophocles' tragedies moving ever since antiquity is nurtured by traditional religion and yet it grows beyond it. It grows to the heights of a piety which is fully aware of the extent of human misery and vulnerability and which, despite this horror and in this horror, worships the divine" (Lesky, *Die tragische Dichtung*, 270, quoted in Budelmann, *Language of Sophocles*, 136, Budelmann's translation).

33. Rabel observes that the word *mythos*, as used in Heracles' own speech and in Philoctetes' response, "signals their mutual recognition of the operation of time-honored methods of heroic persuasion characteristic of the world of epic" ("Sophocles' *Philoctetes*," 301). This idea is shared by Podlecki and Pucci. While a sound observation, it may also lead us to overlook the destructiveness of heroic passions both in the epic and in mythology.

34. "The essence of dramatic tragedy is not unhappiness. It resides in the solemnity of the remorseless working of things. This inevitableness of destiny can only be illustrated in terms of human life by incidents which in fact involve unhappiness. For it is only by them that the futility of escape can be made evident in drama. This remorseless inevitableness is what pervades scientific thought" (Whitehead, *Science and the Modern World*, 10–11).

35. Kierkegaard, *Sickness unto Death*, 68.

36. Ibid.

37. Whitman, *Sophocles*, 188.

38. See Sophocles, *Trachiniae* 1046–63.

39. Sophocles, *Trachiniae* 1259–63. On this Heracles, see Zeitlin, *Playing the Other*, 347, who reminds us Deianeira and her misfortunes are a foil for the heroizing process by which Heracles comes to fulfill his tragic destiny.

40. Foley, *Female Acts in Greek Tragedy*, 95.

41. Carracci's painting *The Choice of Heracles* is now in Galleria Nazionale di Capodimonte in Naples, Italy. Those who are uncomfortable seeing Heracles dressed in Christian garb can easily translate him into a different idiom and see him perhaps as the gnostic pneuma or as "the luminous companion," whom Wallace Stevens seems to have found in the last years of his life, "the completely answering voice." I am grateful to Harold Bloom for these suggestions.

His *Agon,* especially the chapter "A Prelude to Gnosis," 3–15, which traces the path of his own gnostic quest for the sublime, is, in my view, one of the best commentaries on Heracles' function in the *Philoctetes*. Compare in this connection Wallace Stevens: the poet "pushes on and lives, or tries to live, as Paul Valéry did, on the verge of consciousness" ("Effects of Analogy," 712).

42. This impeccable Heracles, as Christian as any saint, seems to be the paradigm accepted by scholars who justify his intervention in this play. For a more complex Heracles, including his monumental transgressions and his ultimate beatification, see chap. 6, n.10.

43. Sophocles, *Plays and Fragments*, Jebb's note at v. 1465; see Webster on the same passage.

44. Greek tragedies often "turn on the sequence of injury, resentment and (as a matter of honor) retaliation. This is not a mere accident of mythology." Underlying this sequence is the moral view that "divine *talio* [retribution] is the sanction behind human *talio*" (Winnington-Ingram, *Sophocles*, 324).

45. Knox, *Heroic Temper*, 141.

46. Pucci, *Filottete*, note on v. 1467.

47. Knox, *Heroic Temper*, 142.

48. The manuscripts give us *glykion* (sweet), but Jebb insists that *Lykion*, as given by a scholiast, must be the true reading.

49. See Jebb's note on. v. 1461, in Sophocles, *Plays and Fragments*.

50. Ibid.

51. Heaney, *Cure at Troy*, 80.

52. Sophocles, *Plays and Fragments*, Jebb's note at v. 1466. On the same passage see also Webster's note at 1466, in Sophocles, *Philoctetes*, and Pucci, *Filottete*. For a discussion of the identity of this Daimon, see Budelmann, *Language of Sophocles*, 148–54.

53. "The sense in Greek tragedy that fate is stronger than the gods really implies that the gods exist to ratify the order of nature" (Frye, *Anatomy of Criticism*, 208).

54. Eur., *Med.*, vv. 1415–18. See also the similar ending for *Bacch.*, vv. 1388–92, and *Hel.*, vv. 1688–92.

Appendix

1. On this problem, see Wilamowitz-Moellendorff, *Die dramatische Technik des Sophocles*; Lloyd-Jones, *Blood for the Ghosts*, 401–18.

2. Easterling, "Philoctetes and Modern Criticism," 224. For further considerations of the prophecy, see Budelmann, *Language of Sophocles*, 109–30, 187–88.

3. For a good discussion of scholarly attitudes toward Sophocles' religion, see Budelmann, *Language of Sophocles*, 133–194. Useful also in this context is Dodds, *Greeks and the Irrational,* chap. 7, "Plato, the Irrational Soul, and the Inherited Conglomerate," 207–35.

4. Wells, "How Did God Get Started?" gives an interesting account of the struggle of monotheism to replace polytheism in the ancient world and of the philosophical absolutism that drove this ambition.

5. For my workaday definition of the Greek gods, which like any definition excludes as much as it includes, I am prepared to accept something akin to what Bloom calls the "modified logocentrism of Protagoras": "meanings for him are presences, not absences, though these are flickering presences, perpetually in flux" (*Agon*, 35). For a modern mathematician's definition of religion, see Whitehead: "Religion is the vision of something that stands beyond, behind, and within, the passing flux of immediate things; something which is real, and yet waiting to be realized; something which is a remote possibility, and yet the greatest of present facts; something that gives meaning to all that passes, and yet eludes apprehension; something whose possession is the final good, and yet is beyond all reach; something which is the ultimate ideal, and the hopeless quest. . . . The fact of religious vision, and its history of persistent expansion, is our one ground for optimism. Apart from it, human life is a flash of occasional enjoyments lighting up a mass of pain and misery, a bagatelle of transient experience" (*Science and the Modern World*, 191–92).

6. For a discussion of how Plato both struggled against the popular religion, what Dodds calls the "Inherited Conglomerate," and came to accept it and incorporate it into his cosmology, see Dodds, *Greeks and the Irrational*, chap. 7, "Plato, the Irrational Soul, and the Inherited Conglomerate," 207–35.

7. A point well made by Herington, *Poetry into Drama*, 60.

8. Nagy discusses at some length the conversion of the hero cult, which is always local, into the larger cult of Epos. He notes that while "*timḗ* 'honor' is conferred by cult, the prestige that *kléos* brings is the undying glory of Epos" (*Best of the Achaeans*, 119). On the cult of Neoptolemus (= Pyrrhus) at Delphi, see his chap. 7, 118–41. On the cult of Heracles and Philoctetes on Mount Oeta, see Finkelberg, "Second Stasimon."

9. It is difficult to suppose that Sophocles, in linking these two heroes together as a team, as they had been linked in the prophecy, would have us to understand, as some modern scholars argue, that only one of them was truly a hero of moral stature and the other was a man with no moral compass whatsoever.

10. See Belfiore, "*Xenia* in Sophocles' *Philoctetes*."

11. Many scholars have addressed the issue of this prophecy and the structural problem it introduces into the play. See, among others, Easterling, "*Philoctetes* and Modern Criticism"; Belfiore, "*Xenia* in Sophocles' *Philoctetes*." Easterling notes that Sophocles could have dispensed with the prophecy altogether. We can imagine a possible treatment in which the delegation from Troy reaches an accord with Philoctetes without ever mentioning the prophecy.

12. Stokes notes how Sophocles is careful to avoid having Neoptolemus commit perjury (in the question regarding whether he formally promised to

take Philoctetes back to Greece): "Sophocles has given us a credibly deceived Philoctetes and a credibly deceitful Neoptolemus" ("Two Questions on Sophocles' *Philoctetes*," 166).

13. Thomson, *Aeschylus and Athens*.

14. Easterling argues that the difference between Neoptolemus's prophecy at the beginning of the play and at the end is "not the factual inconsistency but Neoptolemus' acquisition of insight" ("*Philoctetes* and Modern Criticism," 223). This is undoubtedly true. The play certainly seems to trend in the direction of Neoptolemus's increasing awareness of the meaning of his mission, but that does not erase the inconsistency, that he knows little or nothing of the prophecy when the play opens but by the exodos acts as if he had read and studied the document. Even beginning in the parodos Neoptolemus plays a double role, as an actor in a drama and as a prophet explaining the ways of the gods to his community.

15. Wilson, "Philoctetes."

16. Waldock, *Sophocles the Dramatist*, 200; Bowra, *Sophoclean Tragedy*, 265.

17. Theog. 805–10, Bowra's translation, in his *Sophoclean Tragedy*.

18. Waldock, *Sophocles the Dramatist*, 201. Bowra's idea of the fidelity to the exact terms of an oracle is well taken. Again we recall that there was no text to which either Sophocles or his audience could refer. The play seems, however, to insinuate that the failure on Lemnos was the result of Odysseus's misapplication of the oracle and his disregard for its religious import.

19. Ibid., 197.

20. Bergson, *Creative Evolution*, 57, 211.

Bibliography

Works of Greek Authors

Aeschylus. *The Oresteia Trilogy*. Translated by George Thomson. Edited by Robert W. Corrigan. New York: Dell, 1965.

Aristotle. *The Art of Rhetoric*. Translated by J. H. Freese. Loeb Classical Library. Cambridge, MA: Harvard University Press, 1926.

———. *Poetics*. Translated by Stephen Halliwell. Loeb Classical Library. Cambridge, MA: Harvard University Press, 1995.

Athenaeus. *Deipnosophists*. Translated by Charles Gulick. 7 vols. Loeb Classical Library. Cambridge, MA: Harvard University Press, 1951–61.

Dio Chrysostom. "The Fifty-second Discourse: On Aeschylus and Sophocles and Euripides or the Bow of Philoktetes." In *Discourses*, vol. 4, translated by H. Lamar Crosby. Cambridge, MA: Harvard University Press, 1946.

Euripides. *Fabulae*. Edited by G. Murray. 3 vols. Oxford: Oxford University Press, 1902.

Gorgias. "Gorgias." In Diels, *Fragmente der Vorsokratiker*, frag. 11 (DK82B11).

Heraclitus. *Heraclitus: Greek Text with a Short Commentary*. Edited by M. Marcovich. Merida, Venezuela: Los Andes University Press, 1967.

Herodotus. *Historiae*. Edited by C. Hude. 3rd ed. Oxford: Oxford University Press, 1927.

Hesiod. *Theogony*. Edited by M. L. West. Oxford: Oxford University Press, 1996.

———. *Works and Days*. Edited by M. L. West. Oxford: Oxford University Press, 1996.

Hippocrates. *Hippocrates*. Translated by W. H. S. Jones. Vol. 2. Loeb Classical Library. Cambridge, MA: Harvard University Press, 1923.

Homer. *The Iliad*. Translated by Richard Lattimore. New York: Harper & Row, 1965.

———. *The Odyssey*. Translated by A. T. Murray. Loeb Classical Library. Cambridge, MA: Harvard University Press, 1919.

Plato. *The Collected Dialogues*. Edited by Edith Hamilton and Huntington Cairns. Bollingen Series 71. Princeton, NJ: Princeton University Press, 1961.

———. *Gorgias*. Edited by E. R. Dodds. Oxford: Clarendon Press, 1959.

———. *The Republic*. Translated by Paul Shorey. In Plato, *Collected Dialogues*, 575–844.

Sophocles. *The Complete Plays*. Translated by Paul Roche. New York: Penguin, 2001.

———. *Fabulae*. Edited by H. Lloyd-Jones and N. G. Wilson. Oxford: Oxford University Press, 1990. All the quotations in Greek are from this edition unless otherwise noted.

———. *Filottete*. Edited by Pietro Pucci. Translated in Italian by Giovanni Cerri. Rome: Fondazione Lorenzo Valla, Arnoldo Mondadori Editore, 2003.

———. *Philoctetes*. Edited and translated by Hugh Lloyd-Jones. Loeb Classical Library. Cambridge, MA: Harvard University Press, 1998.

———. *Philoctetes*. Translated by Judith Affleck. Cambridge: Cambridge, University Press, 2001.

———. *Philoctetes*. Translated by Keith Dewhurst. London: Oberon Books, 2000.

———. *Philoctetes*. Translated by Carl Phillips. Introduction and notes by Diskin Clay. Oxford: Oxford University Press, 2002.

———. *Philoctetes*. Edited by T. B. L. Webster. Cambridge: Cambridge University Press, 1970.

———. *The Plays and Fragments: Part IV: The Philoctetes*. Edited and translated by Richard C. Jebb. 2nd ed. Cambridge, 1931. First published 1898.

Secondary Literature

Adkins, A. W. H. *From the Many to the One: A Study of Personality and Views of Human Nature in the Context of Ancient Greek Society, Values, and Beliefs*. Ithaca, NY: Cornell University Press, 1970.

———. *Moral Values and Political Behavior in Ancient Greece*. New York: Norton, 1972.

Annas, Julia. *An Introduction to Plato's Republic*. Oxford: Oxford University Press, 1981.

Arendt, Hannah. *The Human Condition*. Chicago: University of Chicago Press, 1958.

Attali, Jacques. *Noise: The Political Economy of Music*. Translated by Brian Massumi. Minneapolis: University of Minnesota Press, 1985.

Aultman-Moore, L. W. J. "Moral Pain and the Choice of Neoptolemos: *Philoktetes* 894." *Classical World* 87 (1994): 309–10.

Austin, Norman. "The Great Soul Robbery in Sophocles' *Philoktetes*." *Arion* 14 (2006): 69–118.

———. "Theocritus 16: Theocritus and Simonides." *Transactions of the American Philological Association* 98 (1967): 1–21.

Belfiore, Elizabeth S. *Tragic Pleasures: Aristotle on Plot and Emotion*. Princeton, NJ: Princeton University Press, 1992.

———. "*Xenia* in Sophocles' *Philoctetes*." *Classical Journal* 89 (1994): 113–29.

Bergson, Henri. *Creative Evolution*. Translated by Arthur Mitchell. New York: Modern Library, 1944.

Bloom, Harold. *Agon: Towards a Theory of Revisionism*. New York: Oxford University Press, 1982.

———. *The Anxiety of Influence*. New York: Oxford University Press, 1973.

———. *A Map of Misreading*. New York: Oxford University Press, 1975.

———. *Where Shall Wisdom Be Found?* New York: Riverhead Books, 2004.

Blundell, Mary Whitlock. *Helping Friends and Harming Enemies: A Study of Sophocles and Greek Ethics*. Cambridge: Cambridge University Press, 1989.

———. "The Moral Character of Odysseus in *Philoktetes*." *Greek, Roman and Byzantine Studies* 28 (1987): 307–29.

———. "The *Phusis* of Neoptolemus in Sophocles' *Philoctetes*." In McAuslan and Walcot, *Greek Tragedy*, 104–15.

Borges, Jorge Luis. "Pierre Menard, Author of Don Quixote." Translated by Anthony Bonner. In *Ficciones*, edited by Anthony Kerrigan, 45–55. New York: Grove Press, 1962.

Bowra, C. M. *Sophoclean Tragedy*. Oxford: Oxford University Press, 1944.

Bremer, J. M. *Hamartia: Tragic Error in the Poetics of Aristotle and in Greek Tragedy*. Amsterdam: Hakkert, 1969.

Buber, Martin. *I and Thou*. Translated by W. Kauffman. New York: Touchstone, 1996.

Budelmann, Felix. *The Language of Sophocles: Communality, Communication and Involvement*. Cambridge: Cambridge University Press, 2000.

Burian, Peter. "Myth into *Muthos*: The Shaping of the Tragic Plot." In Easterling, *Cambridge Companion to Greek Tragedy*, 178–208.

Burkert, Walter. *Greek Religion*. Translated by John Raffan. Cambridge, MA: Harvard University Press, 1985.

———. *Homo Necans*. Translated by Peter Bing. Berkeley: University of California Press, 1983.

Burnet, John. "The Socratic Doctrine of the Soul." *Proceedings of the British Academy* (1916): 235–59. Reprinted in *Essays and Addresses*, 126–62. London: Chatto & Windus, 1929.

Buxton, R. G. A. *Persuasion in Greek Tragedy: A Study of Peitho*. Cambridge: Cambridge University Press, 1982.

Cairns, Douglas. *AIDOS: The Psychology and Ethics of Honour and Shame in Ancient Greek Literature*. Oxford: Oxford University Press, 1993.

Calder, William. "Sophoclean Apologia." *Greek, Roman and Byzantine Studies* 12 (1971): 154–69.

The Cambridge Ancient History. Edited by J. B. Bury, S. A. Cook, and F. E. Adcock. Cambridge: Cambridge University Press, 1958.

Carlevale, John. "Education, *Phusis*, and Freedom in Sophocles' *Philoctetes*." *Arion*, 3rd ser., 8, no. 1 (2000): 26–60.

Cartledge, Paul. "Deep Plays: Theater as Process in Greek Civic Life." In Easterling, *Cambridge Companion to Greek Theater*, 3–35.

Claus, David B. *Toward the Soul: An Inquiry into the Meaning of ψυχή before Plato*. New Haven, CT : Yale University Press, 1981.

Craik, E. M. "*Philoctetes:* Sophoclean Melodrama." *Antiquité Classique* 48 (1979): 15–29.

Dickinson, Emily. *The Poems of Emily Dickinson*. Edited by R. W. Franklin. Cambridge, MA: Harvard University Press, 1999.

Diels, Hermann. *Die Fragmente der Vorsokratiker*. Edited by Walther Kranz. 6th ed. 3 vols. Berlin: Weidmann, 1951–52

Dillon, John, and Tania Gergel, trans. and eds. *The Greek Sophists*. New York: Penguin, 2003.

Dodds, E. R. *The Greeks and the Irrational*. Berkeley: University of California Press, 1951.

Dworkin, Craig. *Reading the Illegible*. Evanston, IL: Northwestern University Press, 2003.

Easterling, P. E., ed. *The Cambridge Companion to Greek Tragedy*. Cambridge: Cambridge University Press, 1997.

———. "Character in Sophocles." In *Greek Tragedy: Modern Essays in Criticism*, edited by Erich Segal, 138-45. New York: Harper Row, 1983.

———. "Constructing Character in Greek Tragedy." In Pelling, *Characterization and Individuality in Greek Literature*, 83–99.

———. "Form and Performance." In Easterling, *Cambridge Companion to Greek Tragedy*, 151–77.

———. "*Philoctetes* and Modern Criticism." In *Greek Tragedy: Modern Essays in Criticism*, edited by Erich Segal, 217–28. New York: Harper & Row, 1983.

Eco, Umberto. *Kant and the Platypus: Essays on Language and Cognition*. Translated by Alistair McEwen. New York: Harcourt Press, 1997.

Eliot, T. S. "Tradition and Individual Talent." In *The Sacred Wood*, 6th ed., 47–59. New York: Barnes & Noble, 1948.

Else, Gerald F. *The Origin and Form of Early Greek Tragedy*. New York: W. W. Norton, 1972.

Finkelberg, Margalit. "The Second Stasimon of the *Trachiniae* and Heracles' Festival on Mount Oeta." *Mnemosyne* 49 (1996): 129–43.

Foley, Helen. *Female Acts in Greek Tragedy*. Princeton, NJ: Princeton University Press, 2001.

Frame, Douglas. *The Myth of Return in Early Greek Epic*. New Haven, CT: Yale University Press, 1978.

Freeman, Kathleen. *Ancilla to the Pre-Socratic Philosophers*. Cambridge, MA: Harvard University Press, 1957.

Freud, Sigmund. "Analysis Terminable and Interminable." In *The Standard Edition of the Complete Psychological Works of Sigmund Freud*, translated by James Strachey in collaboration with Anna Freud, vol. 13, 209–53. London: Hogarth Press, 1964.

———. *Totem and Taboo: Some Points of Agreement between the Mental Lives of Savages and Neurotics*. Translated by James Strachey. New York: Norton, 1950.

Frye, Northrop. *Anatomy of Criticism*. Princeton, NJ: Princeton University Press, 1967.

Gadamer, Hans-Georg. *Truth and Method*. Translated by Garrett Barden and John Cumming. New York: Seabury Press, 1975.

Gill, Christopher. "Bow, Oracle, and Epiphany in Sophocles' *Philoctetes*." In McAuslan and Walcot, *Greek Tragedy*, 95–103.

Goldhill, Simon. "The Audience of Athenian Tragedy." In Easterling, *Cambridge Companion to Greek Tragedy*, 54–68.

———. "The Great Dionysia and Civic Ideology." In *Nothing to Do with Dionysos? Athenian Drama in Its Social Context*, edited by John J. Winkler and Froma I. Zeitlin, 97–129. Princeton, NJ: Princeton University Press, 1990.

———. "The Language of Tragedy: Rhetoric and Communication." In Easterling, *Cambridge Companion to Greek Tragedy*, 127–50.

———. *Reading Greek Tragedy*. Cambridge: Cambridge University Press, 1986.

Gould, Carol. "Moral Dilemma and Integrity in Sophocles' *Philoctetes*." In *Essays in Ancient Greek Philosophy: Philosophy before Plato*, edited by Anthony Preus, 6 vols., 6:199–218. Albany: State University of New York Press, 2001.

Gould, Thomas. *The Ancient Quarrel between Poetry and Philosophy*. Princeton, NJ: Princeton University Press, 1990.

Greengard, Carola. *Theater in Crisis: Sophocles' Reconstruction of Genre and Politics in* Philoktetes. Amsterdam: Hakkert, 1987.

Griffin, Jasper. "Sophocles and the Democratic City." In *Sophocles Revisited: Essays Presented to Sir Hugh Lloyd-Jones*, edited by Jasper Griffin, 73–94. Oxford: Oxford University Press, 1999.

Hall, Edith. *Inventing the Barbarian: Greek Self-Definition through Tragedy*. New York: Oxford University Press, 1989.

———. "The Sociology of Athenian Tragedy." In Easterling, *Cambridge Companion to Greek Tragedy*, 93–126.

Hamilton, Richard. "Neoptolemos' Story in the *Philoktetes*." *American Journal of Philology* 96 (1975): 131–37.

Harsh, Philip W. "The Role of the Bow in the *Philoctetes* of Sophocles." *American Journal of Philology* 81 (1960): 405–14.

Havelock, Eric A. *Preface to Plato*. Cambridge, MA: Harvard University Press, 1963.

Hawkins, Anne Hunsaker. "Ethical Tragedy and Sophocles' 'Philoctetes.'" *Classical World* 92 (1999): 337–57.

Heaney, Seamus. *The Cure at Troy: A Version of Sophocles'* Philoctetes. New York: Noonday Press, 1991.
Heath, Malcolm. *The Poetics of Greek Tragedy*. Stanford, CA: Stanford University Press, 1987.
———. "Sophocles' Philoctetes: A Problem Play?" In *Sophocles Revisited: Essays Presented to Sir Hugh Lloyd-Jones*, edited by Jasper Griffin, 137–60. Oxford: Oxford University Press, 1999.
Hegel, G. W. F. *Hegel on Tragedy*. Edited and translated by Anne and Henry Paolucci. Smyrna, DE: Griffon House, 2001.
Herington, John. *Poetry into Drama: Early Tragedy and the Greek Poetic Tradition*. Berkeley: University of California Press, 1985.
Jaeger, Werner. *Paideia: The Ideals of Greek Culture*. Translated by Gilbert Highet. 2nd ed. New York: Oxford University Press, 1945.
Jameson, M. H. "Politics and the 'Philoctetes.'" *Classical Philology* 51 (1956): 217–27.
Johnston, S. I. *Restless Dead: Encounters between the Living and the Dead in Ancient Greece*. Berkeley: University of California Press, 1999.
Kahn, Charles H. *The Art and Thought of Heraclitus*. Cambridge: Cambridge University Press, 1979.
Kierkegaard, Søren. *The Sickness unto Death*. Translated by Alistair Hannay. New York: Penguin, 2004.
Kirk, G. S., and J. E. Raven. *The Presocratic Philosophers: A Critical History with a Selection of Texts*. Cambridge: Cambridge University Press, 1957.
Kirkwood, G. M. "Persuasion and Allusion in Sophocles' *Philoctetes*." *Hermes* 122 (1994): 425–36.
———. *A Study of Sophoclean Drama*. Ithaca, NY: Cornell University Press, 1958.
Kittel, Gerhard. *Theological Dictionary of the New Testament*. Vol. 1. Translated by Geoffrey William Bromiley. Grand Rapids, MI: Eerdmans, 1964.
Kitto, H. D. F. *Greek Tragedy*. 3rd ed. New York: Methuen, 1961.
Knox, B. M. W. *The Heroic Temper: Studies in Sophoclean Tragedy*. Berkeley: University of California Press, 1966.
Kohut, Heinz. *Self Psychology and the Humanities*. Edited by C. B. Strozier. New York: Norton, 1985.
———. "Thoughts on Narcissism and Narcissistic Rage." In Kohut, *Self Psychology and the Humanities*, 124–60.
Konstan, David. *The Emotions of the Ancient Greeks: Studies in Aristotle and Classical Literature*. Toronto: University of Toronto Press, 2001.
Kosak, Jennifer Clarke. "Therapeutic Touch and Sophokles' *Philoktetes*." *Harvard Studies in Classical Philology* 99 (1999): 93–124.
Kott, Jan. *The Eating of the Gods*. Translated by Boleslaw Taborski and Edward J. Czerwinski. New York: Random House, 1970.
Lacan, Jacques. *The Four Fundamental Concepts of Psycho-analysis*. Edited by Jacques-Alain Miller. Translated by Alan Sheridan. New York: Penguin, 1979.

Lada-Richards, Ismene. "Neoptolemos and the Bow: Ritual Theater and Theatrical Vision in Sophocles' *Philoctetes.*" *Journal of Hellenic Studies* 117 (1997): 179–83.

Lesky, Albin. *Die tragische Dichtung der Hellenen.* 3rd ed. Göttingen: Vandenhoeck & Ruprecht, 1972.

Levi, Peter. "Greek Drama." In *Oxford History of the Classical World,* edited by John Boardman, Jasper Griffin, and Oswyn Murray, 156–85. Oxford: Oxford University Press, 1986.

Lloyd-Jones, Hugh. *Blood for the Ghosts: Classical Influences in the Nineteenth and Twentieth Centuries.* Baltimore: Johns Hopkins University Press, 1982.

———. *Greek Epic, Lyric, and Tragedy.* Cambridge: Cambridge University Press, 1990.

———. *The Justice of Zeus.* Berkeley: University of California Press, 1983.

Mandel, Oscar. *Philoctetes and the Fall of Troy.* Lincoln: University of Nebraska Press, 1981.

McAuslan, Ian, and Walcot, Peter, eds. *Greek Tragedy.* Oxford: Oxford University Press, 1993.

Nagy, Gregory. *The Best of the Achaeans: Concepts of the Hero in Archaic Greek Poetry.* Baltimore: Johns Hopkins University Press, 1979.

Nestle, Wilhelm. *Von Mythos zum Logos.* Stuttgart: Aalen, Scientia-Verlag, 1966.

Nietzsche, Friedrich. "Homeric Contests." In *The Portable Nietzsche,* translated by Walter Kaufman, 32–39. New York: Penguin, 1954.

Nussbaum, Martha C. "Consequences and Character in Sophocles' *Philoctetes.*" *Philosophy and Literature* 1 (1976–77): 25–53.

Padel, Ruth. *Whom Gods Destroy.* Princeton, NJ: Princeton University Press, 1995.

Pelling, Christopher, ed. *Characterization and Individuality in Greek Literature.* Oxford: Oxford University Press, 1990.

Pickard-Cambridge, Arthur. *Dithyramb, Tragedy and Comedy.* 2nd ed. Revised by T. B. L. Webster. Oxford: Oxford University Press, 1962.

———. *The Theater of Dionysus in Athens.* Oxford: Oxford University Press, 1946.

Podlecki, Anthony J. "The Power of the Word in Sophocles' *Philoktetes.*" *Greek, Roman and Byzantine Studies* 7 (1966): 233–50.

Pucci, Pietro. "Gods' Intervention and Epiphany in Sophocles." *American Journal of Philology* 115 (1994): 15–46.

Puhvel, Jaan. *Comparative Mythology.* Baltimore: Johns Hopkins University Press, 1987.

Rabel, Robert J. "Sophocles' *Philoctetes* and the Interpretations of *Iliad* 9." *Arethusa* 30 (1997): 297–307.

Reinhardt, Karl. *Sophocles.* Translated by Hazel Harvey and David Harvey. New York: Barnes & Noble, 1979.

Ringer, Mark. *Electra and the Empty Urn: Metatheater and Role Playing in Sophocles.* Chapel Hill: University of North Carolina Press, 1998.

Robinson, D. M. "Topics in Sophocles' *Philoctetes*." *Classical Quarterly* 19 (1969): 34–56.

Rohde, Erwin. *Psyche: The Cult of Souls and the Belief in Immortality among the Greeks*. 8th ed. Translated by W. B. Hillis. London: Kegan Paul, 1925.

Rose, Peter W. *Sons of the Gods, Children of Earth: Ideology and Literary Form in Ancient Greece*. Ithaca, NY: Cornell University Press, 1992.

———. "Sophocles' *Philoctetes* and the Teaching of the Sophists." *Harvard Studies in Classical Philology* 80 (1976): 49–105.

Rosenmeyer, T. G. "Decision-Making." In *The Poetics of Therapy*, edited by Martha C. Nussbaum, 187-218. Edmonton, AB: Academic Printing & Publishing, 1990.

Santayana, George. *Interpretations of Poetry and Religion*. New York: Harper, 1957.

———. *The Life of Reason*. Vol. 3 of *Reason in Religion*. New York: Charles Scribner's Sons, 1936.

Segal, Charles. *Interpreting Greek Tragedy: Myth, Poetry, Text*. Ithaca, NY: Cornell University Press, 1986.

———. *Tragedy and Civilization: An Interpretation of Sophocles*. Cambridge, MA: Harvard University Press, 1981.

Shay, Jonathan. *Achilles in Vietnam*. New York: Athenaeum, 1994.

Sheppard, J. T. "Attic Drama in the Fifth Century." In *The Cambridge Ancient History*, vol. 5, *Athens, 478–401 B.C.*, edited by J. B. Bury, S. A. Cook, and F. E. Adcock, 113–44. Cambridge: Cambridge University Press, 1958.

Shorey, Paul. *What Plato Said*. Chicago: University of Chicago Press, 1933.

Silk, M. S. "Heracles and Greek Tragedy." In McAuslan and Walcot, *Greek Tragedy*, 116–37.

Slater, Philip. *The Glory of Hera*. Boston: Beacon Press, 1968.

Snell, Bruno. *The Discovery of the Mind*. Translated by T. G. Rosenmeyer. Oxford: Blackwell, 1953.

Stanford, W. B. *The Ulysses Theme*. Oxford: Blackwell, 1954.

Stephens, J. Ceri. "The Wound of Philoctetes." *Mnemosyne* 48 (1995): 153–68.

Stevens, Wallace. *Collected Poetry and Prose*. New York: Library of America, 1997.

———. "The Comedian as the Letter C." In *Collected Poetry and Prose*, 22–36.

———. "Effects of Analogy." In *Collected Poetry and Prose*, 707–23.

———. "The Sail of Ulysses." In *Collected Poetry and Prose*, 462–67.

Stokes, Michael C. "Two Questions on Sophocles' *Philoctetes*." In *Language and the Tragic Hero*, edited by Pietro Pucci, 155–73. Atlanta: Scholars Press, 1988.

Taplin, Oliver. *Greek Tragedy in Action*. London: Routledge, 1985.

———. "Significant Actions in Sophocles' *Philoctetes*." *Greek, Roman and Byzantine Studies* 12 (1971): 25–44.

Thomson, George. *Aeschylus and Athens: A Study in the Social Origins of Drama*. 2nd ed. New York: Haskell House, 1967.

The Upanishads. Translated by Eknath Easwaran. 2nd ed. Tomales, CA: Nilgiri, 2007.

Vernant, Jean-Pierre, and Pierre Vidal-Naquet, eds. *Myth and Tragedy in Ancient Greece*. Translated by Janet Lloyd. New York: Zone Books, 1988.

Waldock, A. J. A. *Sophocles the Dramatist*. Cambridge: Cambridge University Press, 1966.

Webster, T. B. L. *The Tragedies of Euripides*. London: Methuen, 1967.

Weiss, Joseph, and Harold Sampson. "Unconscious Pathogenic Beliefs." In *The Psychoanalytic Process*, 68–83. New York: Guildford, 1986.

Wells, Colin. "How Did God Get Started?" *Arion* 18 (2010): 1–27.

Whitehead, Alfred North. *Science and the Modern World*. New York: Free Press, 1967.

Whitman, Cedric H. *Sophocles: A Study of Heroic Humanism*. Cambridge, MA: Harvard University Press, 1951.

Wilamowitz-Moellendorff, Tycho von. *Die dramatische Technik des Sophokles*. Philologische Untersuchungen 22. Berlin, 1917.

Williams, Bernard. *Shame and Necessity*. Berkeley: University of California Press, 1993.

Wilson, Edmund. "Philoctetes: The Wound and the Bow." In *The Wound and the Bow*, 272–95. New York: Oxford University Press, 1959.

Winnington-Ingram, R. P. *Sophocles: An Interpretation*. Cambridge: Cambridge University Press, 1980.

Woolf, Virginia. "On Not Knowing Greek." In *Collected Essays*, 1:1–13. New York: Harcourt Brace & World, 1925.

———. *To the Lighthouse*. New York: Harcourt, 1927.

Zeitlin, Froma. *Playing the Other: Gender and Society in Classical Greek Literature*. Chicago: University of Chicago Press, 1996.

Index

Note: When there is no playwright gloss in a subentry, it is assumed to refer to Sophocles; for example:

Odysseus: character/nature of, refers to Odysseus in *Philoctetes* (Sophocles)

however,

Odysseus: character/nature of (Aeschylus), refers to Odysseus in *Philoctetes* (Aeschylus).

WISCONSIN STUDIES IN CLASSICS

General Editors
William Aylward and Patricia A. Rosenmeyer

E. A. THOMPSON
Romans and Barbarians: The Decline of the Western Empire

JENNIFER TOLBERT ROBERTS
Accountability in Athenian Government

H. I. MARROU
A History of Education in Antiquity
Histoire de l'Education dans l'Antiquité, translated by George Lamb

ERIKA SIMON
Festivals of Attica: An Archaeological Commentary

G. MICHAEL WOLOCH
Roman Cities: Les villes romaines by Pierre Grimal, translated and edited by G. Michael Woloch, together with A Descriptive Catalogue of Roman Cities by G. Michael Woloch

WARREN G. MOON, editor
Ancient Greek Art and Iconography

KATHERINE DOHAN MORROW
Greek Footwear and the Dating of Sculpture

JOHN KEVIN NEWMAN
The Classical Epic Tradition

JEANNY VORYS CANBY, EDITH PORADA, BRUNILDE SISMONDO RIDGWAY, and TAMARA STECH, editors
Ancient Anatolia: Aspects of Change and Cultural Development

ANN NORRIS MICHELINI
Euripides and the Tragic Tradition

WENDY J. RASCHKE, editor
The Archaeology of the Olympics: The Olympics and Other Festivals in Antiquity

PAUL PLASS
Wit and the Writing of History: The Rhetoric of Historiography in Imperial Rome

BARBARA HUGHES FOWLER
The Hellenistic Aesthetic

F. M. CLOVER and R. S. HUMPHREYS, editors
Tradition and Innovation in Late Antiquity

BRUNILDE SISMONDO RIDGWAY
Hellenistic Sculpture I: The Styles of ca. 331–200 B.C.

BARBARA HUGHES FOWLER, editor and translator
Hellenistic Poetry: An Anthology

KATHRYN J. GUTZWILLER
Theocritus' Pastoral Analogies: The Formation of a Genre

VIMALA BEGLEY and RICHARD DANIEL DE PUMA, editors
Rome and India: The Ancient Sea Trade

RUDOLF BLUM
HANS H. WELLISCH, translator
Kallimachos: The Alexandrian Library and the Origins of Bibliography

DAVID CASTRIOTA
Myth, Ethos, and Actuality: Official Art in Fifth Century B.C. Athens

BARBARA HUGHES FOWLER, editor and translator
Archaic Greek Poetry: An Anthology

JOHN H. OAKLEY and REBECCA H. SINOS
The Wedding in Ancient Athens

RICHARD DANIEL DE PUMA and JOCELYN PENNY SMALL, editors
Murlo and the Etruscans: Art and Society in Ancient Etruria

JUDITH LYNN SEBESTA and LARISSA BONFANTE, editors
The World of Roman Costume

JENNIFER LARSON
Greek Heroine Cults

WARREN G. MOON, editor
Polykleitos, the Doryphoros, and Tradition

PAUL PLASS
The Game of Death in Ancient Rome: Arena Sport and Political Suicide

MARGARET S. DROWER
Flinders Petrie: A Life in Archaeology

SUSAN B. MATHESON
Polygnotos and Vase Painting in Classical Athens

JENIFER NEILS, editor
Worshipping Athena: Panathenaia and Parthenon

PAMELA A. WEBB
Hellenistic Architectural Sculpture: Figural Motifs in Western Anatolia and the Aegean Islands

BRUNILDE SISMONDO RIDGWAY
Fourth-Century Styles in Greek Sculpture

LUCY GOODISON and CHRISTINE MORRIS, editors
Ancient Goddesses: The Myths and the Evidence

JO-MARIE CLAASSEN
Displaced Persons: The Literature of Exile from Cicero to Boethius

BRUNILDE SISMONDO RIDGWAY
Hellenistic Sculpture II: The Styles of ca. 200–100 B.C.

PAT GETZ-GENTLE
Personal Styles in Early Cycladic Sculpture

CATULLUS
DAVID MULROY, translator and commentator
The Complete Poetry of Catullus

BRUNILDE SISMONDO RIDGWAY
Hellenistic Sculpture III: The Styles of ca. 100–31 B.C.

ANGELIKI KOSMOPOULOU
The Iconography of Sculptured Statue Bases in the Archaic and Classical Periods

SARA H. LINDHEIM
Mail and Female: Epistolary Narrative and Desire in Ovid's Heroides

GRAHAM ZANKER
Modes of Viewing in Hellenistic Poetry and Art

ALEXANDRA ANN CARPINO
Discs of Splendor: The Relief Mirrors of the Etruscans

TIMOTHY S. JOHNSON
A Symposion of Praise: Horace Returns to Lyric in Odes *IV*

JEAN-RENÉ JANNOT
Religion in Ancient Etruria
Devins, Dieux et Démons: Regards sur la religion de l'Etrurie antique, translated by Jane K. Whitehead

CATHERINE SCHLEGEL
Satire and the Threat of Speech: Horace's Satires, *Book 1*

CHRISTOPHER A. FARAONE and LAURA K. MCCLURE, editors
Prostitutes and Courtesans in the Ancient World

PLAUTUS
JOHN HENDERSON, translator and commentator
Asinaria: The One about the Asses

PATRICE D. RANKINE
Ulysses in Black: Ralph Ellison, Classicism, and African American Literature

PAUL REHAK
JOHN G. YOUNGER, editor
Imperium and Cosmos: Augustus and the Northern Campus Martius

PATRICIA J. JOHNSON
Ovid before Exile: Art and Punishment in the Metamorphoses

VERED LEV KENAAN
Pandora's Senses: The Feminine Character of the Ancient Text

ERIK GUNDERSON
Nox Philologiae: Aulus Gellius and the Fantasy of the Roman Library

SINCLAIR BELL and HELEN NAGY, editors
New Perspectives on Etruria and Early Rome

BARBARA PAVLOCK
The Image of the Poet in Ovid's Metamorphoses

PAUL CARTLEDGE and FIONA ROSE GREENLAND, editors
Responses to Oliver Stone's Alexander*: Film, History, and Cultural Studies*

AMALIA AVRAMIDOU
The Codrus Painter: Iconography and Reception of Athenian Vases in the Age of Pericles

SHANE BUTLER
The Matter of the Page: Essays in Search of Ancient and Medieval Authors

ALLISON GLAZEBROOK and MADELEINE HENRY, editors
Greek Prostitutes in the Ancient Mediterranean, 800 BCE–200 CE

NORMAN AUSTIN
Sophocles' Philoctetes *and the Great Soul Robbery*

SOPHOCLES
A verse translation by DAVID D. MULROY, with introduction and notes
Oedipus Rex